Portable Storage
Nine

COVER—BY CARL JUAREZ

PORTABLE STORAGE NINE

Edited by William M. Breiding

Portable Storage

4...**Editorial**

7...**Selva Broceliandis**
Donald Sidney-Fryer

8...**Style Gives Substance**
Gregory Benford

17...**Reasons for the Visit**
Cy Chauvin

20...**Women in Science Fiction**
Darrell Schweitzer

27...**A Wild Talent & Fine Friend**
Casey Wolf

36...**A New Golden Age?**
Bob Jennings

50...**Smart Dummies**
William M. Breiding

53...**Visible Darkness**
Rich Coad

57...**Down These Mean Trails**
Cheryl Cline

68...**A Fist Full of *Nuggets***
John Fugazzi

74...**My Serial Number Is**
Sandra Bond

NFTs and A.I. Art...77
carl juarez

Original Staples...83
Andy Hooper

Portrait Portfolio...94
John R. Benson

A Pleasure Full Grown...102
Dale Nelson

The Lark Ascended...109
Bruce Gillespie

War of the Worlds...122
Joe Pearson

The Cracked Eye...146
Gary Hubbard

A Mixtape...152
Alva Svoboda

Hidden Machines...157
Jeanne N. Bowman

A Few Moments...160
Chris Sherman

Letters of Comment...164

The Gorgon of Poses...180
G. Sutton Breiding

As far back as the late 1990s I had the urge to collect my writing together, an omnibus of an amateur scribbler. I got as far as printing out pieces from my computer, researching old Apa-50 mailings, rekeying from paper. A collected mess. I can't give you a reason, a motivating factor. I hold very little ego-attachment to my writing. I'm not that good at either writing or thinking. More perhaps a scream in the void: *I was here*. Twenty years later this scream manifest as *Rose Motel*. My dad used to say I had ink in my blood. The itch to pub my ish would not go away. And then in 2014 at Corflu, the convention for fanzine fans, I found both the prompt and the method.

While the progenitors of *Rose Motel* (blatant huckstering: available at Amazon!) were the unlikely pair of Andy Hooper, who was unilaterally encouraging all fanzine writers to edit collections of their work before it was too late, and Michael Dobson, who had begun experimenting with print-on-demand fanzines, the mother of *Portable Storage* was my wife, AC Kolthoff. Without her persistent nudging this fanzine would have never come into being. I was resistant, too lazy and uninspired to even think about it. However, she had planted a seed. Ideas for a certain type of fanzine had begun to form. The evolution of *Portable Storage* from an earnest slender fanzine to a mammoth wild and wooly genzine happened easy, naturally. As Gail predicted, everyone was saying *yes* to my invitations to contribute. Bluntly, it was fucking amazing. At first all that new software was a pain, Gail translating my hardcopy ideas of layout to computer screen. But with the third issue we began hitting our stride. I'd never intended *Portable Storage* to look like anything other than a fanzine. Consistency and perfectionism went against the grain—for both of us. As the issues continued Gail's sensibility emerged and merged with my own and we were fully partnered. Indeed, as I have told her over and over, *Portable Storage* would have never existed without her insistence that it was important and then her willingness to put up with me as we struggled to get it all on to the computer and into print.

Four years later we come to the ninth and final issue. It has been a roller coaster ride, as any fanzine that's published with passion will inevitably be. Perhaps the most pervasive and interesting discussion that *Portable Storage* created has been *what is a fanzine*. Because I chose to use the most advanced (and turns out, the cheapest, by far) bulk printing processes available to publish my fanzine *in hard copy*, print on demand technology, and an odd size (7x10), the look and feel of this fanzine confused most traditional fanzine fans and publishers. It seems most can't quite get their heads around its presentation because it reminds them of the snooty literary quarterlies of their youth. Even though Michael Dobson got here first. Somehow Michael's fanzine *Random Jottings* maintained its sense of "amateur" that most

fanzine fans associate with the term *fanzine*. How he did that I've never quite figured out. Perhaps using the traditional fanzine size, eight and a half by eleven, and a certain informality and spaciousness that I was never able to, er, achieve. Historically if you go back to my fanzine from the 1970s when I was a teenager you'll see the same jam-packed non-perfectionist jumble mixed with pretension to unattainable misty heights. Further, general discussion of what actually constitutes a fanzine began to crop up elsewhere, then winding down, as it must, to it's inevitable conclusion that a fanzine is whatever its creator says it is. All the earmarks are here, some were just bamboozled by the production. Personally, I see *Portable Storage* as an example of a late-stage dying subculture. The curious thing was that it was me that was doing it. Who knew that I, a semi-obscure and wobbly-footed fan, could bring you all together to create this wonderful thing? Thank you, every last one of you, the writers and artists who had faith in me, the faithful loc-hacks, those who stepped forward to help monetarily, and you, the silent readers, scanners, and flippers-through—thank you for a hell of a ride!

William and Gail

Thank you!

Simon K. Agree

Doug Bell

Gregory Benford

John R. Benson

Steven Bieler

Michael Bishop

D.S. Black

James C. Bodie

Sandra Bond

Bill Bowers (RIP)

Jeanne N. Bowman

Michael Bracken

G. Sutton Breiding

Joan Breiding

Michael Breiding

Claire Brialey

Austin Bronson

Bill Burns

Justin E.A. Busch (RIP)

Grant Canfield

Gary Casey

Cy Chauvin

Cheryl Cline

Rich Coad

F. Brett Cox

Richard Dengrove

Paul di Filippo

Ditmar (Dick Jenssen)

Leigh Edmonds

Kurt Erichsen

Nic Farey

Terry Floyd

Brad Foster

John Fugazzi

Gil Gailer (RIP)

Kennedy Gammage

Bruce Gillespie

Michael Gorra

Teddy Harvia

Don Herron

John Hertz

Craig Hilton (Jenner)

Andy Hooper

Gary Hubbard

Tom Jackson

Steve Jeffrey

Bob Jennings

Kent Johnson (RIP)

Jim Jones

carl juarez

Kim Kerbis

L. Jim Khennedy

Jay Kinney

Tim Kirk

Lynn Kuehl

Christina Lake

David Langford

Fred Lerner

Robert Lichtman (RIP)

Craig W. Lion

Ken Love

Miguel Marqueda

Gary Mattingly

Michael McClure

Vincent McHardy

Jim McLeod

Perry Middlemiss

Janet K. Miller

Harry O. Morris

Dale Nelson

Ray Nelson (RIP)

Alec Nevala-Lee

Tracy Nusser

Ulrika O'Brien

Phil Paine

Joe Pearson

Mark Plummer

Andy Porter

James Ru

Jeff Schalles

Marc Schirmeister

Darrell Schweitzer

Stacy Scott

David M. Shea

Chris Sherman

Donald Sidney-Fryer

Al Sirois

Craig Smith

Jon Sommer

Dan Steffan

Steve Stiles (RIP)

Alva Svoboda

Roger D. Sween

Bruce Townley

Frank Vacanti

Fernando Villa Senor

Pat Virzi

Howard Waldrop

Taral Wayne

Alan White

Kip Williams

Charlie Williams (RIP)

Casey June Wolf

Billy Wolfenbarger (RIP)

Peter Young

Gene Young

And to all of our loc-hacks, without you we are nothing!
And to those who valued this fanzine enough to financially
support it, there is a special place reserved for you in that
great fanzine in the sky.

6

Selva Broceliandis
(Broceliaunde: Brittany's real forest of Paimpont)

Within the Forest of Broceliaunde
Inside the borders of the shoes of Brittany,
So choice a place as Edmund Spenser's Faerie-lond;
Behold that herb, in Greek Diktamon or Dittany,
The name: a chant, a lyric, or a litany—
Is that what Lady Viven employed, to live with her
Lord Merlin inside the bole of that ancient oak?
Was that his grave, his coffin, or his sepulture?—
One only of three things that made up his own trinity.

Has he now slept a thousand years and more by half?
When shall he make right the wrong that she awoke?
So we miscalculate, or make an error, elsewise a gaffe?

Unless we have become too subtle, devious or daft—
Shall we not turn our ships around, and steer it full abaft?
—*Donald Sidney-Fryer*
  Thursday morning
  6 October 2022

STYLE GIVE SUBSTANCE

OR

STYLE, SUBSTANCE AND OTHER ILLUSIONS

GREGORY BENFORD

Listen. Here's a story.

There was a desert wind blowing that night. It was one of those hot dry Santa Anas that come down through the mountain passes and curl your hair and make your nerves jump and your skin itch. On nights like that every booze party ends in a fight. Meek little wives feel the edge of the carving knife and study their husbands' necks. Anything can happen. You can even get a full glass of beer at a cocktail lounge.

That is the classic opening of Raymond Chandler's hardboiled novelette, "Red Wind." Here's another story:

The trunks of the trees too were dusty and the leaves fell early that year and we saw the troops marching along the road and the dust rising and leaves, stirred by the breeze, falling and the soldiers marching and afterward the road bare and white except for the leaves.

That's the fourth and concluding sentence in the first paragraph of Hemingway's *A Farewell to Arms*, with its curious catch midway through, *stirred by the breeze*, which defeats the monotony you have by now come to expect from the repeated *ands*. This last sentence finishes the work that paragraph had to do, calling our attention to the momentary stirring before the living leaves fall, then yielding in turn a premonition of early death. Fear of death drives the narrator to abandon combat and in the end the early death comes not to him but to his beloved wife, while giving birth. This early image haunts the entire novel.

Listen. Here's another story:

The place stank. A queer, mingled stench that only the ice-buried cabins of the Antarctic camp know, compounded of reeking human sweat, and the heavy, fish-oil stench of melted sea blubber.

Claustrophobia and revulsion at close contact, the prevailing emotions that run through all of John W. Campbell Jr.'s novella, "Who Goes There?"—later made twice into films titled *The Thing*. Now listen to an opposite encounter with the alien:

The ship came down from space. It carne from the stars and the black velocities, and the shining movements, and the silent gulfs of space.

Abstractions link lyrically with sensations in Bradbury's "Mars is Heaven!"—alliteration-saturated, and grand and doomed in its black velocities.

Listen to Alfred Bester in "Fondly Fahrenheit" scramble your preconceptions immediately by fidgeting with grammar:

He doesn't know which of us I am these days, but they know one truth.

I submit that often and powerfully, the essence of the story appears in the tone, the style, of these opening passages. One of the signatures of particularly effective fiction is just such implication-rich beginnings. Grab the reader early, tell him by suggestion what's

in store, invite him to the fray.

And what of closings? Sometimes this tells us what a writer thinks and feels after writing the story. Suppose you wish to evoke, at a story's recessional, the feelings of resignation:

It was years before he saw her again. But they spent the last days of '99 together, shooting dodos under the shadow of mighty Kilimanjaro.

That is from Robert Silverberg's "Born with the Dead," and echoes Raymond Chandler's ending for *The Big Sleep*,

All they did was make me think of Silver-Wig, and I never saw her again.

That pale, resigned voice quietly closes the door on a story, maybe on a life. And William Gibson used it again in *Neuromancer*:

He never saw Molly again.

But by now it has become a cliche genre signature, yanking you out of the narrative's world and into your own. Gestures tire and wear out. Or so I read it.

Authors often concentrate their themes into stylistic turns, often near the opening. The manner of telling tells us much. You can see the story implicit in the style. Substance dances with style, and the dance is what we see, seldom the dancers. To separate them is to falsify the reading experience.

I suspect authors often don't quite realize what they're doing; certainly, I don't. Their styles tell us matters beyond their conscious control. So the unconscious gets its voice, too. I contend that style is not just an important element in fiction, but is especially so in science fiction. Style can be crucial in determining matters that the author cannot say any other way. Somewhat oddly, this seems true even in this supposedly analytical, science-based literature, its rational underpinnings so often displayed for all too see like a lady's scarlet bloomers. We might well agree with the opening of a great sf novel, Le Guin's *The Left Hand of Darkness*:

I'll make my report as if I told a story, for I was taught as a child on my home world that Truth is a matter of the imagination. The soundest fact may fail or prevail in the style of its telling: like that singular organic jewel of our seas, which grows brighter as one woman wears it and, worn by another, dulls and goes to dust.

Note that "Truth is a matter of the imagination"—a deliberate contrary to conventional wisdom.

"Style is the man himself," says Buffon. Indeed there is nothing more personal, no better way for our subconscious to gain its voice. For our words are chosen, all right, but not by "us"—that consensual, passing parliament of the mind we call consciousness. The subconscious lines up our words for us, so that even as I begin this sentence, not all of me knows how it's going to end—hence, style samples the dark netherworlds, the swamp we cannot see but do sense—with its nuances, allusions, illusions, and Freudian slips on embarrassing banana peels.

When discussing sf, indulge not in glossy generalities. We must quote. Voice is crucial, even in mere book reviews. There a reader will not truly know what we're talking about unless we give examples. You must let writers speak for themselves! It's exactly what they long to do, after all.

Style-less Style

Of course, for long decades the prevailing opinion among fans and even writers of sf was that the best style is one that appears to be no style whatsoever.

The theory here was that the scientific ideas and wrenchings of social perceptions were so great, so alarming, that to mingle any of these with the flourishes, ambiguities and outright flummery of stylistics demanded too much of the reader. This was the ideology of hard sf especially, and largely remains so in the hands of Robert Forward, David Brin and

Charles Sheffield, for example. There appears to be much to be said for this point of view, but the key words here are *appears to be*. Style is partly about appearances, after all.

No style is in fact transparent except to a certain kind of reader, with whom it shares plenty of assumptions. To become even translucent, a manner of telling must agree with the worldview of the reader. It gains transparency by supporting his or her basic assumptions about mechanism and roles. It even defers to the most superficial, ordinary views of the objective labyrinth of sense impressions.

Take the sun, for example. We see it every day, and throughout human history we largely agreed to forget about what it was, and what made it burn. It was so strange, if you thought about it, that everybody agreed to *not* think about it. *Not* thinking about things is the essence of the style-less style. Nobody knew what the sun was, so we slapped essentially religious assumptions into place and, understanding nothing, nonetheless made possible many reassuring phrases.

Think about "as sure as the sunrise." After all, the sun might have gone out while we were on the other side of the Earth from it. Worse, it might go nova, as in Larry Niven's "Inconstant Moon." Indeed, Niven got the striking idea for his story by questioning the obvious. The sun always has come up again, after all.

Now we know pretty much how the sun works through nuclear fusion, so we forget it again. But suppose aliens arrive who believe our sun is divine? The stylistics of dealing with this must be different. Gordon Eklund and I, in "If the Stars are Gods," used Swiftian references and humor, combined with stylistic immersion in the actual experience of merging with the divine sun:

Colder than cold, more terrifying than hate, *more sordid than fear, blacker than evil. The vast inner whole nothingness of everything that was anything, of all.*

I must say that this passage now seems to me rather overwritten. I can hope that Gordon wrote it, but that's a dodge. I at least let it pass, after all. I recall that we meant to amp the character's emotions—and thus the reader's—with a rush of hard adjectiv3es attacking solid nouns.

That passage is an example of what I call *effing the ineffable*, a literary holy grail in sf, usually accomplished by what I call *stylistic blowout*. Overpower the reader with adjectives, throw apparently incompatible analogies at him, mingle senses ("he sounded green down the analytic corridors," to make up one on the spot). Give that already blurry-eyed reader rushes of prose, quiet pauses of apparent contradictions, tweaks and allusions to ideas he already knows but will find topsy-turvy here.

An opposite approach is the lofty Mandarin sentiments of Evelyn Waugh, who said,

"Properly understood, style is not a seductive decoration added to a functional structure; it is of the essence of the work of art. The necessary elements of style are lucidity, elegance, and individuality..."

Elegance is a tricky word, for Hemingway achieves it, but Hemingway himself said that "Prose is architecture, not interior decoration." -- which seems to contradict much of Waugh. Hemingway's elegance was that of Melville's "Call me Ishmael" and the Bible's "Jesus wept..."—the short, declarative sentence, elegance in simplicity. Much emotional muscle behind few words. English is the largest of all languages, and style depends on that immense vocabulary. We have only a few puny tools to manage all this. First, positioning on the page, which has severe limits. The odd uses of this, as in Harlan Ellison's patchwork compositions and a single, spiraling sentence, are typically used only once: we have a curious resistance to spatial invention. And there are only a handful of punctuation marks, with some, such as the exclamation mark, virtually unused.

I remember a conversation with Samuel Delany and Quinn Yarbro about a new punctuation mark we'd like to have—the sarcasm mark. You could simply begin a sentence with it to denote sarcasm by yourself or your character, letting the voice being implicit. But we decided it probably wouldn't catch on; few prose inventions do. One might think that genre authors pay less attention to style, relying on swift plots to enrapture their audiences, but I don't believe so. Witness Raymond Chandler:

In the long run, however little you talk or even think about it, the most durable thing in writing is style, and style is the most valuable investment a writer can make with his time. It pays off slowly, your agent will sneer at it, your publisher will misunderstand it, and it will take people you never heard of to convince them by slow degrees that the writer who puts his individual mark on the way he writes will always payoff. He can't do it by trying, because the kind of style I'm thinking of is a projection of personality and you have to have a personality before you can project it. But granted you have one, you can only project it on paper by thinking of something else. This is ironical in a way: it is the reason, I suppose, why in a generation of 'made' writers I still say you can't make a writer. Preoccupation with style will not produce it. No amount of editing and polishing will have any appreciable effect on the flavor of how a man writes. It is the product of the quality of his emotion and perception: it is the ability to transfer these to paper which makes him a writer, in contrast to the great number of people who have just as good emotions and just as keen perceptions, but cannot come with a googol of miles of putting them on paper.

This given, what is special about style in science fiction?

The Constraints of the Fantastic

I feel that the essential task we face as science fiction writers is to enlist the devices of realism in the cause of the fantastic. Yet this is not so simple as it seemed to be to writers of sf before the 1960s. We ground our flights in the reality we already see and feel. So Joe Haldeman opens *The Forever War* with:

"Tonight we're going to show you eight silent way to kill a man..." The guy who said that was a sergeant who didn't look five years older than me.

—and we are in boot camp, learning only when the word *brainwipes* comes along at the end of the third paragraph that something has changed: this is a future in which people can have their minds erased. But by then we've bought into the reality of this world. Similarly, near the beginning Sheila Finch's *Infinity's Web* the narrator announces, *She would never forgive herself for not being there when her son was born.* And we know we are in a world of strangeness. Establishing that confidence is crucial. Hard sf has done it with a choice of voices, all suggesting possible postures toward the material. Most common is the distant, analytical tone. Arthur Clarke often uses a third person point of view with the lead characters' reactions described from outside, so that the true intelligence of the story is often embodied in the narrative voice. Sometimes this is even an historian, looking back upon events. This mirrors the scientific literature, gathering strength from its association with the unbiased texture of scientific papers--but at times inheriting its dulling mannerisms, such as the passive voice. It can also convey quiet certainty, underplaying its lines, as in *Overhead, without any fuss, the stars were going out.* from Clarke's famous "The Nine Billion Names of God."

Another approach, the voice of Cosmic Mysticism. It's there in the work of James Blish, Arthur Clarke especially, Olaf Stapledon, Poul Anderson (*Tau Zero*)—and yes, myself, among others. This voice assumes an even grander perspective, often with lofty sentiments untied to overt theology, but paralleling the cool immensities of physical law. Clarke's novel *2001* opens:

The drought had lasted now for ten million years, and the reign of the terrible lizards had long since ended.

A third and opposite tone is the Wise Guy Insider. Heinlein used this heavily, as has Fred Pohl, John Varley, and Joe Haldeman. Its cocky savvy plays well to technophiles who, I suspect, feel that they understand rather better than most just how the gritty, hard-edged and unforgiving world works. Sometimes the propensity for one-liners compresses into lists, as in Heinlein's *Notebooks of Lazarus Long*, which proposes this standard for Renaissance humanhood:

A human being should be able to change a diaper, plan an invasion, butcher a hog, conn a ship, design a building, write a sonnet, balance accounts, build a wall, set a bone, comfort the dying, take orders, give orders, cooperate, act alone, solve equations, analyze a new problem, pitch manure, program a computer, cook a tasty meal, fight effectively, die gallantly. Specialization is for insects.

Even Roger Zelazny uses an urbane variant, as in *Isle of the Dead*:

I boosted the Model T into the sky and kept going until space and time ended for a space and a time. I continued.

Elizabeth Bowen has said of modern fiction generally, "We want the naturalistic surface, but with a kind of internal burning." I think we can describe the stylistic aims of many sf writers as seeking to make our sentences burn with an inner reality--often a changed one, not consensual, and often proceeding from striking ideas—our most persistent tribute to the Idea As Hero in sf, perhaps. Those dicta to the writer by Henry James--Select, Contemplate, Render—must contain also the

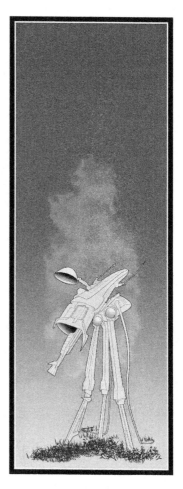

vital infusion of Imagination (notably not a strong trait in James). The Idea must shine through. So when Bradbury conjures up his boyhood Midwest, he cannot simply salt his sentences with the lore of times lost, its musky memorabilia. He must cast the old into the new, as he did in *The Martian Chronicles*. Delany had a more difficult task, as we see in the opening of *Dahlgren*:

to wound the autumnal city. So howled out for the world to give him a name. The in-dark answered with wind.

These lines ride alone on the page, each one like a howl itself, lonely. Of course, style isn't simply word choice: it includes position of words on a page, always remembering that the eye proceeds forward from left to right in the linear lines of print. Then Delany hits you with specifics. One of the universals of style is *be concrete*. Smooth, glossy generalities conjure up little. Pick hairy words, those which arrive with baggage of associations. "Chevy" is better than "car, "brassy" better than "metallic". So Delany goes on:

All you know I know: careening astronauts and bank clerks glancing at the clock before lunch: actresses scowling at light-ringed mirrors and freight elevator operators grinding a thumbful of grease on a steel handle: student riots: know that dark women in bodegas shook their heads last week because in six months prices have risen outlandishly: how coffee tastes after you've held it in your mouth, cold, a whole minute.

He loads all that fine description in one long paragraph burning with detail, a sinker below those high-riding opening lines. The novel ends with "I have come to"—and the seamless connection to the first phrase comes, a cyclic turn.

Or at least I believe I have understood Delany's methods. In the end I can only speak for myself.

The Most Personal of Elements

Of all literary elements, style is the most personal and the hardest to analyze. I don't subscribe to the ideology of transparent style. Style seems to me to be another tool in the narrative game. I use style unremittingly, trying to get at elements not approachable with any of the tones I listed for the hard sf writer, though I am for the most part a member of that club. I used Joycean rhythms and methods in an early novel, *In the Ocean of Niaht*, though for different purposes. My point is that he inventions of modernism, particularly its shattering of consensual reality, now lie open to use by sf. But in using them we mean something quite different from the rather limited goals of the modernists.

We really do talk about the grandly discordant, the truly alien; we're not just viewing the ordinary with discordant methods. Stream of consciousness as in Ulysses is now a *technique*, which taken over into a wildly different sf context can mean very different things--the choice is up to the writer, who can trim his stylistic canvas

and sail where he likes, before these mainstream winds. That I have tried to do.

William Faulkner said that a writer who has plenty to say—"a great deal pushing to get out" as he put it -- can't take time with style. Yet he mastered the most gnarled, surprising style of this century in English. His long sentences, connected by little *ands* suggest the diction and authority of the King James Bible (a device Hemingway knew, too). This method seems to me to arise not so much from a conscious working of voice but rather from a heritage: the storytelling arts of the deep south, where I grew up as well. I heard stories told this way around the fire in my grandparents' house on the Fish River, after the Grand Ol' Opry had been turned off and everybody was too zesty to go right to bed. So when it came to mind to write a novel about the persistence of basic human modes, even in the face of vast, fresh, alien environments, prickly with bizarre technology, I naturally adopted that voice. But I knew that the conventional literary world thought of such oral constructions as a literary signature, so in employing them I made deliberate use of Faulkner himself, and especially of his novella, "The Bear." I structured the first third my novel, *Against Infinity*, after Faulkner, because I was again telling the age-old hunting yarn, variants of which I had heard from my father and grandfather a decade before I ever read Faulkner.

Why? The truest answer lies in the pages of the novel, for I am acutely aware of how little I can truly say about a book. Once written, I am free of its grip. Years have passed now. I trail the novel on a thin line, towing it behind my career, while critics have at it like the sharks in *The Old Man and the Sea*, and now it is hard for me to see through all the blood in the water. There is a further problem, a universal one in discussing style alone: often the choices are made by your unconscious, and now my conscious, critical self fumbles at fathoming them. Nevertheless, why? My devices evolved as I tried to use the reemergence on far Ganymede of ancient human activities, the hunting and going-out, the bond between animals and men. I glimpsed also that aliens would know these features of us, would see in us our true origins, and would play to them. Our modern theories of ourselves are as matchsticks to these great, lumbering truths. I also wanted to talk about the frontier, which most sf is about, as in Heinlein--essentially a human stage. There has not yet been much sf about the wilderness, that territory we do not rule and which cannot be housed inside some human paradigm. Thoreau wrote of it, and Faulkner, sometimes. In sf, Stapledon and Clarke have sung of the grand, natural perspectives beyond humanity. The encounter with that wilderness is a basic event (all too rare nowadays) that propagates through human history, shedding sparks into our literature and lives. Sf brushes against that experience. Finding it unsettling and alien, many turn away. Space opera is more like opera, an urban human activity, than like the huge spaces which await only a hundred kilometers above our heads.

Critic Gary Wolfe examined my possible motives in deploying an ornate style, concluding that I was "adopting a heightened rhetoric that serves to distance us equally from both the mundane action of the novel (family relationships, economics, etc.) and the scientific adventure." (*Fantasy Review* 96, 1986.) Well, yes--and no. Using verbal storytelling cadences does "defamiliarize the iconography of hard sf without sacrificing its sense of wonder." That was indeed a crucial reason to choose such an unusual maneuver. Deliberately choosing a Southern voice, one I learned as a boy but set aside when I entered the Nawthern Intellectu'l realm of university discourse, accomplished several tasks. Personally, it got me back to the world of my own growing up--quite appropriate for a tale of maturation.

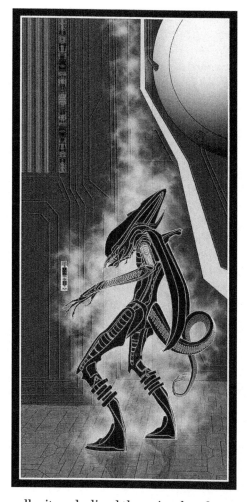

Generally, it underlined the point that there are deep processes and rituals laid down in us, such as hunting, and these will emerge again in circumstances wildly different. The heart-stirring thrill of tracking in piney woods may be quite like the pursuit of the unknowable among icy wastes, I thought. In *Against Infinity* the alien Aleph which draws humans out may well be using this simple fact. To study us? We don't know. But we will go, of that I am sure. So I tried to use a Faulknerian perspective on the irreducibly alien, to see it as both strange and natural and unknowable, and to do it in a voice that recalled prior human encounters. So here are two sentences:

Some Jew had given it that, a blank name that was the first letter of the Hebrew alphabet: a neutral vowel that bespoke the opaque nature of the blocky, gravid thing, the bulk that humans had tried to write upon with their cutters and tractors and on which they had left no mark. A neutral name, and yet it was the source of long legend of domes cracked open and rifled, of walker and crawlers and even whole outposts caught up and crushed and trampled as it moved forward on its own oblivious missions, or else homes and sheds ripped apart as the thing rose up out of the ice where it dwelt, walls split by the heaving of the land as it broke free of ice and poked its angular face --eyeless, with only saw-toothed openings to mark what men chose in their ignorance to call a face and so to take away some fragment of its strangeness -- breaking freshly again into the dim sunlight, seeking, always seeking materials men also needed and had compacted into their homes and factories, and thus were forced to futilely defend against the legend that came for the metals and rare rock, the Aleph making no distinction between what men held and what the bare plains offered, so that it took where it found and thus engendered the continuing legend of alarms ignored and traps brushed aside and servo'd armaments smashed and animals mangled and men and women injured and laser and even electron beam bolts delivered at point-blank range as though into nothing, the alien absorbing all and giving nothing, shrugging off the puny attempts of men to deliver death to it, and without pause it kept going -- down a corridor of ruin and destruction starting back before Manuel's birth and even before Old Matt, the massive thing lumbered, not swift but with a ruthless determination, like a machine and yet like a man too; moving onward eternally on some course humans could not guess, it ran forever in the boy's dreams, a vast immemorial alabaster shape.

Of all passages, this most nearly echoes Faulkner, pointing directly to a constellation of associations --to "modernism," to Biblical storytelling rhythms, to science as a lived-in activity and not just metaphor (as in the New Wave). Though this sentence appears in the novel's first chapter, it attempts (among other aims) something I suspect much sf does, though perhaps unconsciously. In this literature we often live in the shadow of natural immensities. Our entire humanistic program dwindles in the perspectives of vast time and space. This is a central fact of our time, one which mainstream literature has reacted to by variously adopting postures of *ennui*, of numbing angst, of rage-- but most often by ignoring it, retreating into the closed geometries of an obsessively human scale, otherwise known as "realism," and in its most reductionist form, "minimalism."

Contrast this quoted passage with the much more austere, impersonal voice used by Arthur C. Clarke. In his balanced, calm sentences we feel the cool analytical view of science, gazing above the tumult of character and incident at the distant, lofty peaks of principle and great time.

Which approach is better? All--and none. Like blind men grappling with an elephant, we bring back what impressions we can. Yet I suspect that, in the end, any sf writer seeks to achieve a telling affect, even using the styleless style.

In many stories' poignant moments, particularly near the conclusion, I often hear the tone of something utterly completed, vying with a sense of something startled into sudden expanding scope and freedom. When a story functions well, one experiences a whole meaning, simultaneously clicking shut and popping open, a momentary illusion (or is it?) that the fulfillments one senses in the ear indeed do spell out completions available in the world--either the world to be, or the one here and now. No matter how much an sf text may insist on the trivial role of ourselves in the universe, its fall toward a valueless limbo is often arrested by the perfectly stretched safety net of literary form itself: which argues perpetually for meaning.

(Copyright 2022 by Gregory Benford)

REASONS FOR THE VISIT
Observation of Fictional Phenomena
(The Voice of Science Fiction)

CY CHAUVIN

Writers often talk about acquiring their own voice, something they often don't get right until after writing for many years. Some 'try on' different voices from others they admire until they settle into their own. Everyone has one, some more distinctive than others. (Think of R.A. Lafferty!) It seems to be something other than style, or perhaps it is style plus something more. I often think of it as the writer's persona. You 'hear' them speak to you, inside. And if you've actually heard them read a story at a convention or bookstore, that may add to this inner voice; or, if you've read them for years prior to a live reading, it may be irrevocably different.

But I've also come to realize that different genres, decades and periods of writing seem

to have their own voice or persona too, and that what may seem unique about one writer is influenced by this 'accent' their writerly voice takes on from others. It seemed that 1950's and 1940's sf had a sort of collective voice, one that I found especially appealing. It seemed unique to me. So I was quite stunned when I came across a similar voice and mindset in *The Ugly American*, by William Lederer and Eugene Burdick, from 1958. The portion I read was about an engineer (of course!) who wants to bring a simple pump to help irrigate rice fields in Indochina.

"Atkins explained that he was an American and an inventor. He had an idea for a pump to lift water. He wants to develop this pump and sell it for a profit. What Atkins wanted the headman to find was a Sarkanse worker with mechanical skill. Each man knew he would eventually have to compromise; and each took pleasure in talking the whole thing out." So the voice is partly a communal one. This seems very disappointing (perhaps I was naïve to expect otherwise). Maybe all the fuss made about style and voice is unnecessary, if people are not going to write how they actually are.

Does the 'reality' or consciousness of a person change over the decades? How they think about themselves, and thus how a writer might express it in a story? I think about Jane Austen's novels, or Elizabeth Gaskell's *Cranford*, since I love those books so much, reading them often, and wonder how they thought about themselves. And then someone like Susanna Clarke adopts Austen's style for *Jonathan Strange & Mr. Norrell*, but they can't ever hope to adopt her consciousness.

During the pandemic, like many, I went through my attic and book shelves. Along with the fanzines, books and sf magazines, I found a number of literary or 'little' magazines, that I re-read more attentively than I did the first time (and some I doubt I read before at all). These date largely from the late 1960's and 1970's. Most of the writers   cultivated a unique, often eccentric voice, especially for *Transatlantic Review* and *Ambit:* and I found contributions from J.G. Ballard and Carol Emshwiller in both. But I was surprised at the focus on people barely making it in life; on alcoholics, casual sex without any apparent meaning, and

bitter humor. I expected more enlightenment, more revelation of the human condition (such as in Doris Lessing), but it was in short supply. It seemed such a contrast to science fiction, where most characters have a purpose and vocation in their life, even if that purpose seems the impossible one of saving the world (and this purpose the only merit of the story). It was the narrowness of the ideas that were suitable for fiction that disappointed.

Does one have no purpose besides love, or drink? Fiction shifted from one precarious extreme to another. And I wondered then – where did these authors get their voice from? Is this how they rate their own lives' purpose? Or is this the voice expected by their average literary reader? Or is this another collective, communal voice speaking through these authors? More a product of their time and genre than anyone would care to admit.

Paul McCartney was asked by one of his aunts when he was going to write a song that wasn't about love (so he wrote "Paperback Writer"). E. M. Forster wrote that love was written about more often in books than it happened in life. Theodore Sturgeon specialized in writing about all the types of love there were. I wonder if he choose the field of sf wisely. Science fiction seems to look more for some other type of relationship, idea or emotion to evoke. Outside of Sturgeon himself, most love in sf seems "tinny".

What happens in a sf story seems more 'important' (and more variable). Other people tell us what's important (sex without love, climate change, a political party, diversity as a percentage), so we imitate them, rather than write eccentrically. I loved the way these writers wrote, but not what they wrote about. One review in *Ambit*, a British literary magazine, describes it thusly: "It isn't that the story is badly written, but more that it lacks any *real* reason for having been written at all."

What can you bear to read? Assuming the writer is effective, how much suffering and pain (as conflict) is necessary for a good story. James Blish wrote that he would ask himself, "now who would this hurt most?" And choose that character as the protagonist for his story. This might keep one glued to their chair (or it might repel you). Blish told Brian Aldiss that sometimes the inevitable fates of his character caused him to weep. But as a reader, my desires and purposes may be quite different. Who do I want to know? I use an author's 'voice', their persona, to determine who I want to invite into my home and mind. This is where I have increasing doubts. If all of what we see and hear, as well as eat and drink, affect us, shouldn't we take more care to read what is truly good?

Perhaps the ultimate question is how do you *use* fiction? As a type of bed time snack, to relax you as you take the sixteen onyx steps into the Land of Deeper Slumber? To give you an insight into someone's life, or a chuckle, or some mystical revelation? As an adventure, since you do not live in very interesting times, unlike the rest of us? As a family substitute, a friend for a moment. Gosh – (because I almost forgot) – to get that wonderful frisson that makes the hair on your neck stand up, when someone hypotheses a nice taunt piece of speculative hard science?

Brian Aldiss gave a famous speech in Rio de Janeiro in 1969, called 'Science Fiction as Empire". He warned that it was a mistake to think of science fiction as a communal body (as an 'empire'), that advanced, or lost ground, or had any mind of its own, when it really consisted of individual writers sitting at home, writing their stories mostly by themselves, completely alone. SF didn't exist outside of its writers. Gregory Benford, in contrast, wrote much later about the joys of 'crosstalk', of sf stories that commented on other stories, that built on ideas introduced by other writers. In the way that scientists collaborate. "Science is the observation of phenomena and the communication of results to others." – Niels Bohr, Danish physicist. It sounds like an ideal use for the voice of science fiction, too.

But in the end I decided it was an author's persona that I craved. Like a friend that you invite home to supper. (Few conversations are as deep and intense as a novel.) That's why I reread so many books, and temper my suffering. It's why so many readers complain, "there's no likeable characters here."

I think of John Crowley's story, "The Reason for the Visit," about the recall of Virginia Woolf from the past to visit for tea. She marvels at his squeezable plastic lemon. Yes, I understand the reason for the visit completely.

Women in Science Fiction
The Death and Persistence of the "Exclusion Myth"

Darrell Schweitzer

Eric Leif Davin's *Partners in Wonder, Women and the Birth of Science Fiction, 1926-1965* should have revolutionized the way we think and talk about the history of science fiction, although clearly it has not. One of the reason it hasn't is that it was published in 2006 by Lexington Books (part of Rowman & Littlefield), which seems to be an academic press devoted to peer-revised monographs, mostly in the sciences. Davin's book is apparently still in print, but the publisher is one of those aiming almost exclusively at university libraries and the books are priced accordingly. As of this writing, *Partners in Wonder* goes for $66.99 for the trade paperback, $63.50 for the e-book. There are copies on eBay for around $75.00. It is effectively priced out of the popular market.

That's a shame, because what Davin does in this particular tome is drive a stake once and for all through the heart of what he calls the "Exclusion Myth" of Women's Science Fiction. This doctrine, which is such an article of faith nowadays that you could probably get kicked out of certain conventions for expressing doubt about it, was expressed succinctly by Shawna McCarthy in an *Asimov's SF* editor in 1983 and is quoted by Davin on page 1:

"Back in the old, old days (gosh fifteen or twenty years or so), there *were* no women in science-fiction. They didn't read it, they didn't write it, and certainly they didn't star in it. . . . . For some reason (no one *really* knows why . . .), in the mid-1960s, this situation began to change. Suddenly women were turning up at science-fiction conventions; names like Joanna [Russ], Ursula [Le Guin], and Joan [Vinge] began appearing on the tables of contents of science-fiction magazines; and real, honest-to-God female characters were showing up in stories . . . To be certain, this sudden influx of women into the onetime hallowed halls of SF did not go unchallenged. . . . But despite all this *sturm and drang* (or maybe even because of it), female writers, readers, and fans hung on. . . . And so it stands. Women have joined the club."

What is wrong with this statement is that *not one single word of it is true.* Anyone with access to a collection of old science-fiction magazines knows it is nonsense. If you have a set of *F&SF* from the 1950s, you know that it tended to contain four or five unambiguous female bylines per issue. If you have older magazines, names like Clare Winger Harris and Sophie Wenzel Ellis may ring a bell. (Ellis was the first woman to appear, under her own name, in *Astounding,* in the *second issue,* February 1930.) But to understand just how off the mark McCarthy is, you don't need to have such a collection, or even to have glanced at the magazines. (Davin claims to have examined every single issue published between 1926 and 1965). You don't even to have read Davin's book. You need only to look at his dedication, which lists 203 "women" published in science-fiction magazines between 1926 and 1960. "Women" is in quotes, because the last six are actually guys writing as women. But that still means 197 unambiguously female writers. This does not include of unknown gender people who just used initials. The appendices drive this point home relentlessly:

"Women writers between 1926 and 1949: 65. Number of stories: 288"

(We will admit that this includes a couple initialed cases like C.L. Moore, but who were known to be women early on, as letters in

letter columns make clear. Number of writers with unambiguously female names in this period: 52. Moore's collaborations with Henry Kuttner after her marriage are included in the story count.)

The stories are listed. The evidence is indisputable. It is hard to argue with a bibliography. Between 1950-1960, we find another 154 writers, 16 of whom debuted before 1950. We also get an additional 127 women writers in *Weird Tales,* 1923-1954. Their stories are listed. We are also told that 40% of the poets in *Weird Tales* were women. That is 63 female poets. 170 poems, all listed. Plus 31 more female fiction writers in other weird fiction magazines, who did not appear in *Weird Tales.* There are 56 "second wave" female writers, 1960-1965. They wrote 133 stories.

Total stories, 1926-1965: 1055. Plus another 365 from *Weird Tales* and another 61 from other weird fiction magazines (a slight stretch; this includes *Magic Carpet* and *Golden* Fleece, which were only marginally fantastic) for a grand total of 1461 stories by known women writers. They are all listed. The appendices of this book are a very useful.

We also encounter 26 female editors from 1928-1960. This includes assistant editors, managing editors, and even Vera Cerutti "Editor-in-Chief" (but actually publisher; she would have been H.L. Gold's boss) of *Galaxy* October 1950-September 1951. Some of these names are well-known to people aware of out field's past: Dorothy McIlwraith, editor of *Weird Tales,* 1940-1954. Mary Gnaedinger, editor of *Famous Fantastic Mysteries, Fantastic Novels,* and *A. Merritt's Fantasy Magazine,* 1939-1953. Beatrice "Bea" Mahaffey, who worked for Ray Palmer variously as managing editor or editor of *Other Worlds, Science Stories,* and *Universe Science Fiction.* (This means that it was Mahaffey who bought Theodore Sturgeon's "A World Well Lost," the first science fiction story about homosexuality, for *Universe* in 1953, although she doubtless did it with Palmer's permission.) Cele Goldsmith, assistant editor, then editor of *Amazing* and *Fan-*

tastic from 1957-1965 is fondly remembered for bringing those magazines to perhaps their highest level ever. Among the new writers she discovered were Ursula K. Le Guin, Roger Zelazny, and Thomas Disch. Some of the other editors are pretty obscure. I confess I did not know that Katherine Dafron edited the last few issues of *Two Complete Science Adventures Books,* 1953-54, or that Beatrice Jones was editor of *Fantastic Universe* between January and March of 1954. It is maybe padding to include female editors (or assistant editors) of *Secret Agent X, Doc Savage, The Shadow,* or *Argosy*, although these magazines certainly partook of the fantastic. The first woman to appear on the masthead of an actual science fiction magazine was Miriam Bourne, associate editor of *Amazing Stories, 1928-1932*. That means she worked for the magazine's founder, Hugo Gernsback, and followed the magazines change of ownership into the T. O'Conor Sloane era.

Clare Winger Harris As Pictured In the 1929 debut issue of Science Wonder Quarterly. Picture cribbed from Wikipedia

Let me digress on Hugo Gernsback for a moment. For all his many faults (he was known as "Hugo the Rat" by H.P. Lovecraft and his circle; a New York lawyer named Ione Weber specialized in collecting Gernsback debts) he was no male-chauvinist. He was the first editor to publish a woman, Clare Winger Harris, in a science fiction magazine, under her own name, in the June 1927 *Amazing*. Gernsback expressed a certain surprise that a woman could write science fiction (probably unaware that she had published a science fiction story in *Weird Tales* in 1926), but he made no attempt to conceal the gender of any of his writers. He published pictures of them, both in *Amazing* Stories and later in *Wonder Stories,* little portraits drawn by Frank R. Paul, taken from photos. Thus there was never any ambiguity that another, slightly later contributor, Leslie F. Stone, was a woman. Harris became a popular contributor to the magazine. So did Stone.

Let us also digress for a moment about C. L. Moore. One of the most commonly repeated pseudo-facts in science fiction history is that Catherine Lucille Moore had to use her initials to conceal her gender. This is not true. She said so many times during her life. She had a job as a teller at a bank and was the sole support of her parents, and was concerned that if her boss found out she had another source of income, she might lose her job. She could not take that risk, in the depths of the Great Depression, on the basis of one sale to *Weird Tales*. Was there a problem with female bylines in *Weird Tales*? No. Women had been appearing since the first issue. She therefore could not have been the first. By Davin's count she was the 116th. There were two others in the same issue that her first story, "Shambleau" appeared. If anybody thought she was a man, this was cleared up quickly, as the letter columns show. When her last novel, *Doomsday Morning*, appeared in 1957, there was a photo of her on the jacket.

There was never much doubt about the gender of Leigh Brackett either. When an early story of hers appeared in Ray Palmer's *Amazing* (July 1941), he published her photo and ran her bio. John Campbell announced her gender in a headline in the *Astounding* letter column when a reader mistakenly referred to her as "he."

Davin goes on to suggest that the "Exclusion Narrative" is actually an "Inclusion Narrative" if you care to look at the facts. He is well aware that there was a great deal of sexism, racism, and anti-Semitism in American society at this time. This understandably led many people to a *presumption of prejudice,* but he concludes that science fiction and its fandom were a haven of tolerance, not an exclusive boys' club to be broken into. There was no feminist Bastille Day in science fiction, when women writers stormed the barricades. They had been there from the beginning. Their numbers increased in every decade, doubling, then tripling. In the 1950s, Anthony Boucher actively sought out women to write for *F&SF* because they had something different to contribute. Boucher certainly did not believe that women had to "write like men" to get into science fiction, or that they should try. He wanted the difference.

Davin states that in the period of 1926-1965, *all science fiction editors, without exception,* bought stories from women at some point in their careers. This last qualification is required to include Harold Hersey, who edited two issues of *Miracle Science Stories* in 1931 with no female writers included. But he published several in *The Thrill Book* in 1919, including Francis Stevens (Gertrude Bennett) and Greye La Spina. (Here I will have to admit that even Jove, and Eric Davin, occasionally nod. I have found two trivial counterexamples. James Blish edited one issue of *Vanguard Science Fiction* in 1958. No women authors. This is also true of *Cosmos Science Fiction and Fantasy Magazine,* 4 issues, 1953-54, although Phyllis Farren is listed as associate editor, so there was at least feminine input.)

Davin is able to document only *one* writer who actually tried to conceal her gender. This was L. (for Lucille) Taylor Hansen, who did so because she was primarily a science-fact writer, and in those days (as any number of women can attest) the pervasive prejudice was that real, serious science was a man's field, and women were discouraged from going into it. So, in order to write science articles with authority, Hansen concealed her gender. But nobody cared about this sort of thing in pulp fiction.

What about Andre Norton? The answer seems to be that her "male" byline was a requirement for juvenile historical novels, which is where she began publishing, and maybe even for juvenile science fiction – the idea that boys won't read a book with a girl's name on it – but ample evidence shows that this was never a requirement in the adult science fiction magazines; and Norton did not write much for the magazines anyway.

Then there is the elephant in the room, John W. Campbell. He is an unperson these days, but he was also the discoverer of Leigh Brackett, Katherine MacLean, Pauline Ashwell (a 2-time Hugo nominee) and the person who did the most to develop Anne McCaffrey. He also published a few holdovers from the earlier era, such as Amelia Reynolds Long. Davin also squelches a rumor about anti-Semitism at Street & Smith, Campbell's publisher during the period in question. One of the first Street and Smith issues of *Astounding,* December 1933 (edited by F. Orlin Tremaine), published a story by Jewish author Nat Schachner called "Ancestral Voices" in which a time-traveler, in late Roman times, kills a Hun, which causes various descendants of that Hun to disappear from the timeline, ranging from a famous Black boxer (Jack Johnson?) to a certain European dictator with a mustache. (This is the first science fiction story to make fun of Hitler, who had just come into power.) Campbell may have published Milton Rothman as "Lee Gregor," but he published Rothman's science articles (he was a nuclear physicist) under his own name, and published H.L. Gold under his own name, not to mention Isaac Asimov and, much later on, a kid named Robert Silverberg. The charge of anti-Semitism in science fiction is the most absurd of any of the various mythologies that Davin stomps flat. Most of the earliest science fiction editors, starting with Hugo Gernsback, and also including Mort Weisinger (*Thrilling Wonder*) and Donald A. Wollheim were Jewish, as were most of the early fans.

Davin does survey fandom. He finds a few women active in the late '30s. There are a lot of them in the letter columns of the SF magazines in the 1940s, some of them making amusing comments about the scantily-clad ladies on the covers of science fiction magazines, few asking for scantily-clad men in the interests of fairness. If the men were wearing space suits and the women were wearing little more than brass brassieres, did that mean that women were tougher and could endure the harsh environments of other planets better? Female readers, of whom there seem to have been a goodly number, wanted to know.

One of the most prolific letterhacks of this period, Marion "Astra" Zimmer, of course became a famous writer later on, as Marion Zimmer Bradley. And in 1952, Julian May, who was then usually known as "Judy Dikty," was chair of the worldcon. She told me once that some people expected her to be a figurehead, but she was not, and fired a few people who weren't doing their jobs.

A few words about naked people in the covers of science-fiction magazines for the benefit of those unfamiliar with SF magazines: *Weird Tales* started it, with Margaret Brundage covers in the 1930s. At this time, the covers of actual science fiction magazines, from Gernsback to Campbell, were pure as the driven snow. *Astounding* never went in for that sort of thing. There are a couple ladies-in-peril from the ultra-pulpy Clayton era (1930- early 1933), but the ladies are modestly clad. While there was an attempt to sex up both the covers and contents of *Marvel Science Stories* a.k.a. *Marvel Tales* in the late 1930s and produce what could only be called *Spicy Science Fiction,* howls of fan protest put a stop to this. The sexy covers (but not content) became ubiquitous on *Thrilling Wonder* and *Startling Stories* and were usually the work of Earle Bergey. These were imitated by other magazines and you can still see traces of that sort of thing on the digests of the 1950s. Special note should be made of *Planet Stories* heroines who, for all they might reveal a bare thigh, were usually quite as capable as any hero of smiting the hideous alien hordes with sword or blasting ray gun. The most iconic of all *Planet Stories* covers is that for Leigh Brackett's "The Black Amazon of Mars" (March 1951). She is fully clad and swinging a battle-axe. As we would say today, *Planet Stories* cover girls seem to have "agency."

So, why do people persist in believing this

mythology, in the face of the mounds of evidence to the contrary? One reason, as I have suggested, is that Davin's book is too expensive and poorly circulated to have had sufficient influence. He explains further. It is basically the same reason that people believe that Eskimos have 100 words for snow or that officials at Ellis Island in the early 20th century anglicized the names of immigrants or that scholars argued against Columbus on the grounds that the Earth is flat. If "everybody knows" a thing, then it does not require evidence. It is received wisdom and is never questioned.

Sometimes it's just ignorance. Davin quotes Philip Klass (William Tenn) as claiming that there were no women in science fiction before Judith Merril published "That Only a Mother" in *Astounding* (June 1948). When challenged on this, he angrily responded, regarding the others, "I've never heard of them!" As if that mattered. Thus he consigned whole generations of female SF writers to oblivion.

Had he ever heard of Margaret St. Clair, the most prolific female SF writer of the pre-1960 period? Maybe not. Collectors are familiar with the Bantam edition of her *The Sign of the Labrys* (1963) with its infamous back cover blurb that proclaimed the astonishing news "Women are writing science fiction!!!" and went on about how they are closer to "the moon pools and the earth tides," whatever that means. St. Clair had been publishing since 1946. *The Sign of the Labrys* was her third novel. Yet somebody thought this was a great novelty in 1963.

When Alice Sheldon decided to become "James Tiptree Jr." in 1968 she apparently thought that her gender would be held against her. She simply should have known better. She was a long-time SF reader and therefore would have been familiar with the magazines in which women appeared under their own names, as Davin has documented, by the hundreds.

Davin expresses only sadness when he quotes Karen Joy Fowler (one of the founders of the Tiptree Award) expressing intense gratitude at the women of the 1970s who made her own career possible, as if the Exclusion Myth were true. She too, out of ignorance presumably, consigned hundreds of women writers to oblivion.

(Ironically, editor Samuel Mines published a "Women are swarming into science fiction and are here to stay" editorial in *Thrilling Wonder* in December 1950. He thought the change had occurred in the middle-1930s. This is much closer to the truth.)

Another factor is that too many critics or writers simply have no first-hand knowledge of early science fiction. The anthologies can be misleading. There are no women at all in the enormously influential *Adventures in Time and Space* ed. Healy and McComas (1946). Groff Conklin's *The Best of Science Fiction* (1946) contains one story by Leslie F. Stone who, if you had not read the blurbs or seen her portraits in the Gernsback magazines, might be taken for a man. There is also (I will add) a widespread assumption that nothing before or outside of John Campbell's "Golden Age" of *Astounding* (1938-1950) really mattered. True, some of the material is really bad; some of those early women writers were less than geniuses, just like their male counterparts, so not everything is worth reprinting, but critics an anthologists have not paid a lot of attention to Gernsback's magazines or to the early *Thrilling Wonder* or to Ray Palmer's *Amazing* and *Fantastic Adventures*. If you only know science fiction from books, and have never looked at an old science fiction magazine, you are going to get a blinkered view.

This amnesia persists. Davin gets sociological about this (he is after all, an academic, a professor of history about why myths continue, and why people want to believe them. The *presumption* of prejudice is a major factor. There is ignorance. There is the deliberate distortion of the historical record. The storming of the imaginary

THE MAGAZINE OF
Fantasy and
Science Fiction

35¢   JANUARY

WILDERNESS
a novelet of The People by
ZENNA HENDERSON

ARTHUR C. CLARKE
POUL ANDERSON
JOHN DICKSON CARR
MILDRED CLINGERMAN

barricades didn't happen, so the date is movable. By 2050, no doubt, we will be learning that it only happened in 2000, or 2020, or whenever. Davin quotes Lloyd Biggle as saying, "Too often history is not what we find out. It is what we want to believe."

But for those of us who actually know better, Eric Leif Davin's *Partners in Wonder* suggests some intriguing things:

Women's SF of the first half of the 20th century is largely unexplored territory. It needs to be examined further. There is a lot of grist for the Ph.D. mills there. Davin has provided us an excellent guide, having listed all the stories. One thought that comes to me is that if C. L. Moore was the 116th woman to sell a story to *Weird Tales* in 1933 and the magazine in its first incarnation continued until 1954, then somebody could do an anthology called *The Women of Weird Ta-*

les. Should I do it? I realize could. Should I do it under a female pseudonym? We egalitarians believe everyone should be treated equally so, no. Right now I am editing a series of *Weird Tales* anthologies for Centipede Press, but not precisely on this theme. Of course there are stories by women in them.

I look back to Davin's dedication. A few of these women I've met or even interviewed. Many of the names are familiar. All published SF before 1960. Karen Anderson, Pauline Ashwell (Pauline Whitby), Leigh Brackett, Marion Zimmer Bradley, Rosel George Brown, Doris Piktin Buck, Mildred Clingerman, Mary Elizabeth Counselman, Betsy Curtis, Catherine de Camp, Miriam Allen DeFord, Leah Bodine Drake, Carol Emshwiller, Phyllis Gotlieb, Clare Winger Harris, Hazel Heald, Zenna Henderson, E (Edna) Mayne Hull, Shirley Jackson, Madeleine L'Engle, Anne McCaffrey, Winona McClintic, Katherine MacLean, Julian May, "Andre Norton," Jane Rice, Joanna Russ, Margaret St. Clair, Wilmar Shiras, Evelyn E. Smith, Helen Weinbaum, Kate Wilhelm. (If you're curious, I interviewed Brackett, Bradley, MacLean, and May.)

And there are lots more you *haven't* heard off, not to mention stories you haven't read. This is where the exploration can begin. Davin tells us that, as Anthony Boucher perceived, there was an entire feminine "counterculture" in SF of the 1950s and that the women of that period wrote in a distinctly different manner, addressing different themes. At this point Davin moves from bibliography to interpretation. Start there. In my case, I've had a nice copy of Clare Winger Harris's 1947 collection *Away from the Here and Now* on my shelves for some years. I think it's time for me to read it.

Eileen Kernaghan:
Wild Talent & Fine Friend

Casey Wolf

Eileen Kernaghan is a good human, one with an incisive and curious mind who loves life and laughter and hard work and whose kindness and good humored outlook on the world make her a pleasure to be around. Add to that Eileen's skill and talent as a writer and her dedication not only to her own literary work but to the arts community itself – including the once marginal world of speculative fiction (science fiction and fantasy, Eileen's primary writing genre) – and you have a woman who has been both an inspiration and a mentor to many.

I had the great good fortune, as a beginning writer and science fiction fan, of befriending Eileen at VCon 11, Vancouver, B.C.'s oldest science fiction convention, in May 1983. She was an established, professional writer and I was still finding my feet, both in writing and in confidence. Eileen's bright energy and easy way of being with people attracted me. I can't recall exactly how it happened – perhaps I'd participated in a writing workshop that Eileen was in – but I glommed onto her, and was soon invited by her to join the Burnaby Writers Society and eventually her own speculative fiction critique group, Helix.

Over time Eileen has had an enormous influence on my writing, and as well, become a very dear friend.

A Life of Words

There are people (like me) who are writers, and there are people like Eileen in whose life nearly every element has something to do with writing. An author, a poet, a teacher and mentor of those learning the craft, a used-bookstore owner (with husband Pat), a host of poetry performances and attendee/participant at many a literary conference, reading and launch, and of course, someone with books of all ages in every corner of her home, Eileen has built a life out of words.

Born Eileen Pritchard in 1939, she grew up on a dairy farm outside of Grindrod, B.C. Many of her childhood memories have to do with reading and writing. Her mother taught her to read at age five and Eileen was soon reading everything she could get her hands on and writing stories of her own. Her webpage lists among her early influences, "[t]he reading material ... on the family shelves – Greek myths, historical novels, G.A. Henty's boys' adventure books, a musty collection of *Weird Tales* and *Thrilling Wonder Stories*..."

Her reminiscences reveal more: her father getting up an hour early so he could read his romance novels before going out to milk the cows; the day her aunt got the creeps when she walked in on a very young Eileen reading the Hansard (parliamentary) reports (which was her habit); her revision of the tale of Peter Rabbit at around six years old; a story she wrote at eight that drew heavily on "Alice in Wonderland" ("Molly in Mouseland"), which her teacher was so taken with he asked for a copy. (When they met thirty years later at a writing conference he mentioned that he still had it.) The pleasure of reading *Cold Comfort Farm* by Stella Gibbons or *Precious Bane* by Mary Webb while waiting in the barn for the next load of hay. (Her job was to raise the hay up into the loft by means of pulleys and draft horses or, later, a tractor.) The kindly vicar and his wife who would bring her novels to read. The fellow in Grindrod with a tiny, private lending library up above a store.

Eileen had parents and teachers who encouraged her literary aspirations. Her parents bought her first typewriter when she was twelve, and her mother acted as her research assistant (making the phone calls to get needed information) when, at about the same age, she worked as a reporter for the *Enderby Commoner.*

Eileen's first professional publication appeared in the *Vancouver Sun* in 1951. Unbeknownst to her publisher, she was twelve years old. A tale of a boy and a wolverine in the backwoods of northern Canada, she confesses she had little real life experience in the matter, but clearly she was able to fake it well enough to convince the editors. Her next story they rejected as being "juvenile." Well, she *was* twelve.

"I began to write seriously when I was twelve. I sold a children's story to *The Vancouver Sun*, for which I was paid twelve dollars and sixty-five cents. What an epiphany—that I could earn money by doing what I liked best! In Grade Seven I wrote a rousing tale of interplanetary adventure in weekly installments, which I handed round to my classmates. There was no pay for that one,

but I learned to keep my audience interested by always ending on a cliff-hanger. Starting around the same time, I was the Grindrod correspondent for *The Enderby Commoner* newspaper, reporting on births, marriages, and other social events in our farming village of 600 people. (It helped to listen in shamelessly on our party line.) In high school I wrote and produced a radio play (*The Legend of Sleepy Hollow*) for the Vernon radio station, joined the debating team (and ended up writing the arguments for both sides), wrote the candidates' speeches for the school elections, and scripted the cheers for the cheerleading squad. (Nobody would have dreamed of making me a cheerleader!)

"The high point of my Grade Twelve English class was our production of *Wild Bill Shakespeare Rides Again* by the Stratford-on-Shuswap Players (script mostly by me). We gave minor roles to both of the English teachers, and conscripted the science teacher to help us create a spectacular (though harmless) explosion for our version of *Macbeth*. We invited the whole community, and played to a full house."

"Interview: Eileen Kernaghan, Poet and Novelist" by C. June Wolf, *Strange Horizons*, (28 March 2005).

Upon completing high school, Eileen left Grindrod to train as a teacher in Vancouver. After finishing her studies, she married Patrick Kernaghan (her university sweetheart) and moved back to the interior of B.C. She taught primary school in small towns briefly and later, for many years, taught adults creative writing at Kyle Centre in Port Moody and Shadbolt Centre for the Arts in Burnaby.

When Eileen and Pat began raising a family, she put her teaching and writing on hold for a few years and focussed on her home and family. Once the children were all in school, she determined that Wednesday mornings from 10 – 12 A.M. would be her time to write.

Since then she has published nine novels and two collections, one of speculative poetry and the other of short stories, as well as contributing to many anthologies and magazines, including *PRISM international*, *On Spec*, *Tesseracts*, *Pulp Literature,* and *The Year's Best Fantasy & Horror*.

Her second professional publication came in 1971, when her novella "Starcult" (available online) was the cover story for the Nov. - Dec. issue of *Galaxy Magazine*. Influenced by everything from Jane Austen to *Weird Tales*, Eileen developed the ability to craft good plots and interesting characters, weave believable magic, and tackle a welcome breadth of subject matter in a consistently fine writing style. Her first novel, *Journey To Aprilioth* (1980) won a silver medal for original paperback fiction from The West Coast Review of Books and *Songs from the Drowned Lands* (1983), its sequel, won the Canadian Science fiction and Fantasy Award (originally the Casper, now the Aurora Award). *Sarsen Witch*, the culminating book in the series, was shortlisted for the same prize. *The Snow Queen* won the Canadian Science Fiction and Fantasy Award (Aurora) for 2001 and was shortlisted for the 2009 Sunburst Award for Excellence in Canadian Literature of the Fantastic. Eileen was inducted into the Canadian Science Fiction and Fantasy Hall of Fame in 2019.

Eileen's first young adult fantasy, *Dance of the Snow Dragon* (1995), was the result of research she did for a non-fiction book on reincarnation. Set in 18th century Bhutan and based on Tibetan Buddhist mythology, *Dance of the Snow Dragon* follows a young boy, Sangay, who embarks on a magic-filled journey to Shambhala. Her next book, *The Snow Queen* (2000), intertwines the Robber Maiden fable, with its echoes of northern shamanism, and the Finnish mythological cycle, the Kalevala, in a retelling of Hans Christian Andersen's classic tale. *The Alchemist's Daughter* followed in 2004. Set in

Elizabethan England, a year before the Armada, *The Alchemist's Daughter* sees its heroine immersed in a world of scrying, alchemy, and natural magic as she sets out to save her father and her country. *Winter on the Plain of Ghosts: a novel of Mohenjo-daro*, published the same year, is possibly my favorite of Eileen's books. It's told through the eyes of a man who had not been intended to survive childhood, and looks back on a long life in the epic times of the collapse of the ancient Indus Valley civilization. In *Wild Talent: a Novel of the Supernatural* (2008), a young Scottish farm worker, Jeannie Guthrie, flees her home country in fear of being burned as a witch. Arriving in London, she encounters the world of the 19th century's greatest students of the occult, while simultaneously discovering her own unwanted powers. A related tale about the now adult Jeannie Guthrie's orphaned ward, *Sophie, in Shadow* (2014), takes place in India in the later years of the British Raj. Against the background of growing unrest in India and a European war, Sophie begins to experience shocking visions from past and future, while spies, kidnappers, and mystics populate her present. Finally, Eileen's speculative poetry was collected in *Tales from the Holograph Woods* (2009), and her short fiction, which ranges from science fiction to dark fantasy and includes several tales linked to her novels, is gathered in *Dragon-Rain and Other Stories* (2013).

The first thing that strikes me whenever I read something of Eileen's is that her writing is so damn beautiful. Much of her fantasy has magic in it, magic that contains the astonishing, the transformative. But half of the magic is her sensory and revelatory perception of the mundane, her way of seeing worlds in their barest details and bringing us right inside that vision.

This may be a good time for a few examples.

Observe these elegant ancient bones

lying composed, in decent order, in their

tombs.

See, here is the lady who was late, and last,

carrying her silver headband in her robe.

Death was quicker than she, and to her shame,

it found her

indifferently prepared.

from "Ur" *Tales from the Holograph Woods*

===

"You must begin by breathing right," Wanjur told him. "Set your bow aside for now – we must begin at the beginning." And he showed Sangay how an archer must breathe: how each action in turn – nocking the arrow, raising and drawing the bow, loosing the shot – began on an in-drawn breath, was sustained on a held breath, and ended with a slow and gentle breathing out. Gradually Sangay mastered the trick of it; and as he learned to control his breathing, so too did he learn to relax the stiff muscles of his arms and shoulders and legs, letting his two hands do all the work. But still, each time he opened his fingers to loose the arrow from the string, the force of recoil made his hand jerk and sent the shot wild.

"That is the last thing any archer learns," Wanjur said.

"It will come, in time."

from *Dance of the Snow Dragon*

===

This morning, when I visited the warehouse, Akalla was breaking the seal on a chest full of luxury goods – among them some jars of unguent imported from the western deserts of

WINTER
ON THE
PLAIN OF GHOSTS
a novel of Mohenjo-daro

EILEEN KERNAGHAN

Meluhha. I took one home with me and opened it in the privacy of my bedchamber. Released from its stone container, the rich, oily perfume awoke a rush of memories.

Once again I breathed the fragrance of oleander, growing high up in a desolate hill pass. I heard the throbbing of the skin drums, the wistful music of the reed-pipes; and the shrill voice of the desert wind, crying across the parched, dun-coloured plain. But underneath the scent of spice and sun and flowers, there was a hint of something darker, muskier – a cloying, sweet-sour odour of the swamp. And there rose in my mind's eye a vision of the great Meluhhan capitals, those once noble cities of the plains. I saw them crouched behind their crumbling walls like enormous stricken animals, choking on their own poisoned breath.

from *Winter on the Plain of Ghosts – a novel of Mohenjo-daro*

===

On Sunday, I went to visit Alexandra. She seemed to me a little pale and subdued. When I asked after her health, she told me, "I am well enough, but I have had a very curious adventure."

One of the guests presently staying at the house of the Supreme Gnosis is a landscape artist from Paris, called M. Jacques Villemain. Alexandra seems quite smitten, although of course she will not admit to this.

She describes him as a tall, pale, rather solemn young man, with an otherworldly air, not at all like an *artiste parisien*. He is *très sérieux*, she says. "I cannot imagine him, dressed it up in a costume at the Beaux Arts Ball."

He was a mystic, he informed Alexandra, though not religious, and he invited Alexandra to his room so that she could see some of his work. His landscapes, he said, had a secret reality that ordinary people could not perceive. Of course Alexandra, who is insatiably curious, was intrigued; though she did not think the English would approve of her visiting a young man alone in his room. However, he reassured her, saying that adepts of the Supreme Gnosis regarded such conventions as absurd, and in any case, all Gnostics were pure in spirit. "Besides," he said in all seriousness, "I will leave the door ajar" – which made Alexandra laugh.

All she saw at first was simple landscapes. "They seemed accomplished enough, with a certain charm, though whether they were anything out of the ordinary, I was not qualified to judge. But M. Villemain urged me to look deeper, and gradually, I began to see the paintings with different eyes. It was, as he said, as though another, stranger reality hovered just beneath the surface."

Everywhere Alexandra looked – rocks, flowers, bushes, mountains – she saw an unsettling double image. In one painting, a vast deserted heath stretched away to the edge of a lake, with snow-capped peaks rising out of the mists beyond. All across the heath were slender, indistinct forms that were at once trees or bushes, and at the same time *something else*. I saw her shiver a little as she went on, "Somehow they had become men, or animals, and as they looked out at me, their faces were full of cunning and dreadful malice. At that moment I felt quite terrified."

But needless to say, Alexandra's quick curiosity overcame her fear, and she reached out to touch the picture. As she did so, M. Villemain suddenly cried out, "Be careful. You could be pulled in."

"Into what?" she asked an alarm.

"Into the landscape. It is dangerous."

By now I was quite caught up in this strange story. I leaned forward in excitement. "And what happened then?"

Alexandra shrugged. "That is all that happened. I felt all at once overcome with a terrible fatigue, and so we went downstairs for toast and tea."

I longed for more. It was as though Alexandra had strayed to the edge of faerie, and returned to tell me only half the tale.

She laughed, as though to dismiss it all as fancy, but there was an edge to her laughter that told me the experience had left her shaken. In truth, I am beginning to fear a little for Alexandra, in case her boldness and her curiosity may take her into places better left unexplored.

from *Wild Talent – a Novel of The Supernatural*

===

I hope that these samples give a sense of the range of Eileen's interests as a writer. From stories of peril and daring to poems of visceral enchantment, from thought-provoking science fiction to gracefully wrought fantasy, from beings of myth and fairy-tale to historical figures like occult luminary Madame Blavatsky and mould-breaking adventurer Alexandra David-Néel, Eileen's adventuresome mind, once seized on an idea, delves deeply into every aspect of the world she is taking us to and the characters she is discovering in her tale. (Eileen is not the sort of writer who works from an outline. She gets an idea, engages in extensive research, determines the ending, and goes on a voyage of discovery.)

I know we tend to feel friendly toward the writing of our comrades, but the substance and quality of everything she has written have made Eileen into one of my favourite writers. She's one of the few authors I will happily reread (always off to the next adventure, me). Her simple but beautiful writing style became the standard I unconsciously aspired to; it was in large part Eileen's influence that moved me to work hard to achieve the best I could in my own writing. In addition, her gentle and humorous way of encouraging me in my writing life, her ability to put up with my anxious and sometimes outright touchy feelings about it, made her an amazing mentor. Her clear concern for the well-being and creative life of not just me but every one of her students and colleagues is unstinting, which leads me to the next topic:

The Alchemist's Daughter

a novel

EILEEN KERNAGHAN

By the author of the Aurora Prize winner, *The Snow Queen*

Public-Spirited Eileen

For someone who has not gone out of her way to call attention to herself, Eileen has done much good in the writing community. She has supported countless people, both in and outside of formal settings, who are trying to find the best ways to express themselves in their writing. She's given advice, critiques, and praise; written endorsements, gone to endless readings and launches, and otherwise provided concrete assistance to other writers.

Burnaby Writers Society

A longstanding member of the Burnaby Writers Society, Eileen faithfully attended their monthly meetings and published their newsletter. Under her captaincy, the newsletter was, in those pre-Internet days particularly, an extremely useful tool. Not only were there updates on who had published what and where, and what prizes members had won, as well as, of course, announcements of BWS competitions and other business, but Eileen included lengthy lists of current markets, and other lists of those that had gone to the publishing graveyard since the previous newsletter. These markets were nearly all culled by Eileen from various sources. Because of its usefulness, the newsletter's reach went well beyond the society, with non-members frequently subscribing to it.

I wish now that I had once thought to save any of these newsletters. I have a clear memory of legal size, coloured pages, beautifully laid out, with a literary and lovely feel to them. (This memory sends me back to my halcyon days with Gestetners, but that's another and only partially fannish story.)

VCon

It may have been at the yearly VCon (Vancouver Con) that I saw the most sides of Eileen. On panels and at readings, depending on their nature, Eileen revealed herself to be a discerning, unpretentious, and gifted woman, sometimes animated, sometimes quiet; playful or serious. At the Turkey Readings, where panelists read out the most abominable scenes they can find in the most tired of science fiction novels, fans zealously perform the parts while other fans pay to make it stop – and start – and stop. Eileen was silly in her earnestness, great at finding appalling scenes, and the laughter was uproarious. She participated as well in The Lonely Cry Theatre, and later, The Pallahaxi Players Readers Theatre. The Lonely Cry Theatre was a readers theatre group with ridiculous scripts (mostly written by fellow SF writer, Mike Coney) and slapdash props. Eileen threw herself into the fun without reserve.

When not on panels, Eileen could generally be found in the Dealers Room, either with husband Pat and their Neville Books used book offerings, or at the SF Canada literature table.

Teacher and Shaper of Writers

After many years of hearing Eileen talk about her writing classes I finally joined one, travelling from Vancouver to the Kyle Centre in Port Moody every Thursday morning, going far out of my way to meet her in New Westminster, where she lived. She would pick me up at the Skytrain station near her home and we would enjoy a half hour of visiting while she drove.

EILEEN KERNAGHAN

WILD TALENT

A Novel of the Supernatural

The classes were excellent. Eileen set a controlled but easy tone that kept us on track but permitted people to relax and take risks in showing their writing, and over time to work toward a high but attainable standard of craft. As a teacher, her approach was even-handed and (usually!) gentle. All points of view on a piece were considered and chewed over, but from time to time her instructor's prerogative was exercised and she would rule on a point of argument. She could see the jewels underneath the crust of her students' writing and found ways to help us steadily polish our work. This allowed us to hone our own critical skills, as well.

A great mix of people attended over the years and everyone was welcomed equally. The affection and respect that her students held her in was obvious, and I was not the only one who was sorry when Eileen left Kyle Centre at last.

Helix/Dangling on the Edge

In our speculative writing group, Helix, which met for many years and is presently on hiatus, Eileen became our grande dame. We were always happy to receive her short, perfect chapters. On the one hand, we wished for more so we could carry on reading, and on the other hand we had to work hard to find anything *to* critique. (We were generally able to find some small thing, and lively discussions would ensue as we disagreed with each other on almost every point.) When it came to her critiques of our work, she was gracious and always fair, treating every manuscript with equal respect and dignity, no matter how the writer might be struggling with his or her work.

At one point, we decided as a group to do performance-y poetry readings at Eileen and Pat's used bookstore in Burnaby. It was a bright, airy place and we were able to clear enough space to pack twenty or so souls in. Eileen took care of making tastefully literate (and often humorous) flyers and bookmarks to advertise the events, using illustrations from old novels, which lent something both dignified and silly at the same time. A good metaphor for our events, I suppose. Maybe it's a good way of describing Eileen, herself.

Eileen's contributions to her literary communities have not gathered fame to her, but they have certainly been appreciated by those around her. In 1992 she received the Canada 124 Medal for community arts activism, and later that decade, under the ruse of going to yet another reading by a burgeoning writer, she was given a surprise celebration, where members of the audience took the stage, speaking of their respect and affection for, and their personal debt to Eileen, as well as reading aloud from her work.

Eileen, Mentor and Friend

Eileen's kindness and generosity extended beyond all of these venues. She has always supported people in their hearts, as well; she certainly did me, encouraging me not to give up when things seemed too hard, helping me to believe in my writing, even when it did not fit with the styles then desired and was difficult to sell.

In her working days, which continued until the COVID lockdown put an end to them, Eileen was wont to listen compassionately to the cares of her colleagues, friends, and protégés whenever called to, and to offer brief and practical advice which could often be boiled down to, "You can do it.

Carry on." Or, "Let it go." With Eileen, the margins between mentor and friend were not severe. I think that many if not most of her students will have come to think of her as a dear friend over time.

I remember her taking in a young writer who found herself in serious difficulties, sheltering her and doing what she could to help. She provided a listening ear for another colleague, over decades, who struggles painfully with her mental health. There was once long ago when I found myself badly frightened by something that had happened and feeling too vulnerable to stay alone. Although we didn't have a practice of staying overnight at each other's places, Eileen was the person I turned to, to ask for a couple of days' respite. She gave it without hesitation, or rather, after the initial hesitation of great surprise. She and her husband, Pat, were very kind in putting me up for a night or two and just being normal with me, which was all I needed. Company and friends, and a moment to come down from the fright I'd experienced. It stands out as one of the kindest things anyone has done for me: to trust that I knew what I needed, and to be welcoming and relaxed enough to say yes. (Of course, Eileen and Pat had raised three children and welcomed their friends into the house. Indeed, they stayed in contact with many of them, themselves, when the grown children moved away. So, I suppose they had quite a bit of practice under their belt when it came to young people [in my case, young*ish*] needing a hand.)

Eileen's contributions to her literary communities have been deeply appreciated by those around her. In 1992 she received the Canada 124 Medal for community arts activism, and later that decade, under the ruse of going to yet another reading by a burgeoning writer (me), she was given a surprise celebration, where members of the audience took the stage and spoke warmly of their respect and affection for, and their personal debt to, Eileen, as well as reading aloud from her work.

My Friend Eileen

I have a heart full of things I could say about Eileen Kernaghan. The world I entered because of her brought me into a sphere of people I could learn from, laugh with, and shape a life with. In large part I have Eileen's friendship to thank for giving me the sense of welcome and belonging that allowed me, a much more socially anxious and shy person than I normally show, to stay long enough for those seeds to bear fruit. The Helix writing group and Eileen's classes allowed me to slowly grow into a writer I can be contented with. Our many, many hours of conversation – about life, about the written word, our shared love – our walks and readings given or attended, books launched and tears shed (mine, generally), our kindly affection toward each other created an enduring friendship.

Over the three years since COVID sprang upon us, till her departure for Saltspring Island in August, I've seen Eileen more than ever. Living alone and far from her family and friends (though surrounded by friendly neighbours), Eileen did not have an obvious "bubble" when COVID restrictions came in. So we became bubble-mates. Instead of the more event-oriented occasions much of our time together had been centered around, or the one or two hour visits that were the normal tea-walk-talk fare of previous years, we spent whole days together. Some of what we had to look at then was hard stuff: the isolation that COVID brought us, the danger for someone like Eileen who is vulnerable to respiratory disease, major life changes we must face as we age. But it was good to talk about those things together. We grew closer as a result.

Confidence is something that was not in big supply in my childhood. Much as I love to write, I doubted myself constantly, and had a shaky sense of belonging in the writing community. Eileen encouraged me not to give up when things felt too hard, helping me to believe in my writing, even when it was not easy to get published stories that did not fit in with the styles of writing commonly sought after. And much as I loved to perform, do readings, sing, and the like, I found myself sick with anxiety every time. For years I would be in tears after every performance, just as I had worked myself to the bone beforehand trying to get each story, each poem, each *word* right.

Eileen was someone who had unflagging belief in me as a writer and as a person. Her presence, her permission for me to be a mess if I had to and be brilliant anyway, to feel pride in what I did instead of embarrassment and shame, made my writing life a possibility. Where twice before in my life unkind words had left me unable to write for years, Eileen's kindness allowed me to write for the rest of my life. I cannot possibly thank her enough for that.

Now that Eileen no longer lives on the Lower Mainland, our bubble has burst. We have phone calls, which are a blessing, but our hours of palling around are over. She is now near to family, which is an exceedingly good thing. But I miss her very much.

Waving at you over on Saltspring, Eileen. Sending lots and lots of love. Thank you for being a friend and a most excellent mentor. Thank you most especially for being you.

Note: To learn more about Eileen's books, and for her bibliography, see https://www.eileenkernaghan.ca

To read "Starcult" in *Galaxy* Nov. – Dec. 1971: https://isfdb.org/cgi-bin/pl.cgi?58608

You can find her *Strange Horizons* interview at: https://web.archive.org/web/20071113232646/http://www.strangehorizons.com/2005/20050328/i-kernaghan-a.shtml

Her 30 May 2019 interview, "Interview with Eileen Kernaghan, Author," on my blog, *Another Fine Day in the Scriptorium*, can be found at: https://finedayscriptorium.blogspot.com/2019/05/interview-with-eileen-kernaghan-author.html

A New Golden Age?

Bob Jennings

While checking the nomination lists from last year's Hugo Awards/Dragon Con/Locus Awards and more I discovered that I had only read one of the novels on the nomination lists of all the big awards (and it was not a winner on any of them either). I was properly shocked. I decided that this year I was going to make a serious effort to keep myself better posted on the field, so I have been reading a lot of the newly released stf titles, all obtained through the local town library or the interlibrary loan system, and I have been pleasantly surprised to find lots of really excellent reading material out there.

The thing about being an old science fiction fan is that over the course of many decades you have read a lot of this stuff, so you tend to notice right away when the same old themes, the same old stereotypes, the same kinds of characters get reused over and over again. It's a truism that the older you get, the more sophisticated your tastes become, because you've encountered so much of the stuff before. It's also a truism that human nature does not change, which is why the plays of

the ancient Greek playwrights are just as interesting and as relevant today as they were when they were originally written thousands of years ago.

Those realities place a pretty heavy burden on modern science fiction writers. They have to not only come up with something new and unusual in the way of plots, but they also have to create characters that will make the setup premises workable while keeping the stories both fresh and interesting.

Well, I am happy to relate that 2022 has been a very successful one for the world of science fiction/fantasy. The new crop of science fiction/fantasy writers has not only managed to come up with a bunch of new ideas, but they have also managed to generate characters that are both interesting and who also successfully keep the plots and adventures moving.

Which naturally leads right in to---

THE EXTRACTIONIST by Kimberly Unger; Tachyon Books; 293 pages; Trade Paperback; July 2022

This is a fantasy novel masquerading as science fiction. The premise is that in the not too distant future computer technology has made significant advances to the point where people can become hard-wired, with complex computer systems built right into their brains. In this future world there is a never ending radio wave flow of information about everything everywhere that savvy computer whizzes, especially people with X-advance

interfaces such as our heroine Eliza McKay has can tap into. The setup says that McKay can also direct and control this at the local level, including writing effective computer code in her mind on the fly, and have it applied immediately to the data flow (the Stream) and seeing its effects become reality immediately (apparently no hard core engineering work is needed in this world).

I'm a firm believer that when reading any kind of science fiction novel you have to Buy The Bit; that is, accept the background and the basic premises the author sets up in order to make the story work, then go with it to see what the author has accomplished with the setup and the plot as it unfolds.

However this was a pretty large pill for me to swallow. Although I am pretty much a computer and mathematical dunce, it was very difficult to accept this setup, even though Ms Unger handles the setup very well and only

rarely steps outside the fictional technological world she has created. I just can't see much difference here between the computer code spinning McKay uses effortlessly to direct and change reality and a mage knight swinging a magical sword or a Doctor Strange character wiggling his fingers around and muttering a few gobbley-gook words to have something he wants magically happen without any rational explanation for any of that besides the generic term "hey, it's all magic!". Except in this case, "Hey, it's all computer-ese!" So far as I can see all the computing stuff in this book might as well be magic too, since it doesn't seem to have any kind of connection with the real world at all.

To be fair, some of the computer-magic in the story is clearly nanotech, and A-I robotics, not computer tech. The things that get done are often the work of nano-robots, the stuff scientists and micro-engineers say can be literally built from molecule molding levels upward and assigned to do specific tasks, like keeping carpets clean of dirt, or eating food spots off dishes. In this story robots from small to large have A-I intelligence built in and are told to handle any number of routine tasks, so there is that much anchorage in the world of science/science fiction.

But, be that as it may, Ms Unger handles the story very well. The X3 enhanced computer designer Eliza McKay has lost her government license to fiddle around designing new computer and nanotech A–I systems because of a never quite disclosed foul up, and now works as an Extractionist. In this world people can send their personas into virtual worlds where they can stay and experience the artificial world of gaming, or pornographic fantasies, or mathematical interfaces, or business extrapolations, or whatever. The costs are cheap, the lure is often addicting, and sometimes the personas get trapped in the digital world and cannot be retrieved by normal means. That's when an Extractionist needs to be called in, to pull the persona out of the virtual universe and moved back into the physical body in the real world.

What starts out as a semi-secret extraction of a government investigator who was in the Stream trying to find information on possible illegal activities his agency is checking on escalates rapidly. First, the persona doesn't want to be extracted, then outside forces, presumably employed by the person who is being investigated, try to break up the operation. Then the plot swiftly surges forward as McKay is physically and cybernetically attacked by people or agencies unknown. Everyone either wants the persona of Mike to be extracted and contained, or allowed to slowly degrade and die. McKay is the only one who seems able to complete the job of actually pulling Mike's persona out, that's if she can live long enough to get the word coding processed properly.

This is a high tension, fast moving, suspenseful story that holds the reader interest from first to last. There are any number of quirks and red herrings along the way to keep the plot twisting in unexpected ways. Ms. Unger is a good writer, and as mentioned, once you Buy The Bit, she remains remarkably consistent with the perimeters of the universe she has created. The heroine is interesting and the plot works very well to keep the reader completely engaged in the story.

Author Kimberly Unger is a computer whiz herself. A designer of computer games going back to the early days of the field, she also has degrees in English and Illustration. In addition to writing computer games, and science fiction, she also gives lectures on the intersection of art and computer code. *The Extractionist* is her second full length novel, and it is a good one, well worth reading. I'm sure it won't be her last.

THE MOONDAY LETTERS by Emmi Itaranta; Titan Books; July 2022, 368 pages

Ms. Itaranta is a Finnish science fiction author who writes in English, and has been both nominated for and received awards for her previous novels and short fiction. This book will definitely enhance her already stellar reputation.

The novel is primarily composed of an ongoing series of letters written by Lumi Salo to her husband Sol Uriarte. She is traveling to meet Sol at a scientific conference held at Datong, on planet Mars, but after giving a short interview to the news media after the conference, he has disappeared. As events develop, it turns out that he and several of his co-workers have vanished from their work site, along with many specimens and much research material. A fully functioning above surface rover vehicle has also been stolen, and the police fear foul play is involved.

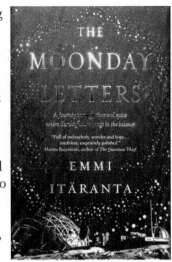

Lumi is a practicing spiritual healer, while Sol is a researcher primarily studying fungi with a goal of creating symbiosis plants that can help purify pollution problems. In this story, set several hundred years in the future, planet Earth is an environmental disaster. Mars, Luna, and some solar moons along with other asteroids are inhabited, but a lot of the off-planet population lives in enormous manufactured space cities, cylinder cities they are called, all self contained and self sustaining. These cylinder cities orbit Mars, Luna and other satellites.

Earth's surviving population is generally treated as pariahs. Only a token limited number of earth dwellers are allowed to emigrate off planet, and none of the governments of the outer planets or their satellites will assist the inhabitants of the home world, who have wrecked their planet through centuries of pollution and unregulated environmental disasters.

As the story unfolds Lumi's peaceful life is shattered by the apparent kidnapping of her spouse and his co-workers. Despite some cryptic messages received from Sol, including several that beg her not to try to look for him, Lumi is relentless in her efforts to locate Sol, and she is also relentless in trying to uncover connections from his past that might have led to his present disappearance.

In the mix we get information about the future space going civilization, and also about Lumi's past. She grew up the only child of an impoverished family in the northern European part of Earth, and through a series of mental flashbacks we learn how she became a healer, able to walk the spirit paths to cure disease and personality disorders. The marriage between Lumi and Sol is an odd one, the spiritual almost magical healing ability of Lumi, and the hard scientific practicability of Sol.

The writing here is sometimes almost lyrical, as the protagonist struggles to be light and upbeat in the face of this horrible personal crisis. In the process we learn a great deal about her background without the necessity of info dumps or other clumsy writing clichés. The book's title comes from their current home, Moonday House, located at Harmonia on Mars.

This is a remarkable book, beautifully written, with an intriguing plot that grows in complexity as it unfolds. The framing device and the method of filling the reader in on the universe its characters inhabit is both subtle yet completely effective, evoking a sense of wonder while maintaining a connecting relationship with our own world. The characterization of Lumi and the supporting characters, primarily Sol's immediate family, is expertly developed, and the prose is both engrossing and compelling as the reader followings along in the events of this unusual adventure.

I highly recommend this book. It is a vol- ume you will remember, and it is a volume I am certain will show up on the nomination lists of all the major awards connected with the science fiction field.

HIDDEN PICTURES by Jason Rekulak; Flatiron Books; April 2022; 384 pages

This book is being advertised and promoted as a horror thriller. It even has a glowing recommendation from Stephen King as a prominent cover blurb. Do not be swayed by this hype. I am well aware that there are lots of people who turn and run the other way when the very mention of a horror novel comes up in conversation.

Hidden Pictures is not a horror novel. It is an unusual story involving supernatural elements, and a mystery story that escalates and becomes a genuine thriller as it nears its climax.

The plot is deceptively simple. Mallory Quinn, 21 years old, is a recovering drug addict. She got hooked on Oxycodone due to injuries and guilt from a car wreck that killed her sister, an accidence she is convinced she caused. She switched to heron because it was lots cheaper than Oxycodone, and the slide downhill was very rapid. But thanks to the intervention of a dedicated brother figure at a half-way house she is well on the road to recovery, or so she believes.

With the help of her mentor she applies for and gets a job as a summer nanny for a five year old boy named Teddy who lives with his parents in a very up-scale community after they recently returned from Barcelona, Spain. Parents Ted and Caroline Maxwell agree to hire her conditionally, with some limitations on her behavior and movement, all of which she readily agrees to. She gets a little converted cottage behind the big house to live in, and soon bonds with young Teddy. She likes the community, goes for nightly runs to stay fit, watches Hallmark movies on her tablet, and hopes that this summer seasonal job will turn into a full time employment situation.

Teddy is very shy and resists socializing with other children, but, like a lot of kids he loves to draw. He is seldom without his pad and set of crayons, but sometimes when he draws there is a black, shaggy, bestial figure in the picture. He says this is his imaginary friend Annie. Confronted he cheerfully admits that he knows Annie isn't a real person, but the images continue to appear in the kid's drawings and then one day there is a picture of a man dragging a woman by the hair through the woods. Then Teddy's drawings began to become more detailed and more sophisticated, demonstrating artistic talent far beyond the ability of a five year old child, while the subjects become increasingly more sinister.

Mallory sets out to discover what these images mean, and why Teddy is drawing this stuff, which leads to information about a decades old murder of a local artist that took place on the property, in the very tool shed that has become her own converted cottage living space.

This is a very well written story that appears to progress at a leisurely fashion with plenty of characterization of the heroine and all the supporting characters, but this is a deceptive skill of the author, because the plots moves very rapidly. Aiding the development of the plot is the able assistance of artists Will Steele and Doogie Horner who provide black and white illustrations to go along with the narrative. These drawings, supposedly done by Teddy and carefully positioned throughout the book, graphically and eerily display the rapidly changing mood that is driving the crux of the story.

Unraveling the mystery, trying to find out why Teddy is being used as the human sketching machine for the unknown seemingly supernatural creature, and what it all means is the ongoing plot of the story. Answers do not come easy, and there are false steps along the way as the tension begins to mount. This is a brilliant mix of ghosts, murder mystery, supernatural possession, high tension thrills, and unusual plot twists, all built around the personal challenges Mallory faces as she tries to rebuild her life. The climax and its aftermath are both realistically and supernaturally satisfying.

This is one terrific book, a title I recommend without hesitation. Just make sure you give yourself plenty of time once you start reading, because this is one of those novels that once you begin you are not going to want to put down until you finish it. I fully expect this book to be among the top contenders for all of the awards in the supernatural/horror/thriller categories, and it is a story that will stay with you long after you have read that final page.

VENOMOUS LUMPSUCKER; by Ned Beauman; Soho; July 2022; ISBN: 978-1641294126; hardcover, 336 pages

Ned Beauman is an award winning British author who is involved in environmental research and environmental activism when he isn't writing science fiction. This novel is a natural extension of his interests.

In the not very distant future thousands of species are going extinct on planet earth every year. When the Chinese panda almost went extinct, a whole new industry sprang up to help the human race preserve those species that remain. Or, as the author suggests several times, maybe this new system is just there to salve our collective guilt. Industries and nations can trade off or sell extinction credits to advance their particular programs, or help advance their national goals.

As a back-up against the ongoing disaster, there are huge BioBanks scattered around the globe, secure archives holding DNA samples from existing and lost organisms that might someday be resurrected. Except, one day, those BioBanks are gone when a mysterious cyber-attack hits every BioBank at the same time, destroying the last traces of the vanished species.

The story focuses on Karin Resaint and Mark Halyard. Karin Resaint is an animal cognition scientist concerned with one particular species, an aquatic fish known as the venomous lumpsucker, a small, ugly creature that happens to be the most intelligent fish on the planet. Resaint is consumed with grief over what human beings have done to nature and is determined to preserve this particular species whose sole breeding ground is right in the way of a major ocean-going industrial mining operation.

Mark Halyard is an executive from the mining company, an expert in the extinction industry economy, who has inadvertently okayed the mining operation that has without warning destroyed the lumpsucker breeding habitat. At the same time he speculated heavily by short-selling extinction credits, and he faces personal bankruptcy, disgrace, and arrest if he cannot salvage the situation.

There is a chance, just a small chance, that the lumpsucker may have survivors, another colony located elsewhere, with a different breeding area. The pair set out to try and locate any survivors and see what can be done to protect them. It's a strange partnership. Halyard wants to save his career and his wealthy lifestyle, Resaint wants to save the lumpsucker and somehow enact revenge on Halyard and the industry he represents.

The journey across an increasingly dysfunctional dystopia carries them to nature preserves full of toxic waste, an outlaw city of rogue scientists and biological engineers floating in arctic waters, the biological operations of a totalitarian state designed solely to enrich its leaders, and perhaps somewhere along the way they might be able to find who or what attacked the BioBanks.

This is a story with multiple facets. It's an environmental warning, an adventure story, a social and political satire, an unfolding tale of the near future that is unraveling in the face of human race's interest in commercial and political supremacy at the expense of every other creature on the planet including our fellow humans. Plus it is an ongoing fictional essay about the economic changes wrought by our planet's environment unraveling out of control. It is also a very witty story that has a good many passages and paragraphs that are laugh out loud funny.

This is also a dense book to read. Some paragraphs take up almost an entire page, but I found it both fascinating and a very fast read, one of those books that you don't want to put down once you get started. Ned Beauman is an excellent writer who has created engaging characters despite the fact that the two protagonists, and most everyone else they encounter, have severe emotional and character flaws. Yet throughout all of this the author presents a story that is not only intensely interesting, but a story that is a clear warning to the readers that unless we start dealing with environmental problems right now we might very well be living this disturbing story in the coming decades.

That is excellent writing, and this is an excellent story. I highly recommend this novel and suggest that it will very likely be among those books nominated for awards in the science fiction community when the WorldCon, Dragon Con and the rest roll around again next year. Do yourself a favor and read this book. It's important, and it's wildly entertaining.

ORDINARY MONSTERS; J.M. Miro; Flatiron Books; 660 pages, June 2022

This is easily the best stf book I have read in the past three years. "J.M. Miro" is a pseudonym of Steven Price, a Canadian poet and writer living in California with his author wife Esi Edugyan and their two children. He has written other science fiction stories, but according to an interview he did recently with Sean Loughran for his Avocado Diaries website, Price adopted a pseudonym for this massive book because he wanted to free his mental state from his past constraints and linkage with the science fiction world to write a story that is a fantasy horror thriller.

This is indeed exactly that, a fantasy horror thriller. It is also a complex story with multiple personalities involved, and many on-going intertwined and sometimes cross conflicting plot threats that unwind and then re-cross in unexpected way. Characterization is an essential part of the plot work, and the author goes to some trouble to effortlessly fill in the reader about the major characters, and most of the minor ones as well, in detail, giving this novel the kind of treatment that first class mainstream novels try to develop. In this case, the merging of unique, deeply interesting characters involved in a fantastic plot works remarkably well.

Set in the early 1880s in the United States and Victorian England, the story revolves around an ongoing mission by agents employed by the Cairndale Institute in Scotland to locate and bring in children with unique, often bizarre special abilities. These "Talents" fall into five distinct classes, and their powers which always first develop in childhood are almost always shocking, and very alarming to ordinary people.

At the same time, an adult talent whose mind and abilities have become aligned with a supernatural entity from beyond the realm of death known as a Drughr, is also seeking the child Talents. Some of the young talents become food for his supernatural mentor, and others are to be used for the purpose of having the Drughr destroy the portal separating the worlds of the living from the strange realm of the dead, so the Drughr can completely cross over and become part of the world of living humans. The forces of supernatural evil are relentless; and in addition they have the services of a few witches, and reanimated death corpses with incredible speed and strength, to aid them.

The story is told through the eyes of multiple characters, but the primary protagonist is a teenage Talent named Charlie Ovid who regenerates when harmed in any way. Charlie is a mulatto who has been convicted of killing a white man in Mississippi and condemned to death. Except he can't be killed. He heals up every time the authorities try to kill him. That doesn't stop them from trying, repeatedly, using more ingenious, savage methods.

The quest leads to other young talents in the United States and in England. All of the young Talents encountered are orphaned and either trying to survive on their own, or living in protected situations where their unique talents are either suppressed or are being used to eek out a precarious living, such as being employed as circus freaks or existing in virtual slavery to malicious adults who use them for their own profit.

The other major Talent in the story is young Marlowe, a child whose abilities are unique, largely unknown, and whose talents partially manifested themselves even as a new born baby.

Everybody wants Marlowe: the Institute, the bad guys, his biological father, who is a wealthy man with great influence in Scotland where he was born, and any number of regular people who want to exploit his peculiar talents for their personal profit.

This is a very fast moving adventure with a great deal of historic background provided. The world of the late Victorian period is largely unknown to modern audiences, so the sights and descriptions of the people and the living conditions will seem as strange and alien to most readers as any science fiction trip to a far away alien planet. The plot and the interwoven characters combine to create an intense, suspenseful story that you will not soon forget.

My sole objection is that this is supposed to be the first of a three part series. This novel could have concluded nicely at the end of page 660 without any additional follow-up at all. Since there will be at least a second book in the series, it is likely that we will have to wait several years, or longer, before it comes out and we can read more about these very interesting characters and their extraordinary world.

Read this book. Do it now. If you can't afford to buy a physical copy yourself, or even to purchase the e-book version, then borrow a copy from your local library. If your local library doesn't have a copy, ask them to order one, or at least get a copy through inter-library loan. You might suggest to your local library that this novel is clearly going to be one of the top contenders for the Hugo, the Nebula, the World Fantasy Award, the Neffy, the Locus Awards, the Bram Stoker Prize, the Dragon Con Awards and any other awards associated with the field. And when those awards come around and it comes your time to cast a ballot, you will be glad indeed that you read this superb novel and had the opportunity to cast your vote for it in the best novel category.

THE LAST BLADE PREIST, W.P. Wiles; Angry Robot Books, 520 pages; Trade Paperback; July 2022.

This is an epic fantasy novel that doesn't seem to want to get into epic adventure territory. It's a dark fantasy that seems oddly reluctant to embrace the full scope of the darkness that is an essential part of the background of this tale. It's a detailed character study that clearly shows the effects of living in a world where magic works, often not to the benefit of the mass of people, and where empire building politics and fanatical religion can corrupt the very foundations on which those principles were built. How does all that fit together to move the story along? Well, it's complicated.

There are several protagonists in this adventure, all of them reluctant actors who would very much prefer that the world beyond their own little corners of it would simply leave them alone. But the world is changing, whether they like it or not, and they have been thrust into the events driving that change.

Inar Astarasso, a young master builder with an affinity for stone has a reputation as someone who can construct walls and buildings with lasting structural integrity. He understands rock, and knows how to successfully work with it at all levels. He lives in the Kingdom of Mishig-Tenh, a land that recently lost a war with the League of the Free Cities, a mercantile federation rapidly turning  into a sprawling empire. He is also the son of a traitor who betrayed one of the kingdom's key cities to the invaders in order to save the lives of everyone from a prolonged and bloody siege, but his father paid the price for his actions, and his son lives in the shadow of that betrayal. So when a female officer of the League, Anzola Stiyitta, wants Inar to come work with her for a mission to Edith-Tenh, known as The Hidden Land, the region wherein lies the God Mountain, he is less than enthusiastic. Unfortunately he is instructed to go by the Kingdom's sinister Lord Chancellor, head of the secret service, and to act as a spy for him.

Meanwhile in Edith-Tenh, Anton, a blade priest for the Living God Mountain, is caught up in swirling religious politics. The Old Religion, The Tzante, is slowly dying out, and meanwhile ancient enemies, the Elves, are regrouping and building their forces to attack the mountain stronghold and slaughter every human being in their path.

An alliance has been proposed between the Tzante and the League to defend against the Elf armies that are already beginning to mass in the outer regions. But internal politics and doctorial schisms are at work within the monastic-like stronghold. Anton himself never had any enthusiasm for chopping the living hearts out of sacrificial victims to offer up to the Custodians, the winged magical servants of the Living Mountain, but in an unexpected move the elder leader of the religion names Anton as his chosen successor; right before he is murdered. Then suddenly Anton is framed for the killing.

Other characters are introduced as the plot unfolds, including Duna a tween girl who is moody and sullen but apparently has some kind of magical ability possibly related to stone just as Inar's miniscule magical talents are. Inar and the League party start on a mission to the Hidden Land to solidify their treaty when things begin to go wrong. A trip along the old Pilgrim's Path, full of deliberate hardships and dangers encounters unexpected perils immediately, with death and betrayal not far behind.

The author is in no hurry to explain any of his extensive world building to the readers. Instead he reveals its boundaries through the ongoing

lives of his all-to-human characters as the events in their lives become more and more complicated. The picture emerging is of a world riddled with dangerous magic on a collision course with multiple competing human ambitions.

Malignant danger looms on the horizon, as the author also deliberately upends the conventional tropes about magic and magical beings. For example, Elves, the dreaded foes that are menacing every human kingdom in this world are actual human beings transformed by the addictive poisonous effects of the elf-bane plant. The plant turns ordinary humans into maniacal psychopaths who believe they are immortal and invincible (they are neither). The plant breaks down the barriers between id and ego so Elves become vicious psychopathic killers who delight in torture and mutilation. They are determined to turn any human they capture into Elves like themselves by forcing them to eat the elf-bane plant. Those that refuse are tortured until they either take the narcotic or die.

Author Will Wiles is a freelance journalist who specializes in articles about architecture and concept design. He has turned out three previous novels, but this is clearly his magnum-opus. This is a well written highly entertaining book. The strength of the novel is its deep characterizations and an overarching sense of near fatalistic darkness, the feeling that human events and magical beings are in a twin race toward disaster, a bloody climax that might be beyond the ability of anyone to stop.

The problem with this book is that even at 520 pages, it is clearly part one of an ongoing story. At the last page there is not even a courtesy attempt at wrapping things up or trying to make it appear that this is a complete novel. Instead things just stop. You turn the page expecting the next chapter but there are only some blank end papers. How long will it take for the next book in this long epic to appear is anybody's guess, it but it is going to be too long a wait for me. I really liked this story and I was pretty damn disappointed when the story simply ran out of paper. It's well worth the read, but be prepared for plenty of frustration when the adventure abruptly stops right in the middle of a significant ongoing event.

I am one of those people who believe in handing out brick-bats as well as bouquets when discussing books read. I feel it is the duty of the reviewer to point out bad books and to warn readers away from literary garbage as much as it is to praise worthy writing efforts. Everybody's time is limited, and life is too short to waste reading crap. Yes, I did encounter a few books this year that were inferior and pretty much a waste of my time, but due to the space limitations with this article I'm not going to mention them this time round. But I will say that they were few and far between. The titles that I would be prepared to kick in the rump were mostly guilty of mundane triteness rather than suffering bad writing or stupid plotting.

Most of the books I have read this year have been excellent. The ratio of really good stuff to mediocre or bad stuff has been astonishing, especially considering some past years in which I have plowed through any number of books and magazine stories that were humdrum or routine at best and pretty boring or downright stupid at worse. But not this year. Despite the current state of the world and the woes of the human race, 2022 was a stellar year for science fiction and fantasy. I am amazed at the consistent high quality of the material, and I continue to be amazed as I read more and more of the new books being released in 2022. Will this wave of excellence continue on into 2023? I dunno. I sure hope so. I also hope you will try the books I have mentioned here for yourself. I am sure you will share my enthusiasm for these titles when you do.

====

Another part of the print science fiction/fantasy scene that many readers of this magazine might not be considering right now is the world of comic books. Funny books have come a long way from the days when you picked up your four color fix from spinner racks at the local drug store.

Today comics cost four bucks a pop or more, and although there are still a few comics (precious few!) aimed at juvenile readers, the bulk of the material is directed at the adult market, the ones who have the money to engage in the hobby.

The overwhelming bulk of modern comic book publishing is directed toward the costumed super hero branch of the industry. Enduring heroes like Superman, Spider-Man, Wonder Woman, Batman, the X-Men and hundreds more comprise the bulk of the industry's production.

But, at the same time, there are worlds beyond super heroes, which is good, because frankly, I'm pretty burned out on super heroes. Just as old fans get tired of the same old-same old in science fiction and fantasy novels, so also do we have old comic fans getting tired of the same old stereotypes being churned out by the super hero crowd.

In the modern world of super hero comics we have now reached what I call the Marvel Epoch. Mere human beings can no longer be counted on to pose any kind of threat or maintain even a semblance of a story plot when it comes to super-powered comic book heroes. Instead, every story has to have a Costumed Super Villain, with malignant powers equal to or superior to those of the hero. These spandex-clad bad guys aren't even interested in cleaning out the local First National Bank vault either. All they want to do is cream the hero and smash his body into hamburger. Long fight scenes fill up most of the pages of these stories (battles in which bruises, broken bones, shredded body parts, or even blood, is never seen).

Long involved soap opera story lines lasting many months or even years are the threads that keep most readers involved with these characters, and in order to inject some degree of excitement to hold onto easily jaded readers, now there are yearly, or twice-yearly cross-universe master menaces where all the characters in the publisher's stable must band together to combat some lethal foe so powerful that he threatens to destroy the entire planet, or perhaps even the known universe, if it isn't somehow neutralized. (Note I don't use the word killed. In the modern comic book bad guys are never killed. They are stopped, thwarted, diverted, or defeated, but never actually slain, because the publisher and editors might want to use that bad apple again for some future multi-zone combat plotline).

These endless repetitious cookie-cutter plots of super heroes vs. super villains vs. universe destroying Ultra-Menace are the primary reason I no longer read most super hero comic books. Fortunately there are plenty of other publishers providing interesting stories with solid involved plots and good artwork to keep me involved in the hobby and many of these non-super hero comics are science fiction and fantasy, featuring complex, interesting tales that often work better in the visual-word mix media of comic books than they might in a straight prose story. Most

of these are being produced by independent comic publishers, since the Big Three Companies are primarily involved with the super hero crowd.

Here are a few recent titles that I found particularly interesting, all of which I can recommend without hesitation. Most of these comics are either graphic novels or will be turned into graphic novel collections in the near future, but you can sample a first issue of each series to test the water. Most of the first issues are available at most comic stores for about twenty-five cents above the original retail price (to cover the price of the backing board and plastic bag), sometimes for less.

NEW THINK a five issue anthology mini-series from AWA Comics, graphic novel $9.99

AWA (formally known as AWA Upshot) produces some of the best written and best drawn comics on the market today, including this one. Each issue of this mini-series takes a particular aspect of modern or past human technology and gives it a unique spin, often reflecting philosophical and cultural viewpoints you might not have even considered. A sort of Black Mirror-style anthology, it examines the cultural and political polarization of the country and the technocrats that have driven us to such extremes that even the present might be viewed as something remarkably futuristic.

I am not going to say much more about this comic series, because if I do I will give away all the plot details of each issue. This is one you will have to take my word for. Get the first issue featuring a story titled "The Coming of the Skreezns." It's a minor masterpiece that will stir your imagination, and your sense of irony. Just do it, then buy the graphic novel that collects the whole series, and you can give your copy of that first issue to a friend to get him hooked on this series as well. You will both thank me.

TELEPATHS a six issue mini-series from AWA Comics; graphic novel $9.99

This is an award winning series written by J. Michael Staczynski, the creator/writer of the Babylon 5 TV series that explores the idea of what might happen if some kind of cosmic energy blip hit planet Earth and suddenly a small percentage of human beings developed psionic powers. What would happen, especially in the first moments after the event took place? Now imagine if some of the people affected were criminals, convicted convicts led by an intelligent, ambitious, narcissistic, charismatic, and ruthless leader. Who would be able to oppose them? If there are a few police officers similarly affected, what would happen if they clashed? More important, what would the government(s) of the world do when faced with this phenomenon? How could it be confronted, let alone controlled? Trust, suspicions, confrontation, destruction, are just a few of the choices. This series explores it all in detail with exceptional art work as well. Highly recommended., or you can sample to first issue from the back issue bins of any comic book store or any of the hundreds of on-line comic dealers and decide for yourself. Read the first issue and you'll soon buy the graphic novel.

TRAVELING TO MARS; Ablaze Comics; ongoing series (8 to 10 issues projected) $3.99/issue

A new innovative comic series mixing science fiction dystopian anxiety with dark humor. The world of the near future has almost run out of fossil fuels, but we still need energy or civilization will collapse. Then, one of those Martian robot probes discovers an incredible reservoir of concentrated natural gas beneath the planet's surface, more than enough to take care of planet Earth's energy needs for centuries to come. Of course, somebody has to get there and claim it for the good of humanity, or maybe just for good old fashioned greed & avarice.

Traveling To Mars tells the story of former pet store manager Roy Livingston, the first human to ever set foot on Mars. Roy was chosen for the unlikely mission for one simple reason: he is terminally ill and has no expectation of returning. Roy is joined on his mission by Leopold and Albert, two Mars rovers equipped with artificial intelligence, who look upon the dying pet store manager as a sort of God. Against the backdrop of his final days Roy has plenty of time to think about where things went wrong with his life and the about the whole human race.

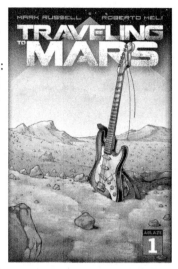

Mark Russell is the writer and he does an exceptional job in a mix of irony, pathos, humor and cynicism, with realistic art by Roberto Meli. Unhesitatingly recommended.

MINDSET; Vault Comics; ongoing series (6 issues projected—graphic novel to follow) $3.99/issue

From the Vault Comics editors: "When an introverted tech geek from Stanford, with dreams of changing the world, accidentally discovers a form of mind control, he and his friends do something unexpected – they put

the science into a meditation app to help users break their addiction to other manipulative technologies and platforms. But after their rags-to-riches rise, a wake of murders and a series of mind games, their Mindset app replaces all rival social media and achieves a cult following of a billion users, and they must ask the question – are they helping people or controlling them?"

Then what happens when Big Money players get wind of this interesting addictive app? Money can be a powerful force, often a destructive one, especially when previously idealistic friends are suddenly faced with unbelievable wealth. Will they stay true to the mission, to make the world better, or are compromises inevitable. This is a technological and psychological tale that explores the possibilities.

I am not particularly fond of the artwork for this series, but it works for the premise, and plenty of other people think it is perfect for the story line. You can check the first issue out or sample a few pages from the first issues for free. Unfortunately the free sample pages are random and do not give you a sense of the actual plot.

THE ARGUS; Action Lab; ongoing series; $3.99/issue; 6 issues followed by a graphic novel $14.99

The Argus is the type of time travel, action adventure story that will either get your imagination revved up, or make your head hurt, or maybe both. Mark Bertolini's story centers on Randall Patton; a smart guy who has just invented a workable theory of time travel. Unfortunately, the theory immediately proves to be a dangerous reality as he's visited by multiple versions of himself from the future. They need him to stop one of his future selves from destroying the very fabric of time after going insane from a freak accident.

The story works as author Bertolini dumps a whole lot of background information on the reader by using the first original Randall Patton as the audience surrogate. Randall is just as confused as we are, so his questions effectively fill in the background. These explanations are necessary for the story to function, getting the reader immersed in the confusing rules of time travel without the feeling that we are reading a physics textbook. Randall is visited by multiple versions of himself, gathered from different points of the timeline. In theory each Randall should look somewhat like the original Randall only aged differently, but some of the Randalls look like completely different people, so the idea of multiple Randalls doesn't make visual sense as presented, however some of that is explained in subsequent issues of the comic. This is an ambitious science fiction time travel story plot that is handled very well with speculative theory imbedded within the ongoing action adventure.

BLINK; Omni Press; 6 issue miniseries; $3.99/issue; graphic novel to come

Okay, here is a series I cannot recommend for everyone. This series is definitely an acquired taste, and I'm not sure whether I've actually acquired the taste or if I just want to see what the hell is going on with all these bizarre events.

Hype from Omni Comics: "Wren Booker was three when she was found alone and covered in blood on the streets of New York. Since that day, she's been haunted by the childhood she can't remember...until decades later when she finds a cryptic website streaming multiple CCT feeds from strange rooms in a ruined building. Something clicks, setting off hidden memories that lead her back to a place she's seen in lifelong nightmares. Hunting for answers, Wren breaks in and finds herself lost in the camera-filled dark mazes of a decayed social experiment known only as BLINK...which she quickly discovers is not abandoned at all. But what should be a foreign nightmare-scape feels all too familiar for Wren as she follows her obsession all the way down, piecing together the story of BLINK—as well as her own ties to it."

And if that sounds confusing, wait until you actually dive into the story. With unusually dark art that bleeds right to the edges of every single page, and a near total lack of traditional paneling, this is a surrealistic journey where there are endless puzzling questions and very few answers. The Blink Building with its secrets, mountains of old TV sets and outdated computer monitors, is a fantasyland and a horrific war zone, with Wren right in the middle trying to find the answers to her existence.

As I say, not for everyone. I would suggest anyone interested try the first issue to see if this is something you will like. Already people are talking about nominations for this series in some of the more prestigious comic book awards, and it's hard not to be impressed with the way the story has been developing.

As the cliché goes, this sampling is just the tip of the iceberg. There are any number of really good science fiction/fantasy related comic book series being produced, most of them coming from the smaller independent comic companies. I appreciate that you might need a native guide to find clear pathways through the jungle of material that is coming out. This year alone literally thousands of new comic books have been published each and every month. I hope my suggestions have been useful.

Birthday Poem: Seventy

The big Seven Oh.
This is a serious number.
I am no more a junior
apprentice assistant geezer,
but the real thing.
For all it doesn't feel
any different from yesterday
or the day before and I don't think
that the stiffness and assorted aches
are any different from sixty-five,
or sixty, or even the distant
and dimly-remembered fifty,
still I know that the numbers
must one day run out,
that the end is coming,
and my words to the Reaper
will inevitably be, "Wait, wait,
I'm not done yet."
But not today, which continues to feel
quite a lot like yesterday.

(part of a continuing series)
                            —*Darrell Schweitzer*

SMART DUMMIES
William M. Breiding

The Alchemy of Stone by Ekaterina Sedia; Prime Books; 2008; 301 pages

The story of a clockwork automaton's struggle with her creator, Ekaterina Sedia's third novel *The Alchemy of Stone*, is an ambiguous steampunk dystopia. Sedia, at 21 years, emigrated to America from Russia. She is an associate professor of biology at Stockton University in Galloway, New Jersey. She co-authored a pivotal paper on the effects that lichen, moss and grass have on the forests of the New Jersey Pine Barrens. She is deeply engaged with fashion. All of this extra-literary life experience plays deeply into Ekaterina Sedia's fiction, the rich description of clothing and furnishings, her views of the uses of alchemy, the look and feel of her city-states.

The Alchemy of Stone's background story is that of the political rivalry between the radically different ideologies of the clockwork Mechanics and the healing Alchemists (apparently there is a gender division—the Mechanics are male, Alchemists female) both whom run the city in uneasy accord with the Duke. The city itself has been grown whole from stone by the Gargoyles who are alive and animate but reverting to stone too quickly to survive as a species.

There is an urban and agrarian class struggle against both the hereditary ruling Duke and the plutocratic Mechanics and Alchemists that has erupted into violent revolution which, with the help of certain palace courtiers, has overthrown the court. Mattie, our automaton, is swept up in these events but cares

Ekaterina Sedia

nothing for them. She is only searching for an alchemical cure to relieve the Gargoyles of their disease of stone, trying to navigate her own consciousness, and to achieve her goals to become an advanced Alchemist, and healer.

Mattie was created by Loharri, a clockwork mechanic. Automatons are common but few are instilled with an autonomous consciousness; they are created essentially as slaves. Mattie was given a self-aware personality but as she gains experience and memory she tries to sort her evolving sense of self from the consciousness and aesthetics instilled by her creator. Mattie's overarching personality is feminine and kind. She suffers from and fights against passivity. We are never told of Loharri's intent in creating Mattie. He seems to have wanted obliging companionship, domestic help (Mattie grew Loharri a fantastic garden), and a kind of sexual gratification that Mattie experiences as visceral groping. Loharri granted Mattie emancipation when requested though she continues to be bound to Loharri. Her clockwork "heart" must occasionally be wound or she becomes inert. Loharri retains the "key to her heart" never intending to pass it on to her. She remains partially indentured by a kindly, even loving, "slaveowner".

This is not an epic tale of the strife between the industrial revolution created by the clockwork mechanics (men) and the softer healers of the earth-magic alchemists (women), or of gender politics. It's not really about the possible extinction of the Gargoyles or their species rescue as the title might suggest, nor is it about slavery, class insurrection, or gender identity. It has all of these components sketched into its curlicue fabric but they remain only tokens to express a larger world. *The Alchemy of Stone* could best be viewed as a coming of age story. But even this is clotted with enigma.

I questioned the veracity of many things in this book. Mattie is both sentient and sapient. She is made of metal and whalebone. She has a clockwork engine in her chest which gives her life but it can wind down. If she is not rewound she will "die", that is, turn off—completely. In Mattie's head there is *something* that acts as a "brain" but we are never told what. At one important juncture her head begins to smoke and she becomes incapacitated. We are later told that this is because she was trying to hide something from her maker, Loharri, who has programmed her this way—not that she would be incapable of lying but that she would damage herself if she did so.

Mattie has a fragile removable porcelain face mask. Behind this mask are more gears and unknowable tiny bits of machinery. The two times her face mask must come off (they

crack easily and must be replaced) she feels both vulnerable and violated. Mattie is capable of not only thinking, but feeling. How does she achieve this thought and feeling? She can also smell and has "taste sensors" on her "lips." Remember—she is wearing a removable porcelain mask that shows no sign of plugging into any clockwork gears in her head. By the sheer presence of a young dynamic man she immediately falls in love. When she reveals her feelings he takes advantage of her—by embracing her whalebone waist and exposing the clockwork heart at her center and sticking his tongue into her keyhole—which she experiences as both erotic sensation and intimate abuse. There is much talk of "souls"; there is an entire subplot about a soul eater. Mattie encompasses everything that makes us human but our flesh and blood yet she has no soul.

I had to wonder. How was all this achievable by a mechanic? It appears more like magic than the clockwork scientific method, more alchemical, like Pinocchio's wood turned flesh. In fact, it makes no sense, you just have to buy into it. This was my first foray into clockwork fiction, a genre closely related to steampunk, so maybe my suspension of disbelief wasn't properly activated, the gears remaining disengaged.

There was also a brief instance in the book where Mattie considers her gender. "Mattie was a woman because of the corset stays and whalebone, because of the heave of metal chest, because of the bone hoops fastened to her hips that held the skirts wide—but also because Loharri told her she was one." Here was something of an interesting moment left unexplored. Is it the body shape, the clothes, and the perceptions of others that dictate gender? Mattie is a woman not only because Loharri tells her so, but because he *made* her that way. Again, I ask, how can a clockwork mechanic imbue his automaton with an iconic feminine psyche? Only through magic, I think.

I remain undecided if Ekaterina Sedia's ambiguity in all of these areas is intentional or merely a lack of vision and craft. There is so much in this

book that is left unexplained, or just hinted at, that I had suspicions that I was actually reading a Young Adult novel. I'm sorry, but yes, labels matter in the approach to reading. These kinds of hinted-at details and half-formed ideas allow a questing young mind to not only deeply extrapolate but to project one's self onto the prose and into the situation.

Something should also be said about the writing which immediately gives *The Alchemy of Stone* it's sensation of a Victorian steampunk cosplay world. "Loharri's room smelled of incense and smoke, the air thick like taffy. Mattie tasted it on her lips." There is habitual languor, spilt glass on thick carpet, a fat black cat, slashes of warm light through heavy drapery, a workbench full of clockwork bits and pieces, Mattie's cracked porcelain face and Victorian garments. Although at times lush and filled with a pervasive sense of dusk and rich sensory details the writing often feels stilted. Again, I am undecided if this was done by intention.

I think Prime Books, an independent book publisher, did a disservice to Sedia's novel by not marketing it to the Young Adult category, where I believe it belongs. (Prime Books may have hung up it's shingle and gone bust, which would be sad, if true. Their webpage was last updated in 2019, though the website is copyrighted for 2023.) *The Alchemy of Stone* may have found a far larger audience if Prime Books had taken advantage of the YA market. But its ending—**spoiler alert!**—may have precluded that YA marketing. Loharri's final sabotage (among many, I might add) is to kill his courtier lover and then allow Mattie to wind down even as he himself dies. For you see, Mattie's key is *special* and cannot be replicated. Only Loharri's key will work and it has been destroyed—or gone missing—in a climatic explosion. Mattie "dies" at the end, gone to fairytale stillness, like Baum's Tin Woodsman rusting under trees in a rainy forest.

52

~~VISIBLE DARKNESS~~
Daniel F. Galouye and the Limits of Perception

RICH COAD

The cinema houselights go down. It's dim, but the audience can still see well enough to quiet down and pay attention as the curtain in front of the screen begins to rise. As it rises the secondary lights start to go out, one row at a time, from the front of the auditorium to the back. Soon the cinema is pitch black. Nobody can see a neighbor, nor even a hand held before their own face. Slowly the audience becomes aware of a sound. A clicking, snapping sound. The sound of two rocks being knocked together. A voice: "I don't hear anything." A different voice: "It's here. Give me an arrow." Suddenly the sound of beating wings, the hum of a taut bowstring released, a hideous scream. "Did you get it?" "Only notched the wing." The screams are decreasing, the sound is moving away when, without

any warning, the screen is awash with intensely bright white light. Each member of the audience, having become accustomed to the dark, turns a head, or looks down, or squints at the screen which is rapidly filling up with dark spots until the light is left to spell out "Guillermo del Toro presents *Dark Universe*" but the words don't last. Soon all is dark again. The clicking of stones can be heard again.

Such was the opening of a 2029 film that restored a reputation tarnished by the big budget flops of *Pacific Rim: Stompers Vs. Chompers* and *Hell Toddler*. Del Toro's return to his roots of low budget (lighting costs were minimal; only a few voice actors and a foley team were needed) science fiction with a unique story restored his reputation with the critics which, in turn, made

the studios willing to finance other projects he had in mind. But it wasn't only Del Toro's career that was revived. Daniel F. Galouye, dead for over fifty years, his books either out of print or available only in cheap print-on-demand editions from publishers with no budget for advertising, suddenly was back in vogue, with matched trade paperbacks of his five novels and one story collection available at bookstores across the nation. What was it about this mid-twentieth-century author that gripped readers in the first third of the twenty-first century?

Daniel F. Galouye was born in New Orleans in 1920 and died there in 1976. In that relatively brief life he was a test pilot during World War Two, a journalist, an early retiree (due to the effects of war injuries), and, during the 1950s and 1960s, a science fiction writer. During the 1950s, Galouye published over 40 short stories in the science fiction magazines of the time. Initially he appeared almost exclusively in *Imagination* with occasional sales to *F&SF* or *Galaxy*. By the latter half of the decade, however, he was appearing in many different publications. As he began to concentrate on novels in the 1960s the number of short stories published

dropped, especially after 1961. Surprisingly, despite over 60 appearances in US sf magazines, no collection of Galouye's short stories was published in the USA until a print-on-demand reprint of the 1968 Gollancz UK collection, *Project Barrier*, was recently made available. The paperback

British publisher Corgi had released an earlier collection, *The Last Leap and Other Stories of the Super-Mind*, in 1964. Of the 60 plus stories, then, only a dozen have ever been collected in English, and only the five in *Project Barrier* can be considered easily accessible.

Fortunately for Galouye's bank account, at least, German publishers were eager to make his stories available. No fewer than eight collections were published in German according to the ISFDB, translations of the two British collections and six original to Germany.

This popularity in Germany probably helps explain why the first visual media adaptation of a Galouye novel was a four hour television film based on *Simulacron-3*, his third novel. Like all of his work, *Simulacrom-3* can be read as a pure SF adventure, with unexplained disappearances, vicious murders, false accusations, and a protagonist desperately trying to save themselves and understand what is going on. Underlying all this action is Galouye's recurring obsession with whether what we perceive as reality is, in fact, reality itself. In this case we have three computer scientists who have built a simulated world in order to provide market research for their clients. It's not giving anything more than what the back cover gives away to tell you that, yes, they are indeed inside an even larger simulated environment. This was in 1964, before the idea that the entire universe could conceivably be a computer simulation had much currency. In Rainier Warner Fassbinder's 1973 adaptation, "Welt am Draht" aka "World on a Wire", the characters slowly become aware that they are trapped in a simulation, although one thinks they have found a way out, to reach the real world. Or have they? This is the sort of plot that people thought mind-blowing when the Wachowski's made "The Matrix" and its sequels, and here it all is in a 1964 novel by an obscure science fiction writer from Louisiana.

The novel was compelling enough to spawn a second film adaptation, "The Thirteenth Floor", in 1999. Simulated reality was big that year. In addition to "The Thirteenth Floor", there was "The Matrix" and (probably the best of the three) David Cronenberg's "eXistenz". In my opinion, "The Thirteenth Floor" deserves better than the 30% rating it is given on Rotten Tomatoes. It's a far from perfect movie but it held my interest and has the advantage of being much shorter, and thus faster-moving, than Fassbinder's turgid epic. The movie lost the Saturn Award to "The Matrix" despite philosopher Slavov Žižek calling the film "much better than *The Matrix.*" I agree with Slavov.

But let us return to the novels. The Hugo nominated *Dark Universe* was undoubtedly Galouye's most successful novel. Published in 1961 it can be read as simply a post-apocalyptic thriller with a plausible explanation and a rewarding resolution. The Survivors are living deep under the earth in a world completely devoid of light. They use their clickstones and echo location to navigate through their world. Other beings exist that seem to manage navigation without needing echoes. And a monstrous new presence is being encountered in the pathways around their world. More or less standard SF fare. The intriguing thing, though, is that the inhabitants of this world do not recognize that they are living in darkness. They have their own version of the fall from grace where once there was an Original World of Light and mankind committed the darkness of Radiation and so on and so forth. Our hero, Jared, is trying to find darkness so that he can better understand light. The culture and technology of the world is quite well worked out and it all seems quite feasible that, as Galouye put it in a later novel, "Consider an entire world that's never known light... (a person) turns a corner and somebody throws a hundred-candlepower beam in their face..."

The limits of perception creating a limited reality is a key theme in all of Galouye's novels.

This theme is overarching in Galouye's penultimate novel, *A Scourge of Screamers* aka *The Lost Perception*. The British title is a giveaway but so is the introduction where it is made quite clear that *zylphing the rault* is something humanity cannot do but other, alien, species can. Once again, the basic plot is standard sf fare. A post nuclear holocaust society is trying to rebuild while a plague of mental illness, "the screamies", is spreading around the world infecting increasing numbers with each passing year. There are aliens moving about the earth, here either to help mankind get past the plague or planning to seize control of the planet for their own uses. They are opposed by an international Security Bureau which is either helping humanity get past the plague or planning to seize control of the planet for their own uses. Over time our hero becomes a victim of the screamies, a recovered screamie victim, before finally achieving transcendence. By the end of the novel what started out with battles using lasers and machine guns has become a battle with fear of new perceptions that are becoming omnipresent as the solar system leaves an area where the rault has been occluded.

Lords of the Psychon, Galouye's second novel published in 1963, also has aliens but these ones do not ever appear benign. The Spheres, as they are known, generally ignore humanity although from time to time individual Spheres seem to take a delight in hunting a hapless human and killing them by electrocution. Everybody, though, lives in fear of Horror Day which comes every year and seems to be getting worse with each passing year. On Horror Day an energy grid appears over earth and humanity is subjected to extreme mental and physical distress. Nobody knows what the Spheres want or what it is they are trying to do on Horror Day. The novel follows a platoon of soldiers, some of the last remnants of the US Army, as they attempt to fight the Spheres. As the novel opens they are transporting a 50 kiloton nuclear bomb into a City of Force, one of a number of such cities that the Spheres have established around the globe. The soldiers succeed in getting the device in place and detonating only to see the city easily absorb every bit of energy released by the bomb and continue to add and remove geometric shapes to itself just as it always has. The bombing does have the effect of infuriating the local civilian population who are afraid it will cause the Spheres to attack and kill more of their own.

Lords of the Psychon is in many ways a very traditional SF novel. Ragtag groups of fighters trying to overcome overwhelming odds against invaders whose motives and technology are incomprehensible. At least incomprehensible until the team meets a woman living on an isolated farm who has what appears to be a small pet Sphere. Despite the somewhat sudden appearance of a deus ex machine, the Spheres, in their alienness and unknowability make interesting reading; sufficiently so that Galouye brought them back for a 1970 novelette published in *If*. The forthcoming Netflix series, jointly produced by Robert Rodriguez and Quentin Tarantino, promises to be enjoyable, sort of like "Spy Kids meets the "Inglorious Basterds", with Spheres.

Galouye's final novel, *The Infinite Man*, was a "fix-up" of two much earlier stories from *Imagina-*

tion. The plot here is somewhat similar to Robert Heinlein's famous short story "They". Milton Bradford has gone from drug-addled bum to owner of a mega-corporation in just a few years. Ostensibly this bit of luck came about because the former owner wrote a will leaving everything to Bradford, his illegitimate son, and then killed himself. In truth, though, the old owner is still kicking and the whole set up is a ruse so that various personnel can keep tabs on Bradford and make sure he remains unaware that he contains within himself the Creative Force, which has decided to go into hiding due to becoming overwhelmed by the complexity of the universe it has created. This concept has, I believe, a lot of comic potential but that is ignored here with a rather standard dawning of awareness coming into play. There is a cult which worships Bradford as the Inverse Vessel and also the Infinite Man. They do silly things like reverse their names and get amazed at how they can traverse a möbius strip in one continuous motion. Since Galouye was pretty obviously aiming at what he hoped would be a best seller amongst the hippies, a-la *Stranger in a Strange Land* or *Steppenwolf*, this novel seems quite badly dated. It has its moments, such as the Creative Force making Pluto disappear and rationalizing pi, but these tend to be throwaway moments used mostly to convince doubting characters that there is real power residing with Bradford (or Drofdarb, as he is known by the cultists). Of his five published novels, the last is definitely the weakest.

For four novels, though, in the 1960s, Galouye created some very memorable science fiction that has stood the test of time. He is certainly deserving of the rediscovery and new readership that Del Toro's film has brought him.

Down These Mean Trails

WESTERN DETECTIVE & MYSTERY FICTION

Cheryl Cline

Bat Durston Rides Again (Again)

When I started reading Westerns with an eye for comparing them to Mysteries, I quickly found I was heading down the wrong trail. I would be reading, for example, *Night of Shadows* by Ed Gorman, and go, hmm. Or *The Gallows Land* by Bill Pronzini and go, huh. By the time I'd read three or four more books labeled "Westerns," a pretty obvious road sign was pointing me down the other fork.

Friends, *there is no difference between Westerns and Mysteries*. Except, as George R.R. Martin says, for the furniture.

To paraphrase B.J. from Karen Joy Fowler's *Sarah Canary* (see my article in *Portable Storage* 8):

> I've heard that story, but instead of a P.I. there was a Sheriff, and instead of the Mob there was a Gang, and instead of a crook there was an outlaw, and instead of gats there were Colts and instead of fast cars there were fast horses and instead of speakeasys there were saloons and instead of bootleggers there were cattle rustlers and instead of a bank tycoon's daughter there was a rancher's daughter and instead of mean streets there was a mean desert. Other than that, it's the same story.

Or we might add another column to Galaxy Magazine's infamous "Bat Durston" ad (see my article in *Portable Storage* 7):

Tires screeching, Bat Durston raced the coupe down the narrow streets of the waterfront. A car lurched from an alley between darkened warehouses and Durston hit the brakes, but before he could spin the coupe out of the trap, a goombah who looked like he'd been quarried from a granite rockface stepped out of the shadows and pointed a gat at him. "Get out of the car, Bat Durston. You don't know it, but you just -- wait, where'd he go? Follow that horse! FOLLLOW THAT HORSE!"

The bit of literary DNA that SF, Westerns, and the Mystery/Detective genres hold in common is Action and Adventure, and it goes all the way back to -- well, all the way back. Some earnest defenders of Westerns will bring up the *Iliad*, but let's just go back to the 19th century. Westerns and detective stories were the two most popular types of the Dime Novels. It was only a matter of time that someone combined them, and once that happened (in basically no time at all), detectives were all over the West. Pinkertons, Secret Service Agents, Itinerant Lawmen, Robin-Hood bandits and even crime-solving boy inventors!

They appeared in titles like *The Secret Service Series No. 24: The Prairie Detective* by Leander P. Richardson (Street & Smith, 1889), *The Dragoon Detective; Or, A Man of Destiny* by Dr. Frank Powell (Beadle's Dime Library, 1893) or even *Deadwood Dick As A Detective: A Story of the Great Carbonate Region* by Edward L. Wheeler (The Deadwood Dick Library 2, 1899).

Science fiction was added to the mix on occasion, and the boy wonder who built the Steam Man of the Plains also stars in *Frank Reade, the Inventor, Chasing the James Boys With His Steam Team: A Thrilling Story from a Lost Diary* (The New York Detective Library, 1890).

If a writer feels the urge to introduce a detective to the Wild West there is, shall we say, precedent.

It's easy enough to do, since a big swath of popular Westerns deal with crime of some kind: shoot-outs, bank heists, train robberies, murders, claim jumping, stagecoach hold-ups, lynchings,

cattle-rustling, small government corruption and land fraud. Their pages are filled with horse thieves, card-sharks, gunslingers, prostitutes, bootleggers, snake-oil salesmen, and outlaws of all kinds, including some famous ones. Whole libraries could be devoted to telling and re-telling the life and times of Billy the Kid alone.

I'm thinking Bat Durston is better used as a guide to mix-and-match genre fiction. Certainly he points the way to how popular fiction genres actually work, rather than how H.L. Gold wanted them to work.

"But down these mean streets a man must go who is not himself mean, who is neither tarnished nor afraid. The detective in this kind of story must be such a man. He is the hero, he is everything. He must be a complete man and a common man and yet an unusual man. He must be, to use a rather weathered phrase, a man of honor, by instinct, by inevitability, without thought of it, and certainly without saying it... He is a relatively poor man, or he would not be a detective at all. He is a common man or he could not go among common people. He has a sense of character, or he would not know his job. He will take no man's money dishonestly and no man's insolence without a due and dispassionate revenge. He is a lonely man and his pride is that you will treat him as a proud man or be very sorry you ever saw him."

Raymond Chandler, "The Simple Art of Murder"

Shorter version:

"When you say that, smile."

Owen Wister, *The Virginian*

Mystery Writers and Western Detectives

Sometimes it seems like every Mystery writer has written a Western. These crossover artists include Erle Stanley Gardner (the

"Whispering Sands" series in Black Mask), John D. MacDonald, Brett Halliday (as Davis Dresser), Alistair Maclean, and Richard Prather (even if the Western in question takes place on a movie set). Before he had a hit with Gorky Park, Martin Cruz Smith wrote a Western (a pretty weird one, at that). James Patterson wrote a Western, because of course he did. By the year 2050, all books will be written by James Patterson.

Donald Hamilton wrote Westerns before he published his Matt Helm spy novels, including *Smoke Valley* (1954), *Mad River* (1956) and *Texas Fever* (1960). In 1967 he edited a pretty good Western anthology, *Iron Men and Silver Stars*.

I was excited to discover that Mickey Spillane had written a Western, *The Legend of Caleb York*. Sadly, it's a posthumous novel, adapted from a screenplay Spillane wrote for John Wayne that was never produced. This is an example of an author continuing a series even though he's dead, a not uncommon phenomenon (though the record is probably held by Edward L. Wheeler, who wrote 33 Deadwood Dick dime novels, died, and then "wrote" 99 more). After writing the initial book, Max Allen Collins went on to publish another half-dozen "Caleb York" novels. While Collins is a Spillane-ish writer, and the series may be good (or at least as good as Spillane), it's not as exciting as finding a trove of Genuine Mickey Spillane Westerns.

Few crime writers went as far as John Creasey, who according to Bill Pronzini "was responsible for 29 bang-bang tales of the Old West, published under a trio of pen-names: Tex Riley, William K. Reilly, and Ken Ranger." Creasey's "bang-bang" Westerns were bad enough for Pronzini to quote a number of them in *Six-Gun in Cheek*. Pronzini writes that Creasey once told an audience he began one of his Westerns with "High in the noonday sky, a lonely coyote circled." He didn't know much about horses, either:

A lone rider, jogging easily along the trail, on a magnificent bay pinto not long from mustang stage. (Tex Riley, *Range War*, quoted in *Six-Gun in Cheek*)

That's some weird horse!

Contemporary Western Mysteries

Western Mysteries can be roughly divided between those set in contemporary settings and those set in the Old West. But sometimes it's hard to know where to draw a line -- if a line is even needed.

Bill Crider, like many of the crossover writers, wrote Mysteries, and both contemporary and historical Westerns. In an excellent essay, "Sleuths and Spurs," Crider draws his lines thus:

> "I've written quite a few Mystery novels, and the ones in the Sheriff Dan Rhodes series sometimes get shelved in the Western section (the books are about a sheriff, and he's from Texas). But I've also written Western novels, and *A Time for Hanging* (1989) is a straight Mystery that just happens to be set in the 1880s instead of the 1980s when it was written."

Or is it a straight Western that happens to be a Mystery? Paco Morales is accused of murdering a young woman, and a bunch of the townspeople want to string him up. But the sheriff, who has up to now been rather mild-mannered and lazy, straightens his spine, squares his shoulders and faces them down because it's the right thing to do. Stop me if you've heard this before.

Relentless by Ed Gorman is another Western that happens to be a Mystery or vice versa. In this one, it's the Sheriff's wife who's accused of murder, so he's got an added spur to get real justice done.

Loren D. Estleman's career is also a mix-and-match collection of urban Mysteries and Mysteries combined with modern or historical Westerns. His first novel, *The Oklahoma Punk* (1976) is described as "a gangster novel set in the West." His own title was *Twister*, and he was so chagrined by publisher's title change that he has insisted on naming rights ever since. Title aside, it perhaps set a pattern for his later works.

Percival Everett is a Black author who has written several Westerns, including *Wounded*, a contemporary Western Mystery with a Black police detective living in rural Wyoming, and an Old West spoof, *God's Country*. He also writes straight Mysteries and not-so-straight Mysteries (his latest Mystery novel, *Trees*, which deals with lynching, has a strong element of magical realism).

Obviously Joe Lansdale isn't a traditional Western author, or any kind of traditional author at all. But he does write straight Westerns, and has edited (more or less) traditional Western anthologies. He writes horror, fantasy and detective stories and mixes them freely – sometimes all in the same story... plus he writes other rather oddball stuff. So he's less like an your old school Western writer and more like an alien from another planet masquerading as a Western writer.

Other authors stick to a modern setting. The Joe Pickett series by C.J. Box and the Longmire series by Craig Johnson are similar enough that fans of one tend to like the other. Pickett is a game warden -- a job that lets him poke his nose into all kinds of cases, from drug smuggling to eco-terrorism. Box says of his protagonist: "Joe doesn't enter every fight with an agenda other than to do the right thing. It's his fatal flaw."

Longmire is the sheriff of the fictitious Absaroka County, Wyoming, which *doesn't* allow him to poke his nose into all kinds of cases, but he does anyway. He too carries the fatal flaw of any detective worth his salt.

Both of these series are what I'd call mildly hard-boiled; The *Longmire* books are a bit stronger, the hero more reckless and with a painful personal life and past (Pickett on the other hand is happily married with a houseful of daughters he dotes on).

Tony Hillerman is known for his Mystery novels featuring Joe Leaphorn and Jim Chee, Navajo Nation policemen, for which he's won both Edgar and Spur Awards. Hillerman's novels are a good example of a Western police procedural transplanted into the West -- a world away from Ed McBain's 87th Precinct in more than just geographical distance.

Western Thrillers

Many Westerns of a criminal bent could be called thrillers rather than Mysteries. There's a crime, and good guys chasing after bad guys (or bad guys going after worse) but there's no *mystery* to solve. The hero knows who the villain is — or if he doesn't, the reader does. Western thriller plots include range wars incited by an evil rancher who wants everybody else's spread; tales of vengeance where our hero tracks down and kills the people who murdered his family, burned his ranch and stole his bible; men blamed for crimes they didn't commit and who must bring the man who did to justice; or just generally a character caught up in a bad situation through no fault of his own and who must see it through to its more or less violent end.

Elmore Leonard's *Three-ten to Yuma* is a thriller. Deputy Marshall Paul Scallen must deliver a fugitive to Tucson to stand trial, fighting off both the townspeople who would lynch him and the gang who would free him. In the same vein, there is no mystery in Leonard's vengeance story *Valdez is Coming*. The town constable Valdez is (for the sake of argument) the good guy, the Rancher Tanner is the bad guy, and we're just here to watch him get his comeuppance.

Richard Matheson's *Journal of the Gun Years* veers towards historical fiction (it's framed by comments by the "editor" of the journal) but it has its thriller-ish moments. Once you get past the idea of a gunslinger writing a journal of his exploits ("we've got his confession, Your Honor, it's right here in his book!") the tale of his long, violent and lonely years as a gunman is filled with misfortune and tragedy, but no mystery.

As for contemporary or "neo" Westerns, Cormac McCarthy's *No Country for Old Men* is definitely a thriller. We know who the psychokiller is, meeting him in the first pages. We just have to watch ~~Tommy Lee Jones~~ Ed Tom Bell suffer through the agony of tracking him down. James Crumley's *The Last Good Kiss* and *Bordersnakes* read as roadtrip thrillers but are at least partly Mysteries, because private investigator C.W. Sughrue takes on the mystery of the missing daughter in the former and the fact that Sughrue doesn't know who is trying to kill him in the latter.

From the Best to the Worst

If genre Westerns and writers have not been before the public and academic eye, it's no fault of Bill Pronzini.

From the 1980s onward, Pronzini edited over a hundred anthologies, many of them co-edited with Martin H. Greenberg. Around thirty of these are anthologies of Western stories. Along with omnibus collections such as *The Western Hall of Fame: An Anthology of Classic Western Stories* (1984) for The Western Writers of America, he worked on anthologies arranged around subjects: *The Cowboys* (1985), *The Gunfighters* (1987), *The Lawmen* (1984), *The Cattlemen* (1986) *The Outlaws* (1984), a regional series: The Texans (1988), The Arizonans (1989), The Californians (1989), The Montanans (1991) and the Northerners and Northwesterners (both 1990); and even a collection of stories about *Christmas out West* (1990).

Again with Martin Harry Greenberg, he worked on two collections of (then) newer stories: New Frontiers (both Volumes 1990), and with Marcia Muller he edited *She Won the West: An Anthology of Western & Frontier Stories by Women* (1985).

On his own he edited collections of Western stories from the pulps, *Wild Westerns: Stories from the Grand Old Pulps* (1986) and

More Wild Westerns (1989), and once more with Greenberg, three volumes of Western short stories that were made into movies: *The Reel West* (1984), *The Second Reel West* (1985) and *The Third Reel West* (1986).

He edited, alone or with Greenberg, 40 author collections, including a series of "The Best Westerns" -- by, among others, Steve Frazee, Lewis B. Patten, Wayne D. Overholser, Ed Gorman -- and himself. On his own he edited a dozen short story collections by Frank Bonham -- some of them longer stories (or shorter novels) collected into "Duos" and "Trios."

He even edited several anthologies of horror and science fiction with Barry Malzberg, including one called *Bug-Eyed Monsters* (1980).

He's written 46 books in his Nameless Detective series, which is chiefly set in California; his Quincannon and Sabina detective series set in gaslight San Francisco, some of them written with his wife Marcia Muller; many standalone Mysteries, Westerns and Western Mysteries, including *Crucifixion River* with Marcia Muller (2007); and a gazillion short stories, including the aforementioned *Best Westerns of Bill Pronzini* (1990), *Coyote and Quarter-Moon* (2006) and short stories in the Quincanon series, *Quincannon's Game: Western Stories* (2005).

And after he did all this work to bring the best of Western genre fiction to the notice of the public, he goes on to show us the *worst*. He has a soft spot for books "so spectacularly awful that they are classics of their kind." He calls them "alternative Westerns."

He'd already dealt with the "alternative" classics of Mystery and Detective fiction in his hilarious books *Gun in Cheek* and *Son of Gun in Cheek*. He followed this with a similar book on Westerns, called, what else? *Six-Gun in Cheek*.

In all these books, Pronzini gleefully quotes some of the worst prose set to print. My favorite from Gun in Cheek is "In plain English, nix on the gat." Some gems from *Six-Gun in Cheek*:

"More bullets trundled across the room." (Oscar Kennard, *Timberline*)

A bullet had found its way to some portion of Brad's anatomy that was resenting it." (Jackson Cole, *The Outlaws of Caja Basin*)

With the cattle there would be close to thirty riders, most longhaired and unkept [sic]. All were fighting men, hired and paid according to the number of notches on their butts. (Tom Roan, *Rawhiders*)

But as in the previous books, *Six Gun in Cheek* isn't *all* about the funny quotes. Here he gives a history of the lending library publishers (LLPs) who filled a niche for cheap, plentiful and sensational Western hardcovers between the pulp era and the paperback era (the same publishers put out a raft of similarly cheap Science Fiction hardcovers). These were meant as disposable reading and cycled in and out of local public libraries as quickly as they were written.

As with the dime novels and pulps before them -- and the paperback originals to come, they were churned out by authors who wrote in any genre that would make them quick money, so there's a fair bit of genre crossover. The LLPs are a good source for Western Mysteries and hard-boiled Westerns. Unfortunately most of them were as terrible as they were popular.

...And the Ugly

While we're on the subject of *bad* Westerns, I suppose I should say something about Adult Westerns. These were popular in the 70s and 80s and carried on the traditions of the dime novels, the pulps and the series paperback originals -- that is, too many books written too quickly, to formula, by writers under a variety of house names and aliases. The British writers reveled in violence and sex while their American counterparts leaned more towards sex and violence. Hardboiled? You betcha.

Inspired by the spaghetti Westerns, the Piccadilly Cowboys were a group of British writers living in London, none of whom had ever been west of

Piccadilly (thus the name). Their real names were Terry Harknett, Angus Wells, Laurence James and John Harvey, but they wrote under a variety of pseudonyms, depending on the series.

"The Most Violent Westerns in Print" was their motto. In the fanzine *Hot Lead #1: The Piccadilly Cowboys* Paul Bishop writes: "... the protagonists created by the Piccadilly Cowboys were not traditional anti-heroes, or even amoral drifters with their own personal code. They were often brutal, violent bullies -- sociopathic villains -- with no thought for anything beyond their own survival or the slaking of their depraved lusts -- killing, vengeance, sadism and prurient rutting."

Between them, the Piccadilly Cowboys wrote over three hundred of these, in 16 series, with names like *Edge* (the leader with 61 titles), *Crow*, *Apache*, *Herne the Hunter* and my favorite that I'll probably never read, *Claw* (yes, he has a creepy mechanical hand).

Terry Harknett, in an interview in *Hot Lead*, describes (a bit hilariously) writing the *Edge* series, which rather wore on him towards the end of its run. "I started to ask myself whether I had written 60 books or one book 60 times."

I've only read one of them, but maybe I've read them all. Efficient!

Hot Lead #3 is devoted to the Adult Western more generally. Paul Bishop provides a good capsule history beginning with the Lassiter series, published by "legendary low-end publisher" Harry Shorten, who went through several imprints and house-name authors to get what he wanted, a character who was "a complete bastard and an unrepentant son-of-a-bitch." But it wasn't until Playboy Press started publishing the Slocum (argh) series under the house name Jake Logan that the term "Adult Western" appeared on the cover -- in a big red circle you can't miss. The "bible" for the series called for three hard-core sex scenes per book.

Other publishers followed with series like Buckskin (Leisure), The Trailsman (Signet), and the hugely popular *Longarm* (Jove). Bishop writes, "If you understandably thought Longarm was a cool nickname for a U.S. Marshall, as in *Long Arm of the law*, you would be wrong." Longarm ran from 1978 to 2015, ending with #436: *Longarm and the Model Prisoner.*

The series with the most titles is *The Gunsmith* series written Robert J. Randisi under the name J.R. Roberts. The series started in 1982 with *Macklin's Women*; #480: *The Friendly Gold Mine,* was published in 2022. Randisi is an odd duck. He's a latter-day pulpster of the old school, with bragging rights to over 600 novels, including the Gunsmith books, which he churned out monthly for years. To round out his career, he's written other Adult Westerns, straight Westerns, and Mysteries.

So *why* were these books so popular? I suppose because, hey -- it was the 70s and what we needed was an oversexed trigger-happy hero with a porn-stache to die for. Or... something.

Hardboiled Westerns

All this is interesting -- and there's lots of good (and bad) reading here, but I found myself wanting a hard-boiled Western. Not a hardboiled Western *Mystery*, or hardboiled Western *porn*, just a plain, gritty, *hardboiled Western*. I ended up with Robert Parker and Elmore Leonard.

Robert Parker wrote only a few Westerns late in his career, *Gunman's Rhapsody* (2001) about Wyatt Earp and an excellent series featuring two "itinerant lawmen," Virgil Cole and Everett Hitch, who clean up towns that badly need it. They're gunslingers, but they're the good guys, and they have standards. In each town, the powers that be are presented with a list of new laws Cole and

Hitch have written up -- which boil down to "stop shooting each other." If they're not adopted, then no deal.

Hitch is Cole's Dr. Watson, chronicling Cole's deeds, and some of his own past, in a laconic style that Parker has used to the same good effect in his detective stories.

The first, *Appaloosa* (2005) was made into a film starring Ed Harris and Viggo Mortensen. Parker wrote three more in the series; *Resolution* (2008), *Brimstone* (2009) and *Blue-Eyed Devil* (2010), which was published shortly before Parker's death. The series has been continued (in the tradition of pulp fiction) by Robert Knott, with six more titles in the series so far.

The ones Parker himself wrote are solid hard-boiled Westerns. Tough, violent and full of ironic wit.

While Elmore Leonard is best known for his crime fiction and thrillers, his earliest novels and stories were Westerns. His first story, "Trail of the Apaches," appeared in *Argosy* in 1951, and he wrote over thirty more, most of them before 1958. His most famous short story, "Three-Ten to Yuma" was published in *Dime Western Magazine* in 1953; his classic Western novels include *Last Stand at Sabre River* (1959), *Hombre* (1961), and *Valdez is Coming* (1970).

Some of his citified novels have been described as "Eastern Westerns," and Leonard agreed. The first of these was *City Primeval: High Noon in Detroit*. The subtitle (added by the publisher) gives the show away. Other Eastern Westerns are *Kill Shot* (1989) and *Cuba Libre* (1998).

Then in 2002 he began publishing a series of neo-Westerns about Raylan Givens, a maverick U.S. Marshall whose exploits get him transferred to his unbeloved home town in Harlan County. The popular TV series *Justified* was based on the story "Fire in the Hole," first published in the collection *When the Women Come Out to Dance* (2002), which was later renamed *Fire in the Hole* to tie in with the TV series.

Leonard wrote two books about Givens before the TV series: *Pronto* (1993) and *Riding the Rap* (1995). He wrote *Raylan* (2012) while the show was running and didn't worry about meshing the story with the show. He told the Daily Beast:

"They made me an executive producer on the show, and executive producers don't really do anything. I thought, 'How can I sit here and collect money and not do anything?' So I wrote a book, *Raylan*. I didn't want to interfere with the writers. I gave it to them and told them to take what they wanted. Someone said that when Graham Yost [the show's creator] read it, he said, 'Strip it and hang it up for parts.'"

In Leonard's *Valdez is Coming* I found my ideal hardboiled Western. It's also a *meta*-Western. At least the *book* is.

The problem with movies is that movies have actors. And actors have a lot to do with how a story is told and how it's received. Sure, the guy's an outlaw but it's *Paul Newman*. The ending of the story has to be changed to be more upbeat because we can't kill *John Wayne*.

Yes, there are real Mexicans living in Mexico who look like Burt Lancaster but casting a lantern-jawed Hollywood hunk as Roberto "Bob" Valdez pretty much ruins the joke before it's set up. Leonard leans hard on stereotypes, so the mild-mannered Mexican Sheriff is (spoiler alert) completely and tragically underestimated by the Anglo Bad Guys. Without that, and other ironic twists, *Valdez is Coming* is merely a violent shoot-em-up thriller. The plot is simple. Valdez is manipulated into killing an innocent man who Tanner, the local ranching bully, claims is an outlaw. Valdez, being an upright kind of Sheriff, requests $200 in damages for the slain man's pregnant wife. Tanner laughs at him and has his 'boys' rough him up. Valdez is determined, and again requests the money, and again is beaten up and humiliated -- this time tied to a cross and driven into the desert. Finally, since he's now asked twice, very politely, he's had all he can stands and can't stands no more and goes into vengeance overdrive. He gut-shoots one of Tanner's men so

he survives just long enough to ride into Tanner's ranch/compound to deliver the message of the title. Meanwhile, he sneaks into the compound and abducts Tanner's fiancée, planning to use her as leverage. Tanner comes after him with a posse, which Valdez picks off one by one. Turns out he's a sharpshooter, a veteran Indian fighter, a brilliant war strategist, and knows the hills like the back of his hands. It all culminates in a confrontation that isn't the shoot-out one expects.

In "A Conversation with Elmore Leonard," with Gregg Sutter, Elmore says "Look what I got away with... In the final scene of Valdez there is no shootout, not even in the film version. Writing this one I found that I could loosen up, concentrate on bringing the characters to life with recognizable traits, and ignore some of the conventions found in most Western stories." (He later did the same thing in *Cuba Libre*.)

The dialog is tough with a dose of black humor. Hardboiled, in other words. Near the end of the book Tanner's second in command turns to Valdez just before the non-shootout.

"Goddam, you do it." The Segundo said. "You know how many of mine you kill?"

"Twelve," Valdez said.

"You count them."

"You better, eh?" Valdez said.

The Segundo watches him, thinking he'd trade four of him for Tanner and his entire crew. *"He could kill a man at six hundred yards, and the son of a bitch kept count."*

The satisfaction of *Valdez is Coming* lies in the familiar worm-turns plot, but also in Leonard's sly tweaks and not-so-small details: A Mexican in the Old Southwest is an unlikely Western hero, just to start. The man Valdez is tricked into shooting is Black; his pregnant wife is Apache; and Tanner's fiancée turns out to be a damsel in distress who just needs a little help to save herself. Leonard doesn't just "ignore" the usual conventions, he tweaked them with glee. He wrote a shoot-em-up novel that's almost but not quite a straight Western; one that's as illuminating as it is entertaining. A meta-Western!

No, But I've Seen the Movie

With every essay on Westerns I've started out with the idea that I could find a few interesting books, write them up, and dust off my hands. Each time I have quickly found myself drowning in books, in over my head, overwhelmed — and delighted, of course. But I have a To Be Read pile tall enough to make a bookaholic turn to drink.

Note that I said *books*. I've been writing about *written* Westerns, because I'm a bookworm, dang it. And I started with the idea to write about some oddball and/or obscure SF/F/Western novels – books like *Six-Gun Planet* by John Jakes and *Lone Star Planet* by H. Beam Piper.

I had no idea I was doing anything unusual. I started doing research, and as long as I was reading commentary by SF critics, nothing went too far amiss. But once I started reading serious criticism about The Western, I was confused for longer than I should have been, because the stuff written *about* Westerns didn't seem to line up with the novels and short stories I was reading. What I needed was somebody to pull me aside and murmur, "Cheryl, dear, nobody *reads* Westerns."

I mean, I know genre Westerns aren't as popular as SF/F, Romances, Mysteries or blockbuster Thrillers. Or possibly books on vacuum tubes or cooking with lard. But I was shocked that academics and popular critics ignored written Westerns. Serious "literary" study or off-the-cuff opinion piece, it's *all* about The Movie.

They'll even slide from writing about *Riders of the Purple Sage* (the book) to writing about *Shane* (the movie) without acknowledging they've made a switch from one medium to another. Yet they make grand pronouncements about "The Western" based on film. That the Western is dead is the most common of these.

Articles that *do* discuss novels tend to move from works considered foundational to the Western genre and then skip over the genre entirely to end up at Literature with a capital L. They'll start with Zane Grey and Owen Wister (sometimes going back to James Fenimore Cooper); may or may not spend much time on Dime Novels; will mention Louis L'Amour in passing; then a handful of the same popular titles will make an appearance – *The Ox-Bow Incident*, *Warlock*, *The Shootist*, *True Grit* -- the list trending more to the literary side until we arrive at *Little Big Man* and *Blood Meridian*.

Except for the brief mention of L'Amour and perhaps a glancing reference to "formula Westerns" dismissed as "sub-literary," the entire swath of popular genre Westerns is just... not there.

All of this feels peculiar to me as a Science Fiction fan. The SF/F genre is so focused on the written word, whether modern novels or '30s pulps or 19th century authors. Not to say film isn't important to SF/F, from *The Blob* to *Star Wars*. But film is just one part of the genre, along with TV shows, graphic novels, videogames... Nothing is left out of the conversation, even if there are strenuous arguments about it. And there are! But nothing is just completely ignored. Especially not most of the genre!

Treating SF/F like Westerns would mean a critical survey of SF would focus on key films (The *Day the Earth Stood Still*, *2001: A Space Odyssey*, *Dune*, *Star Wars*) without mentioning any SF authors, not even the ones who wrote the novels the films were based on.

Or writing about SF/F by noting a few foundational written works -- Verne, Wells, Orwell; maybe briefly noting the pulps; followed by a short discussion of the modern period – Asimov, Clarke, Heinlein; moving on to some of the "serious" authors – Le Guin, Bradbury, Delany --

trending towards Literature until arriving at Vonnegut, Atwood and Murakami. Leaving out almost everybody else from Anthony to Zelazny.

Weird, right?

The irony is, once you tear yourself away from Western films and Literary Westerns and look more closely at popular Western novels and short stories, you can find all kinds of interesting things in the genre Westerns — including the very things that critics claim the Western lacks.

Including some *really good* writers. To add insult to irony, the authors who write this interesting stuff are disregarded and overlooked, when by rights they should interest serious critics. If you're worried that Westerns are too white, why wouldn't you want to consider Percival Everett, a Black author of Westerns, Mysteries and literary fiction, all with Black characters and from a Black sensibility? Why wouldn't you want to hear what Robert J. Conley had to say about writing Westerns while Cherokee (it's fascinating!) or explore Stephen Graham Jones's desire to "put Indians everywhere?" If you're worried Westerns are too male, why wouldn't you explore the women Western writers -- Dorothy M. Johnson, Anna North, Marcia Muller, Leigh Brackett, Lee Hoffman, Eli(za) Colter? Why wouldn't you want to delve into the novels of Elmer Kelton or Rudolfo Anaya that deal with the tensions, historical and present-day, between Whites and Mexicans?

Thomas J. Roberts, in his book with the irritating title *The Aesthetics of Junk Fiction*, writes that it's important to recognize that genre fiction comes in different media and these have different aims, meanings and even histories *within* a genre. "Westerns" includes "the Western in film, in print, on television, in comic books, in commercials, in tourist attractions, in song, and no doubt other mediums as well..." (I would add videogames). The differences between these are not trivial, Roberts says. Confusing one part of a genre with the whole "is a continuing source of error -- most notoriously, perhaps, in the impressions people form of prose science fiction from their experiences with film science fiction."

Prose Western fiction suffers the same kind of error. And this is really too bad, because there is a lot of good prose Western fiction out there. And a lot of this good stuff is genre fiction of some kind. Straight-out Westerns. Space Westerns. Post-apocalyptic Westerns. Westerns full of ghosts and pale riders, magic wagons and vengeful deer spirits. Gaslight San Francisco detective Westerns. Hardboiled detective Westerns. Hardboiled outlaw Westerns. Modern-day cop Westerns -- Marshalls whose beat includes Yellowstone, Small-town Texas sheriffs, Navajo reservation detectives. Road trip Westerns, whether across the prairie by horse and wagon, or down the highways of Texas or California.

And finally... there's another branch of the modern Western that gets absolutely no respect at all: The cowboy Romance. These are extremely popular -- Romances outsell all other categories of popular fiction -- and some of them feature a Mystery plot alongside the Romance alongside the Western. I have not read many of them, but these strike me as a counterpart to "Cozy Mysteries." They may be tough and even violent, but the plots focus on romance, and so they always, *always* have a happy ending.

So it seems the Western is not dead. It's just moved into other genres. These — Mysteries, Detective Fiction, Thrillers, Science Fiction, Horror and Fantasy, even Romances — are all more respectable than paperbacks labeled as WESTERN on the spine.

Even though that's what they are.

Recommended Reading

Bill Crider, "Five of a Kind: Sleuths in Spurs," January Magazine [no date given] https://www.januarymagazine.com/features/westernmyst.html

Hot Lead fanzine. Edited by Justin Marriott, thepaperbackfanatic@sky.com. Issue One: *The Piccadilly Cowboys*, May 2018. Issue Two: *The Art of the Western (The Western in Vintage Paperback)*, June 2018. *Hot Lead Most Wanted All Review Special*, May 2020. (Available through Amazon)

Edward Gorman and Martin H. Greenberg, eds. *The Fatal Frontier*. New York, NY: Kensington Pub. Corp./Pinnacle Books, 1998. Originally published: Carroll & Graf, 1997.

Edward Gorman, Dave Zeltserman and Martin H. Greenberg, eds. *On Dangerous Ground: Stories of Western Noir*. Baltimore, Cemetery Dance Publications, 2011.

Donald Hamilton, ed. *Iron Men and Silver Stars*. Greenwich, Conn.: Fawcett, 1967. Includes his own weird Western ghost story, "The Guns of William Longley."

Tony Hillerman, ed. *The Mysterious West*. New York: Harper Collins, 1994.

Joe R. Lansdale, ed. *The New Frontier: The Best of Today's Western Fiction*. New York: Doubleday, 1989

Elmore Leonard. *The Complete Western Stories of Elmore Leonard*. New York: William Morrow, 2004. Includes the short story "Only Good Ones," that Leonard turned into *Valdez is Coming*.

Billie Sue Mosiman and Martin H. Greenberg, eds. *Blowout in Little Man Flats: And Other Spine-Tingling Stories of Murder in the West*. Nashville: Rutledge Hill Press, 1998.

Bill Pronzini, ed. *Wild Westerns: Stories from The Grand Old Pulps*. New York: Walker and Company, 2001; and *More Wild Westerns*. New York: Walker and Company, 1989.

Robert J. Randisi, ed. *Black Hats*. New York: Berkeley Books, 2003.

Just to complicate things, there's another superior-looking fanzine entitled <u>Starfire</u>. This seventh issue is almost as big, with its 64 similar-sized pages, I wouldn't want to have to decide which fanzine has the better art; the offset reproduction is perfect although a typewriter face is used, and the contents are perhaps more calculated to appeal to both the active fan and the reader whose interest is solely in professional science-fiction. Miraculously, it's mostly the accomplishment of one person, Bill Breiding, with the help of a handful of friends, not the achievement of most of the non-football players at a major university. Don D'Ammassa on Clifford Simak's fiction and a George Barr interview are particularly noteworthy.

—Harry Warner, Jr. from Riverside Quarterly, 1977

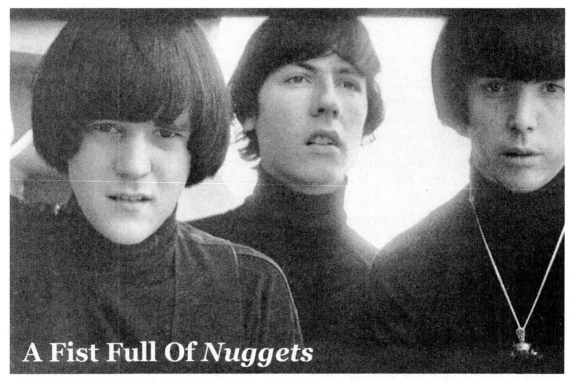

A Fist Full Of *Nuggets*

I write reviews mostly for movies and music on Amazon as johnf. *The movies are usually classic films and the music is classic rock and pop as well as classical music. Last year my musical focus was largely on the 1960s garage band phenomenon. This short piece is based on my review of "Nuggets from Nuggets" without the focus on the individual songs on that disc or its sound, more a general summary of the development of the genre.*

They came from all over the country: New England (Barbarians), Mississippi (Gentrys, Gants), Texas (Five Americans, 13th Floor Elevators), the Upper Midwest (Castaways, ? and the Mysterians), San Francisco Bay Area (Beau Brummels, Count Five, Chocolate Watchband), New York (Blues Magoos, Strangeloves), and a whole wave from L.A. (Standells, Seeds, Leaves, Love). The L.A. Bands were the second wave, appearing from mid-1966 on and marked the new importance of Los Angeles as a center of pop culture. They were initially responding to the British Invasion which above all showed that a self-

contained quartet or quintet was a viable hit maker. Some had names that suggested a British origin (Beau Brummels, Sir Douglas Quintet) and some used British Invasion harmonies (Knickerbockers, Gants) while others followed the British Blues Revival (Shadows of Knight).

The British Invasion was unanticipated and had a gigantic effect on American pop music and teen culture. Like a bomb, it completely blew away most of the previous American pop scene. The teen idols of the day completely vanished as did most of the American Bandstand scene. Even superstars like Connie Francis never had another hit and Elvis had only minor chart success with the exception of "Crying in the Chapel". The ones who survived were mostly the new performers of 1962 and 1963: the Beach Boys and Jan & Dean, the Four Seasons and newer singers like Gene Pitney, Del Shannon and Leslie Gore. Motown stayed around, though their future success would be with new groups like the Supremes and the Temptations. The Girl

The

Music

John Fugazzi Machine

Group Sound continued, but not with the Shirelles or the Phil Spector groups but with new groups like the Shangri-Las and the Dixie Cups. Though these big names thrived as usual in the transition year of 1964, they were all diminished afterwards, with only the Beach Boys and Four Seasons regularly making the Top 10.The R&B scene changed with the triumph of Motown and later the rise of Memphis and Atlantic Records. Like the pop scene, many of the early stars, Brook Benton, Dinah Washington, Chubby Checker, Clyde McPhatter virtually disappeared. All along this time it must be noted that at no time did the British groups completely dominate the charts. There were always a few of them with hits, but never more than a handful at any given time.

The Folk Music Revival had reached its peak in 1963 with some radio stations going all-folk but would quickly disappear as fast as the old pop scene only to resurface not long afterward with many of its members entering the folk-rock and sunshine pop scenes. They brought into the pop scene a whole new set of values in which the lyrics were important and the album was the thing more than the single. They also added a sense of seriousness about their art, which became more about creating great music than becoming a pop star. That took until 1967-1968 but it changed the scene forever. The garage bands for the most part arose in the old world where the single was everything and the album was a hit single, a follow-up and some filler. This had a negative effect on the garage bands, most of whom were one hit wonders. The importance of a string of hits cannot be overestimated: you were only as big as your last single. It was also true that the teen market was mostly a singles market economically and though American teens bought albums, they could only buy so many at least until the late sixties when they were more grown up. Many of these bands would have thrived in the FM radio and album scene that established itself by 1969.

This is all long enough ago to require an explanation of the basics. The current scene is absolutely overflowing with information: interviews and photos on every available social media platform, blog and fan site; songs are streamed, often free, without the need of buying a record. Performances are available 24/7 on YouTube and similar sites. In the 60s it was all about the AM radio. There were a few TV shows, but AM radio was how you heard music. This was all "Top 40 Music" so you generally had only one or two stations that would play it. "Rock and Roll" as all of it was still called by an adult world that made it the fodder of standup comedians and withering newspaper articles, was left to the kids and otherwise ignored (something that was actually positive). Unlike Britain, there was no New Musical Express or other serious critical publications, only trade magazines like Billboard and Teen magazines that mainly featured pictures of cute pop stars for the girls. Early magazines like Crawdaddy had extremely limited circulation and Jazz and Pop tended to ignore top 40 artists. The result was that many people had no idea, short of the Beatles or the Rolling Stones, of what a group or singer looked like, much less know anything about them. It was all just songs on the radio.

Into this moment stepped the garage bands. They were high school bands who played local dances and whose parents had to sign contracts for them (Gants, Gentrys, McCoys), college bands who played frat parties (Swingin' Medallions, Five Americans), club bands (Sam the Sham & the Pharaohs, Knickerbockers) and one band that was a put-on by three Brill Building songwriters (Strangeloves). The first wave had many things in common. Most were teens or early twenties from the suburbs, most were one-hit-wonders, often they were signed to small local labels that didn't have the resources to properly support a hit group and few saw any real money from their endeavors. Some of these bands were really talented and should have thrived for at least another year or two in the right hands while some just lucked into a hit song. For all of them it must have been a really heady experience to go from local dances to having a major hit on the Billboard Hot 100 and appearing on national televi-

sion shows, but a real letdown when they couldn't follow up their hit.

There were, of course, local bands all over the country who played everything from school dances to weddings. As teen clubs began to spring up, they were more rock oriented than the usual local bands. And in the Pacific Northwest in particular, a thriving band scene arose that produced the pre-British Invasion Kingsmen with their seminal garage band anthem, "Louie, Louie". There was also the surf band scene in Southern California, which never seems to get its due. These were mostly instrumental bands and not the vocal groups that later had the hits. They played huge "Surfer Stomps", dances with a thousand or more in attendance, which required really loud music. Leo Fender worked with them in L.A. to provide the guitars and amps they needed, creating the technology that the later bands would need to get their music across.

With the British Invasion as an inspiration, the first successful garage band was the Beau Brummels ("Laugh Laugh") in late 1964, though most people thought they actually were an Invasion band; their name had been chosen to actually convey this. They had their own sound and couldn't possibly be confused with Merseybeat, but shared a folk-like sound with strummed guitars a bit like the Searchers, a beat consistent with most British groups and an interplay of solo and harmony vocal parts similar to the Beatles. It was also true that the latest actual British band, The Zombies, were similar in sound. Both group's hits were melancholy songs in minor keys and the lead vocals of the Beau Brummels Sal Valentino and the Zombies Colin Blunstone were similar in a distant, foggy, mournful way. The fact that they were from San Francisco remained mostly unknown.

The summer and fall of '65 brought in the first bumper crop of bands beginning with The Strangeloves, who were not the usual garage band material, but three Brill Building composers under the wing of Bert Berns (who wrote "Twist and Shout", "Hang On Sloopy"). They made up a zany, zebra striped vest-wearing band allegedly from Australia because their fake English accents were terrible and were surprised when their "I Want Candy" became a national hit. Still. Most people thought they were British. They, however, passed the torch to the McCoys, a Dayton, Ohio teen band with whom they shared a bill as openers for the Dave Clark Five. A surprising number of the early garage bands opened for the DC5, who seemed to tour endlessly, and they all hated them except for keyboardist Mike Smith; it seems the rest were very condescending and unfriendly. The DC5 wanted to make "Hang On Sloopy" their next single and even taped it from the Strangeloves set. Determined that the British Band wouldn't get the song, they gave it to the McCoys (along with their own backing track; the McCoys could play it but this was a rush-release) and flew the band to New York for the vocals. It was a major hit but has never been acknowledged as the true garage hit it was. It came off later as a bubble-gum tune, but in the summer of '65 it was perceived as a hard rock song.

The Gentrys were a seven member band whose "Keep On Dancing" with its sparse arrangement sat in the Top 5 for a month with heavyweights like "Yesterday" and "Turn! Turn! Turn!". One of the three singers, Jimmy Hart became better known as the pro-wrestler known as "The Mouth of the South". Another Mississippi Group. The Gants had a major regional hit with Bo Diddley's "Roadrunner", which gathered more fans on the Nuggets collection than on its first release (peak #43). It was very different from their usual British Invasion sound but when wanting to get time off school with their parents' consent, they were told by their school officials that the local draft board would be informed and their next tour would

be in Vietnam. In Mississippi this was a serious threat. Texas-originated, Memphis club band, Sam the Sham & the Pharaohs had a monster hit earlier that year with "Wooly Bully" but the original Pharaohs split when Sam decided they were just hired backup players and not part of a group. Texas child instrumental prodigy Doug Sahm had a hit with "She's About a Mover" with the rest of the legitimately good Sir Douglas Quintet, but drug busts broke up the band. Worst off were Minnesota's Castaways. They had a national hit with "Liar, Liar" but were signed by a polka label whose big act was the Jolly Lumberjacks, and which never even put out an album for them.

The bands kept coming in early 1966. The Knickerbockers sang just like a British band but were a New Jersey club band whose album showed they could imitate any style including the Four Seasons. The Five Americans came on with the dark and snarling "I See the Light" but later became a sunshine pop band, giving them a second hit with "Western Union". The Bobby Fuller Four briefly brought back a West Texas Buddy Holly feeling ("I Fought the Law"), and the Swingin' Medallions were an all-out Frat Rock party in "Double Shot (Of My Baby's Love)". The Yardbirds-influenced Count Five came out of the high school band scene of San Jose and had a massive hit with "Psychotic Reaction". The first wave was an entirely unexpected flowering of local talent on local labels, each band arriving independently with little to connect them.

Then a new attitude began to emerge, largely influenced by the Rolling Stones. It appeared initially with the Barbarians' "Are You a Boy or a Girl". The Cape Cod bar band had an in your face attitude that later would be called punk, but at this time were thrown in with folk rock, possibly because it arrived at the peak of that movement and of a surface similarity to Barry McGuire . This attitude became dominant in 1966 in songs like "Little Girl", "Gloria", "96 Tears", and most of all the Standells' "Dirty Water". One of the two big garage hits of the summer (the other was "Wild Thing" but the Troggs were British and couldn't be counted as part of the American bands) it was more completely in your face than any song yet. This was the work of songwriter-producer Ed Cobb, who wrote the song after being mugged in Boston; before this the Standells had been a clean cut club band that appeared on television shows (The Bing Crosby Show, The Munsters) when the shows needed a mock British Invasion band.

Afterward the Standells became a proficient garage band, the beginning of a new wave of Los Angeles based bands. The L.A. scene was active and about to boil over. This time they would be more similar than the motley innocents of the first wave, and a little too far ahead of the curve to produce any big hits. They also represented something new that was happening, the beginnings of what would later be dubbed the counterculture, vaguely united by a disenchantment with the dominant culture and the growing use of drugs. Of course these developments were happening in San Francisco, New York and other large cities and college towns, but musically, it was the L.A. bands who first made the airwaves. If most of the first wave wore suits like their British idols, the new guys wore funky, outlandish clothes guaranteed to get them escorted out of many places.

The Leaves succeeded the Byrds at Ciros, and often sounded like them, but their "Hey Joe" in a fast speed with an electrifying guitar riff took intensity to a new level. The Seeds developed a snarling, about to boil over sound in "Pushin' Too Hard". Lead singer Sky Saxon had been trying to make it in the teen pop scene since 1959 and finally found a genre that fit his unique voice; album tracks like "Girl I Want You' were a new level of wild and crazy intensity. The supreme band was Love, led by singer-composer Arthur Lee, and was into wherever Lee's mind was at any given time. Beginning with a Byrds-influenced sound, they next did the apogee of intense, aggressive garage songs, "7 and & Is", and put it in the basically mellow, jazzy LP, "Da Capo". The elusive and enigmatic Lee came up with a masterpiece with 1967's "Forever Changes", an album that took decades to be finally appreciated. Late

1966 brought Sean Bonniwell's band, the Music Machine, whose rough, gravel-voiced "Talk Talk" was instantly added to the song list of every rock band in the country.

This second wave did not have the big hits of the first. Most of these songs, while often #1 in Southern California cities, all peaked only midway in the national charts. L.A. had leapt ahead of the rest of the country where songs like these were often judged too harsh for AM radio playlists and not played at all. Media people were also becoming aware of drugs gaining in popularity among rock musicians and a minor panic happened in 1966 over possible drug references in songs. This reached absurd heights with songs like "Green Grass" by Gary Lewis and the Playboys and "Sugartown" by Nancy Sinatra being banned by some stations. The banning even spread beyond drugs when the Beach Boys "Wouldn't It Be Nice", a celebration of marriage, was banned for mentioning spending the night together and its flip side, "God Only Knows" for taking the Lord's name in vain. Every band was put under suspicion and a split began to rapidly develop between this emerging new music and the culture at large.

The psychedelic music movement was the final phase of the garage bands and it began more or less (it's both difficult and wrong to claim this "started" something that was actually going on in a lot of places) with the 13th Floor Elevators. A Texas band whose lyricist prominently promoted the widespread use of (then still legal) LSD and even insisted that the band be tripping on it at every rehearsal and performance. Needless to say what such a regimen would do to a band, but at least they got one album out before numerous troubles set in. New York's Blues Magoos and L.A.'s Electric Prunes would do better with it, as did the whole San Francisco scene. By mid -1967 most of the garage band phenomenon would end, though you could add 1968's Rugbys and Bubble Puppy. Since it was never acknowledged at the time, it wasn't mourned or for that matter, even commented upon.

It may have gone unnoticed, at least for a long time, but for the sensibility of Lenny Kaye a freelance writer for the emerging American rock press and future member of the Patti Smith Group. Working at the Village Oldies record store in New York and being part of the band scene there exposed him to this music and also to albums of garage bands who never even had that one big hit. He went to Elektra Records Jac Holzman who understood and approved the idea, even though aside from Love, the Doors and Badfinger, Elektra was known as one of the great folk music labels. The project had the added complexity of the songs being scattered among many tiny labels all over the country, some of them no longer around. A daunting project to be sure, including sound engineering having to be done with so many different masters. It was nevertheless done. This is what happens when record labels are run by people really into music and are not gigantic entertainment conglomerates run by lawyers and accountants.

The 2-record set was a big hit in 1972 and later Rhino made it into a 4-CD, 91 song Box Set that became definitive of the genre. The box set not only collected and preserved the hits, but included follow up singles, album tracks and songs by many bands who never had a hit. Some of them, like the Chocolate Watchband, gained more fans than they had ever had when recording. Rhino subsequently released many single CD's from the set and also added material that expanded its scope to include British bands and genres like Sunshine Pop. The box set, now sadly out of print, generally sells above $100.00. The original 2-LP set is available as a 2-CD set. To start out, I recommend the single disc "Nuggets From Nuggets". It compiles the songs that were hit singles, giving someone who didn't grow up then, a sample of the songs everybody knew. The longer version 2-cd and box set give you much more with which to explore the genre, but much of it was unknown to the average teen at the time.

All in all, garage rock was one of the most vibrant and unexpected developments of the sixties. It was able to develop because of the existence of many small labels that might sign them as opposed to trying to get an audition at Columbia or RCA. On the other hand it's true that many of these labels had rather obscure accounting that deprived bands of money, which often went to the label's management or the band's own manager. Often band's composers signed away the publishing, not knowing that it was where the royalties were. Even bands with honest labels had trouble. Usually these labels did not have the promotional staff, salesmen in different markets or clout to promote a band that had a hit. Their albums were avidly bought by other guys in bands, who listened to everything they could to develop a sound, but there weren't enough of these. In fact, the fans of these generally harder edged bands were mostly boys, which meant much of the pop audience was not that interested. Part of the dynamic of the post 1963 pop scene was bringing a lot of boys back into pop/rock music. The pre-1964 American Bandstand Top 40 world was enjoyed by all teens, but just look at the show and you can see that the girls were the predominant audience. Many of the groups were a bit too ahead of the times and more like what was popular in 1969 and after. Though they were never destined to become big hit artists in their day, the garage bands eventually had a major influence on the music to follow.

(The band Love, above.)

73

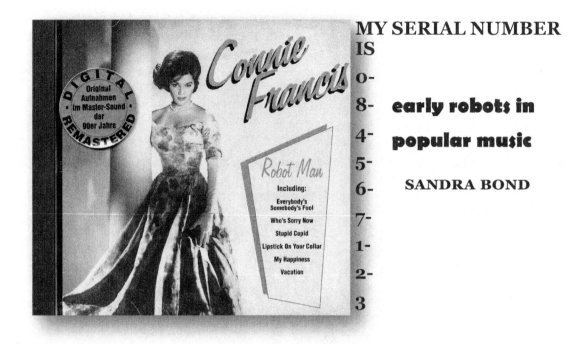

early robots in popular music

SANDRA BOND

I suppose I hardly need to inform the readership of a science fiction fanzine that the word "robot" was coined by Czech writer Karel Čapek in 1921. Nor do I expect most readers will be unaware that Čapek invented the word, but not the concept. Before the word "robot" gained traction, they were generally known by the more ungainly term "automata".

There is no answer to the questions "who invented robots?" or "What was the first robot"; in order to even attempt to answer them, one would first need to define the term. Robotic dancers, musicians, and chess-players are found all over history; Mary Shelley was supposedly inspired to write "Frankenstein" by the automata of Swiss watchmaker Pierre Jaquet-Droz.

Given the fascination which humans have always found in the concept of robotic creations, it is scant surprise that they became a trope of genre science fiction almost as soon as that field came into existence. Equally, robots have featured in popular recorded music for many years.

The ring modulator (patented 1934), vocoder (1938),and the speech generating device (1960) have all found their place in recorded sound. It's a curious trait of these devices that where music is concerned, they tend to fall into two categories a long way apart; the serious avant-garde field, and the novelty. (No doubt some would argue that these two categories, like the extreme left and right wings of politics, go round in a circle and meet each other at the far side.)

Whilst the avant-garde school can claim such illustrious members as Karl-Heinz Stockhausen, it is hard to deny that the novelty pop field has had a wider reach and a greater impact across society in general. Here, of course, the alleged "robot" is very seldom an actual automaton, and is usually a human artiste whose voice and/or instruments have been altered by technology to make them sound robotic. This is a necessity, of course; for how else is the listener meant to discern that the music is supposedly the product of a robot?

Pondering that question, it is unsurprising that the rise of the robot in recorded music coincides with the rise of the robot in the visual medium. Gort in "This Island Earth" made a stir; Robbi in "Forbidden Planet" made a larger one. This is not to mention the motley crowd of robots who strutted their moment on the screen in 1950s B movies. The time was clearly right for robots to make the leap from celluloid to vinyl.

While it doesn't feature a robot itself, I can't pass over what may be the first pop hit to reference robots. It was written by a pair of Brill Building songwriters in New York, Sylvia Dee and George Goehring.

In 1960, Dee was already highly experienced and had a number of decent hits under her belt. Born in 1914, she would have seen the rise of the robots from its start. George Goehring was also a journeyman in the songwriting stakes, and had co-written "Lipstick On Your Collar", an enormous hit for Connie Francis in 1959. Both were well used to collaborating with others, and they had teamed up previously on "Satin Shoes", recorded by the Joy label (owned by publishers Joy Music Ltd), again in 1959.

1960 saw them collaborate on "Robot Man", once more writing for Joy Music Ltd. Perhaps because of the previous link between Goehring and Connie Francis, Francis recorded the song, and it became an enormous hit in Britain, Australia and New Zealand, with Francis claiming that she had had enough of human lovers and wanted a nice, reliable robotic guy instead; a catchy number, concealing a surprisingly transgressive narrative within it. Robots – like aliens – were seen again and again in less ambitious science fiction as being a danger to mankind, either because they simply wanted to destroy us, or because they aimed to steal women. And here was Connie, nice wholesome Connie, seeming to quite relish the idea of being able to "depend upon his robot love."

Perhaps this was why her label, MGM, chose not to release it as an American single, and finding them wrong-footed when it became a worldwide hit. Joy Music were quick to pounce on the lacuna, and their singer Jamie Horton released a slightly belated US single of the number, with advertising pointedly remarking that it was "the original American version of Robot Man, and the only version for sale in the USA." Horton didn't achieve the smash hit that she'd had as a child singer with "I Want A Hippopotamus for Christmas", but her version still reached the lower levels of the charts.

Another, unrelated, song called "Robot Man" was to be released in 1963 in the UK. Behind this one was Barry Gray, a familiar name to science fiction fans because of his long career providing music for Gerry and Sylvia Anderson's epic puppet dramas. The singer went under the anodyne name of "Mary Jane", but appears to have been UK-based Australian singer Eula Parker. Parker was no mean songwriter herself – she penned the highly successful song "The Village of St. Bernardette", and collaborated with Pete Townshend of the Who on his first ever composition, "It Was You", which was written at Barry Gray's house.

1963 also saw, of course, the rise of the Daleks, the unexpected smash success from the BBC's "Doctor Who". Before anyone complains – no, the Daleks were (and are) not robots; they have a small but pugnacious alien inside their metal casing which controls them. The schoolyards of 1963 Britain doubtless cared little for such hairsplitting; what won them over was the easily imitated Dalek voice.

Given the amount of merchandise that was hastily cranked out to capitalise upon Dalekmania, we should hardly be surprised that a record was among them. For many years, one of Doctor Who fandom's holy grails was the supposed Christmas 1963 single, "I'm Gonna Spend My Christmas With A Dalek", by a group whose name was usually given as "The Go Jos". With the rise of the internet, it became clear that this was an oft-perpetuated error and that the group were actually named The Go Gos – not, of course, the outfit who included a young Belinda Carlisle a couple of decades down the line. This syrupy song, far from featuring the Daleks' usual cry of "Exterminate!", had them declare their love for the singer and ask for plum pudding and custard through their ring-modulator. Perhaps this explains why it was not among the merchandising successes of Dalekmania, despite being both written and produced by "Les Vandyke" (Johnny Worth), who counted among his successes most of the songs taken into the charts by British star Adam Faith.

But what the Go Gos' misfire did provide was a template for subsequent robotic record releases; the template of having the song performed by somebody with an electronically altered voice, often referring to, and almost as often credited to, an actual robot – and generally aimed squarely at the novelty end of the market.

Perhaps the earliest robot record actually credited to a robot may be "Mechanical Man", which appeared from MGM at Christmas 1966, with the artiste given as "Bent Bolt and the Nuts". This transparent pseudonym concealed journeyman singer-songwriter Teddy Randazzo, who appeared on the record's flip under his own name. MGM must have thought highly of its chances, since they afforded the release a picture sleeve with a photograph of "Bent Bolt"; it sold well in Chicago, but poorly elsewhere, and didn't reach the national charts.

"Mechanical Man" once again sees a robot go against all logic and wish for a romantic partner; this one, however, pines for a "robot girl who wants to meet a mechanical man". This robot is fixed foursquare in the image of American family life of the day:

> *"I'm looking for someone*
> *who could help me to charge my coils,*
> *and fill me up with bat-ter-ies*
> *and feed me my daily oil"*

The record ends with the hapless narrator expiring in a medley of sound effects, love doomed to be unrequited. Not, though, in vain; in an interview many years later, German avant-gardsters Kraftwerk stated that without "Bent Bolt", their music would never have taken the form it did.

More success tended to greet records where the robotic singer already had a following from the screen, big or small. Thus Marvin the Paranoid Android from "The Hitch Hiker's Guide to the Galaxy", and Metal Mickey from the children's show of the same name, both did well with record releases; Metal Mickey even gained his own record label, Mickeypops.

More interesting robots, however, were to be found away from the cut and thrust of chart hits. Some musicians have taken on – or claimed to take on – the actual personas of robots. In the 1970s, British Christian prog-rockers, Thruaglas Darkly, had (they claimed) a robot member; probably the logical conclusion of this trend was the 1990s band Servotron, who billed themselves as having serial numbers rather than names, and maintained this fiction offstage as well as on. That they were well versed in the genre of science fiction was evident from the fact that they reused an Ed Emsh cover from *Galaxy* magazine on their "There Is No Santa Claus" EP.

Their overt theme was – yet again – pro-robot at the expense of being anti-human, and while a certain amount of tongue in cheek was probably going on, it's telling to note that the same theme we find in robot music time and again makes yet another appearance here – writ large, yes, but still the old chestnut of robots versus humans.

It is hard not to reach the conclusion that robots in popular music have tended to remain within well-trodden thematic paths rather than breaking any new ground. And now that robots have become more than a little *passe* in science fiction, it would seem likely that we will never see a robot artiste who really pushes the envelope of music. Too bad.

carl juarez

Much More than Ugly Ass Apes and Instant Van Gogh: NFTs and A.I. Art

If I tell the average person I make art NFTs I am instantly three steps behind where I was when I started. Aren't those all scams? In fact, aren't they Ponzi schemes layered on top of cryptocurrency scams with a side of insane energy consumption? I saw some NFTs once, they looked like cartoon chimps wearing stupid hats, and some of them were worth millions of dollars!

It takes a lot of work to untangle all that to the point where I can talk about the art and not the medium of distribution, which is what NFTs are. For me it's a way to distribute art — images, videos, short animations, music, words — via the Internet for extraordinarily cheap, under $1 in fact. Making it possible to see my work on any smartphone on the planet seems worth the effort of buying/earning cryptocash (in this case Tezos, aka tez) and maintaining a cloud-based wallet for it with an incomprehensible ID starting tz + 32 letters/digits.

Several cryptocurrencies are used for NFTs, including some that seem to have been created for the purpose. I got into Tezos as part of a wave in 2021 associated with a pioneering website/market known as *Hic et Nunc* ("Here and Now"). In general, each cryptocurrency runs off a blockchain, a publicly-available online ledger that tracks who gave what to whom, and NFTs are a kind of digital contract plugged into a blockchain, saying this image file belongs to that wallet, and this payment was given in exchange. To move funds from one currency's blockchain to another involves exchange rates and fees not unlike exchanging foreign currency in the real world, and I'm not sure it's even possible, just now, to move NFTs from one to another.

Hic et Nunc and afterwards

NFTs are new, but buying digital goods isn't. Some video games, for example, have developed their own economies where you can earn or purchase tools and other goods; this has evolved in

Math for secrecy: The tech behind NFTs

Much of the challenge of getting one's head around NFTs comes from its being the combination, or collision, of multiple emerging technologies.

We start with *cryptography*, which is hardly emerging, it's true — everybody knows it's the basis of private communication on the Internet. If your order for a pillow wasn't encoded into what ideally looks like random gibberish, everyone who saw the message would know what you were buying (complete with payment details) and, worse, could change it into an order for three million chopsticks without leaving a trace.

Encoding data is useful not only for secrecy, but for identification. A password, a fingerprint or face image — all are encoded and compared to an encoded "original". Sophisticated cryptography makes it so there's nothing to read on your smartphone but gibberish without that key; erase it, and without the backing of a nation–state or major corporation you've effectively returned it to random chaos. A variation of that technique allows us to encode individual files so our key is necessary to see the contents.

Next, there's *cryptocurrency and blockchains* — digital alternatives to cash and centralized economies, based on predefined mathematical scarcities and a ton of number-crunching. Transactions are basically anonymous (though accessible via the public blockchain). As the recent crash in value reminds us, cryptocurrency is rarely a viable investment if you're expecting to buy some and let it sit and accumulate. As an

some cases to the point where poorer people are hired to do repetitive in-game tasks to earn the local currency, which can be transferred to other players whose time is presumably more valuable. The difference with NFTs is federation and decentralization — funds earned in one game weren't usable in another, and if that gamemaker went out of business or shut down their servers, it all went poof.

In the case of *Hic et Nunc*, I don't purport to know what was going on behind the scenes, but the website, hicetnunc.xyz, was the work of one developer, who ultimately decided to delete it in November 2021. What was left behind were the ledgers on the blockchain and the NFT files themselves, hosted on IPFS, a next-generation distributed file system accessible via the Internet.

Ordinarily, the marketplace would have vanished like so much digital smoke or campaign promises. But an assistant to the original creator was able to recreate a marketplace, hicetnunc.art, maintaining all that had come before, eventually becoming teia.art. Another site, objkt.com, evolved that not only had all the old *Hic et Nunc* art, but also allowed you to create your own collections, and that's where I do most of my work.

Tezos, after eighteen months, seems to have been a good choice, with a small ton of good artists and a currency not reliant on ruinous power use. There are much larger, more famous NFT markets using Ethereum, but their fees for posting art are three orders of magnitude higher, and they seem to attract more of the negative, scammy behavior that gives the whole field such a bad name.

NFTs at present come in two main flavors: profile pictures (aka PFPs, sometimes called avatars), which are 95 to 98% of the market, and everything else, which I'll call fine art (though that includes pop, folk, and amateur work as well). PFPs resemble collectibles in real life, mass-produced but with distinguishing marks that each is a unique combination of, like one of a kind Beanie Babies. Their appeal is beyond my ken, but the real annoyance is all the wannabees and money-chasers trying to duplicate the successes of earlier PFP projects, Bored Apes and others you may have heard of. I can appreciate the many skills involved in making 10,000 variations of, say, zombie faces by combining degrees of eye protrusion, skin rot, wounds, etc, but it's not art to me...

The fine art NFT market, on the other hand, imitates the real-world art market, both as inspiration and as the inevitable result of masses of artists interacting with masses of collectors on the internet. About 10% of these NFTs are photographs of physical paintings or other art objects, and the rest started out as digital images. Sturgeon's Law applies — there's a lot of mediocre crap — but the law of large numbers does as well, and the non-crap 10–15% comes out to at least hundreds of pieces a day from all over the world.

Who put these fingerprints on my imagination?

Bill Gibson's *Neuromancer* described cyberspace as a consensual mass hallucination, which at this late date naturally leads us to wonder what mass phenomenon, from fascism to the free market, isn't.[1] And the number of layers of consensus here are worth noting.

To collect NFT art, you are using cryptocash to purchase encoded works of art — two layers right there. If you merely want a copy of the image you're looking at, saving it (like nearly anything else on the net) is just a click away, no transaction required, so participation in the marketplace is a socially-supportive intentional choice. When you "purchase" the NFT you're buying a license to say via blockchain, "hey, I own this"; some artists offer physical copies or more traditional reproduction rights but that's purely interpersonal and cannot be enforced other than via the legal system, if at all.

experiment I earned $15 of Bitcoin a year ago, last I checked it was worth $5.

Cryptocash is better thought of as a medium of digital exchange, not speculation. You and others have agreed to use it; the value goes up, the value goes down, and eventually you change it into cash.

Then there's *"smart" contracts* — ways of encoding legal obligations into bits and (hopefully) enforce them without requiring lawyers and courts for action. Its ideal is the copy protection on DVDs and BluRay discs, where the strictures are automatically applied via technology; a world where all the media around you — photos in frames, media on screens, books on your phone — knows who you are and if you're authorized to view it (and maybe cough up some service fee).

Combining the above enables the creation of *NFT*s, non-fungible tokens (as opposed to fungible cryptocash tokens — one Tezos or Ethercoin is indistinguishable from another). We take a file — could be an image, animation, video, text, music — and encode it with a smart contract, resulting in an OBJKT file that we can upload to a marketplace such as Teia, Objkt.com, or many others. The contract includes metadata like title, artist name, description, the total number of copies in the edition, a resale royalty percentage and a wallet or wallets to whom it should be paid.

At this point the artwork has been "minted" and can be seen online, but no price has been set. From here the creator can set the price, accept offers, or start various kinds of auctions, depending on the platform they minted on and its features.

Here we go again: some historical considerations

The world is wide and vasty, and while history never quite repeats, it does rhyme. A.I.-assisted art may be new, but most if not all of the issues it raises echo previous developments in art and technology, not least of which is the fundamental question, is it art?

Is photography art? I happen to think so, and you may too, but there are those for whom it is still debatable. The Romantic notion of art that we all grew up with, where the artist's devotion is to The Work to the exclusion of all else (society, sanity, comfort, bodily safety, etc), often includes a narrative flow of striving and near-total effort that usually ends in tragic loss, a narrative that's undermined when the artist can "merely" click a button to make a piece of art. If substantial physical effort is a requirement of "real" art, then photography doesn't make the cut, and any real art that relies on photography as an aid is deeply suspect as well.

Still, A.I. art can't be art because the A.I. doesn't know what it's doing, right? You can't make art without *trying* to make art, and the A.I. has no consciousness of what art is, much less any intention. Yet Marcel Duchamp, over a hundred years ago, created his "readymades" (of which the upside-down urinal is perhaps the most notorious) from already-manufactured objects, objects mass-produced by people who never thought they were making art. The objects "became" art when the artist signed them and placed them in the context of art.

On top of that, what is a "digital painting"? An ever-increasing number of NFT images are *simulations* of paintings by artists (or non-sentient A.I.s) that involve no paint, no canvas, no brushes even as they imitate their effects. Yet we instinctively perceive and respond to these images as if they were paintings, the same way we shed tears watching sequences of still images portraying imaginary people doing imaginary things in movies or on TV. [2]

So we're "buying" ownership of notional "paintings" portraying imaginary things, using imaginary money marked in a digital ledger spread through a network all over the planet. Seems legit.

Chance takes a hand: Generative art

As a sprouting technophilic teen I was captivated by *Switched-On Bach* and other electronic music, but the math geek inside me was also fascinated by indeterminacy and generative systems. Fractals, non-equilibrium dynamics, chaos theory, all exploring the tensions between incalculable (yet potentially deterministic) randomness and information.

Aleatoric (chance-based) music goes back centuries, and the application of industrial techniques to capturing and reproducing music (player pianos, magnetic tape, vinyl) naturally led to using them to electronically manipulate and, later, compose music, with the sequencer (hardware or software) being the equivalent of a word processor for composition.[3]

Today's computers are essentially very powerful and enthusiastic zombies. There is no consciousness, no "laws" beyond those of physics and digital logic, no self-preservation instinct, no *self* to preserve.

The efforts to add some intelligence into our software have after decades of fitful progress began this century to see results, benefiting from the confluence of the vasty Internet (for raw data) and the ever-more-efficient computations of specialized chips (to process it). Google in particular was the first to bet that useful information could be gleaned from huge data streams (starting with voice recordings from their phone service, used to train speech-recognition systems) without trying to imitate mental structures like consciousness or self in the classic "hard" A.I. sense, and the results have been surprisingly effective.

First (human) speech to text and sentiment analysis (is the text happy? sad? mad?), then visual analysis like object recognition (is this a hot dog? 97% likelihood) and style transfer (draw me this hot dog like van Gogh) have achieved general usefulness. More recently, these techniques have been harnessed to generate new text and images.

Current state of the art takes training data and deconstructs the images mathematically into a multi-dimensional form (about 750,000 dimensions, if anyone's counting). For ease of analysis, math developed to represent diffusion processes (think a droplet of ink spreading throughout a glass of water) is used to consolidate and reduce all those dimensions to a smaller notional "latent space" that can be sampled.

Similar funky math is performed on vectorized representations of the input images' captions, and once all the parts are assembled it's possible to reverse the process, feeding image descriptions into the system and getting new images out.

The results are uncanny but also deeply weird, especially as regards human representation. It knows that fingers tend to appear next to other fingers, for example, but not how many make up a full set. Anatomy in three dimensions is pretty much a mystery, sometimes nonchalantly producing surreal aggregations of flesh that make most body horror look like pleasant illustrations for a children's book.

Yet there are glimpses of new vistas here. Non-abstract painting has thoroughly explored the spectrum of visual representation, from the simplicity of a child's crude daubs through the abstracted sophistication of an "artist's rendering" to a meticulous photorealism that is theoretically

Surely, though, art requires an artist to make it. But in John Cage's seminal work *4'33"* the performer sits at the piano without playing it, and as the audience listens all the accidental and unintended sounds (squeaks, coughs, air movement) in the concert hall become the piece. Perhaps the ultimate indispensable element of a work of art is someone to *experience* it as art, to perceive and consider their response.

A.I. art does raise some novel issues. For one thing, there's a moral and quasi-legal controversy concerning the millions of images (with captions) scraped from the web that are used to train the networks, most (if not all) gathered without the permission of their creators. Moreover, prompts often reference particular artists in order to imitate their styles. Personally, I think it's crass to use a single artist, especially a living one, in one's prompts, notwithstanding the tendency for some systems to spit up a pastiche of van Gogh's Starry Night whenever "starry" and "night" coincide.

There's also the question of copyright. Images can only be copyrighted by humans (including, alas, corporations), and images by non-humans, including that famous monkey selfie, cannot (though the guy who gave the camera to the monkey is happy to take your money as if it were). Current law says A.I.s can't get copyrights or patents, and it seems unlikely that that will change for some time. This leaves the ability to copyright A.I.-assisted art somewhat indeterminate; what amount of human interaction with the results of a generative process is sufficient for the human to be considered its creator?

indistinguishable from being there. There's a suggestive overlap between the circles of human artistic style (informed by a lifetime of embodiment and perceptions) and the naïve malformations of these machine dreams.

As might be expected, the social and especially legal world has plenty to say about the ramifications of all this, exacerbated by the tendency for the state of the technology to develop daily. But the genie is well out of the bottle. Where earlier generators required more graphics power than your average PC could supply, leading many to use cloud-based solutions, in the last few months versions have emerged that can be run on a recent Macintosh or even some tablets.

As to the future? A.I. has a long history of overselling its capabilities, and there's a real danger of being sucked into the usual hype cycle of bold new claims, but some general technical progress seems reasonably predictable.

Get ready for more simulations — hearing words people never said while doing things they never did. Voice emulation is nearly a commercial

product, and the ability to generate albums of music in a given style seems likely in the next 3–5 years. In 10 to 15 years it may be possible to easily create entirely natural-looking video of real people doing fake things, like something from John Brunner's *The Jagged Orbit*.

The next major step will be when the A.I.s are given more autonomy and begin to interact. Perhaps some will start collecting NFT art and develop their own aesthetics in the course of competitive status-seeking. The implications of all this are quite extensive but alas the space-time available here is too small for me to fit them in.

_____

[1] Answer: Most of them, like race and class, are non-consensual.

[2] See my forthcoming work *Into the Valley of the Uncanny: Similitudes, Simulations, Seemings and Substitutes*. "Confusing and deeply disturbed" — A test reader.

[3] I am one of three people who in late 1984 were likely the first to hear one of Bach's Brandenberg Concertos performed on synthetic log drum.

Goodbye Ray Nelson!

ONWARD AND / UPWARD.!

Andy Hooper's

Original Staples

A Column about Fanzines

FOUR STAPLES IN every fanzine!

Falling Through a Trap Door

As I can submit just one more column for *Portable Storage*, I have decided to go out writing about two of my favorite people in fandom. This may have been what I was trying to illustrate to Bill Breiding since he first asked me to write a column about fanzines – that when we think or talk about fanzines, we are really remembering the people who create them.

Fanzine criticism, when it is worth doing at all, is an intensely personal activity. There's

really no point in trying to look at the work impartially or measuring its success or failure by its own objectives. Fans approach a newly received fanzine with a mixture of jealousy, trepidation and unrealistic hopes, and a great fanzine by someone you dislike can be a bitter pill to take. Writing a fanzine review is akin to assessing your relationship with a fan editor, then making your feelings public.

So it's always easier to review a zine by a fan you generally like, even if you don't especially like their fanzine – it becomes an incident in an ongoing relationship, rather than a Molotov cocktail thrown from a speeding car. You tell yourself, and your friend, that they will do better next time and they usually do.

This is not meant to discount those heady few months when a fan first connects with the fanzine publishing community and knows everyone only by their return address. That is an exciting time, when you only suspect the meaning of so many jokes and can't figure out why people spend so many inches talking about other fanzines. Aren't these things supposed to be about science fiction? Your first few fanzine reviews will inevitably provide hilarious entertainment a decade later when someone reads them aloud at the Hugo-Loser's party. Because you will **lose** that Hugo, bruh.

Robert Lichtman did as much as anyone to make that hour of enthusiastic ignorance as brief as possible for me. He wrote letters of comment on my early fanzines, patiently explaining some of the things I just didn't recognize in the fanzine canon. And he went on doing essentially the same thing for over 30 years, pointing out that an ancient fanzine I offered for bid on eBay was in fact a hoax perpetrated by Burbee and Laney while the putative editor was wearing a metal hat in Korea.

Robert died in July of 2022, following a protracted argument with cancer. Our communication waned a bit over his last year; he published two memorable issues of his SAPS fanzine *Door Knob* in late 2021 and early 2022, talking about the aftermath of his wife Carol Carr's death, and reconnecting with his old community on The Farm. As one of six or seven then-living members of

SAPS, I was able to reply in my SAPS fanzine *Henchman,* but of course I wish I had written more.

I mentioned Robert in my last column, and I won't rehash all of his virtues here. But the salient point that I would make about him is that he edited the best fannish fanzine of the last 40 years, which roughly corresponds to my presence in the field. *Trap Door*#1 appeared in October of 1983; the last issue, #34, was published in December of 2018. He had some extremely vague ideas about issue #35 but abandoned them when Steve Stiles died in early 2020. Stiles had become *Trap Door*'s resident artist, drawing title headings for most of the contents for more than a decade. There was honestly no replacing Steve, and Robert could not imagine trying.

Going Back to Cali

35 years is a long time for any fanzine to persist. After the first two decades, it strains credulity to characterize the editor's fanactivity as a mere phase of extended adolescence. Bob was 41 when he began publishing it; he had taken his time coming back to fanzine fandom and had a very good idea of what he wanted to do there. Some fan editors would have started thirty different fanzines over that span of time, but Robert was faithful to *Trap Door*.

He made his first pass at fandom in his very late teens and early twenties, part of the swirling west coast fandom of the 1960s. He was an enthusiastic member of several APAs and published 8 issues of a well-regarded general-interest fanzine titled *Frap*. He didn't cut himself off from fandom in an angry tantrum or by insistent isolation; but it eroded from his life quickly and he replaced its social contacts with the circle he joined at The Farm, an intentional community outside Summertown, Tennessee.

Ironically, Robert had more involvement with commercial publishing through his work for The Farm than he ever did in fandom. Maybe this co-operative experience had some effect on *Trap Door*, because every issue seemed to be crammed with artists, contributors and correspondents, as crowded as a family reunion.

Trap Door's unique feature was continuity, a natural disposition toward the fannish pastime known as "timebinding." Many issues had a contribution from someone who entered fandom in the 1930s or 1940s, people like Elmer Perdue, Redd Boggs, Ray Nelson and Harry Warner Jr. His letter column, entertainingly titled "The Ether Still Vibrates," always featured correspondence from friends that Robert had known in the 1960s, such as Sid Birchby, Jean Young, Boyd Raeburn and Lenny Kaye. Most had done very little in fandom for the past decade, but Robert tickled them into replying. And he published their mailing addresses, as one does, allowing me to expand my mailing list.

Beyond these revenants, Robert gathered contributions from several other California fans, including Greg Benford, Jeanne Bowman, Carol Carr. Calvin Demmon, Bruce Townley and Paul Williams. *Trap Door* often featured writers that were not found in any

other fanzine, like novelist Chester Anderson and writer and divine avatar Grania Davis. Many of the best contemporary fan writers also submitted material to *Trap Door* and Robert was happy to publish them. Early numbers featured contributions from Richard Brandt, Lucy Huntzinger, Dave Langford and Allyn Cadogan, who found themselves rubbing elbows with Fred Pohl, Bob Tucker and James White.

Robert's own contributions were generally contained in his editorial column "Doorway," which often provided the most contemporary material in the issue. He kept readers up to date on major events in his own life but also frequently covered notable fannish gatherings, like Corflu, Westercon or World Conventions in the bay area. He also kept a running tally of the fanzines which *Trap Door* had received in trade across the calendar year, which began a kind of shorthand report on the overall health of the field. (One reason I started the bi-weekly *Apparatchik* in 1994 was to pad out the fanzines documented in Robert's tally.)

He also tended to share his editorial pages with obituaries for notable friends and contributors and enlisted someone particularly close to the decedent to provide some appreciation of them. As the fanzine initially appeared twice per year, there were times when practically no one died between issues. But as Robert settled into an annual schedule, most issues included at least one memorial, as well as a letter from someone who had died waiting to see it published. Such were the realities of participation in such a mature subculture.

Although *Trap Door* frequently published writing on distant experiences of youth, it did not have the same self-consciously "fan historical" quality exemplified by Richard and Nicki Lynch's *Mimo-*

sa. Mimosa was *Trap Door*'s respected contemporary and won the Hugo awards that *Trap Door* never got, although it was nominated in 1987 and 1992.

When the Lynches asked pioneers of fandom like Dave Kyle and Forry Ackerman to contribute, I assume they expected to receive something about fandom's early decades. But I don't think Robert was that thematically focused – he just wanted to publish something by writers he had respected since he first read them, sometimes 30 or 40 years before. If they wanted to write about the modern world, that was all right with him.

Redd Boggs' column "Penseroso" (which Robert cribbed from Boggs' similarly titled SAPS fanzine), was as likely to ruminate on contemporary Berkeley characters as something comical uttered by his grandparents or a wartime quest for ice cream. F. M. Busby's "Scenario" in

#11 (February 1992) was a completely current piece of political paranoia, starring George H. W. Bush, Nancy Reagan, Mario Cuomo and Dan Quayle. Hawaii was to be annexed by Japan!

A Sense of Beatnik

However, the impression that *Trap Door* was largely concerned with our past was hard to escape. In #12 (March 1993), Andi Shechter openly titled her contribution "One of Those Dreaded Beatnik Memoirs," My own first contribution, also in #12, seemed to look back even farther in "On the Road to 1885." Christopher Priest's contribution to #21 (March 2002) was a simple appreciation of the long era in which typewriters generated most of the world's copy; not so long ago, but Chris didn't help by titling it "The Lost Years." "Revisiting Nydahl's Disease," written by Joel Nydahl himself, naturally, appeared in the same issue.

Perhaps this reputation as fandom's version of an elephant's graveyard tweaked Robert; in

May 2003 he published an issue with one major feature, a faan fictional novel by fellow SAP Gordon Eklund. "Sense of Wonder" featured familiar-seeming characters, time travel and the dawn of science fiction as we know it. It was an entertaining story by any standard but oh so much more so if you are familiar with the earliest fans and their publishing ambitions.

Travel was another recurring topic, both to various nations of the world and in wild places closer to home. John D. Berry, an acknowledged master of the form, contributed to several issues. Jeff Schalles' "Looking for Sunrise Mountain" and "Beyond Sunrise Mountain" were models of the form, worthy of a Breiding brother. Jean Young, in a letter of comment published in #9, enthused: "Jeff Schalles' 'Looking for Sunrise Mountain' was not aggressively humorous, yet not sappy Nature Lore. It came near being the sort of thing I like best: True (pretty much) encounters between land and people who love it."

While *Trap Door* certainly had recurring columnists – Gary Hubbard's "The Cracked Eye" probably answered the bell most often – the sheer number of writers who contributed would likely fill much of a page. That doesn't even consider the letter-column, which was known to publish replies from more than two dozen readers in a single issue.

And a last and often unnoticed strength was

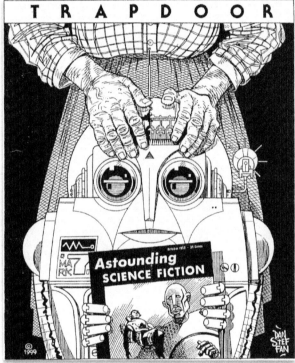

the fanzine's use of graphic art. *Trap Door* was configured in an affordable "digest-size" format, which did not allow for the lavish application of art in the model of an *Outworlds* or *Science Fiction Commentary*. But every issue had memorable graphics, the great majority of which were created specifically by the artist to decorate the article with which it appeared. Over roughly the last half of *Trap Door*'s run, most of its covers were contributed by either Dan Steffan or Steve Stiles. Stiles' covers were consistently funnier and he created a series of them connected by the same gag on a door into or out of nothing. Steffan's work was more stylistically varied and some of his covers are among my favorites across 40 years as a fanzine reader. Every issue had cartoons and illos from a half-dozen creators, including Harry Bell, Grant Canfield, Ross Chamberlain, Brad Foster, Lee Hoffman, Jay Kinney, Donna Nassar, Ray Nelson, Bill Rotsler, Craig Smith, Arthur Thomson and D. West.

As I mentioned earlier, I was also a contributor to *Trap Door* and my assessment must be considered in that light. When the fan history bug finally got under my skin and I began working on my series on the first World SF convention of 1939, *Trap Door* was the fanzine where I wanted to see it published. Robert gave me large chunks of five issues in which to share my findings on Campbell, Bradbury, Weissinger and other convention members and organizers. When he told me he didn't think he would be able to publish Chapter 6, "Sykora's Worldcon," I was quite heartsick. The piece found a home in Kaufman & Tompkins' fine fanzine *Lit-*

tlebrook, but I am still in mourning for the loss of *Trap Door*.

Every publishing jiant of Robert's stature deserves a memorial anthology; my understanding is that a group including Bob's longtime friends Lenny Bailes and John D. Berry are working on publishing a collection of his work. They certainly will have a wide catalog to cover; while Robert is very closely identified with *Trap Door*, he also published dozens of other titles in the two halves of his fannish life. Many of these were composed for submission to an amateur press association; Robert must have been a member of a dozen apas, some of which were private and restricted copies to the membership only. A complete catalog of his fan output would be a thick fanzine in its own right.

Robert was my friend; we had the kind of friendship that requires decades of correspondence to create. We traded letters, certainly; but we traded fanzines even more enthusiastically. I felt like all the work I've done since the early 1980s, well beyond a hundred fanzines, was barely adequate as a trade for the 34 sublime issues of *Trap Door*. Future cultural historians will surely marvel at these expressions of devotion, fascination and love.

The Chance of a Lifetime

As one of Robert's more ardent readers, I found it very satisfying when he received a Lifetime Achievement Award from the committee of Corflu Heatwave in early 2020. The award was introduced at the 2010 Corflu in Winchester, UK and has gone to fans known as fanzine editors, artists and writers, who have inspired the people who organize the convention. Honorees have included Earl Kemp, Ray Nelson, John Bangsund and Elinor Busby; you can find the full list online with the rest of the convention's history at Corflu.org.

Sadly, while the award is always given to a living person, many of its recipients have left us in the years since they were recognized. Since so many of them were above the age of 80 when they received the award, this was probably inevitable. But in the past five years, the committee has begun to recognize fans who are just slightly younger, including Paul Skelton, Bruce Gillespie and Dave Langford. And then in 2022, we chose the "youngest" recipient to date, at least in fannish terms, by presenting the award to Geri Sullivan.

Geri's credentials as a fan writer, publisher, convention organizer, freelance publican, traveling jiant and speaker to elder fen tower among her admiring peers. And her recognition represents a personal transition to me: Geri is the first fan honored whose entire fan career has taken place after I attended my first convention in 1978.

Some of our earlier recipients conducted their first fanactivity decades before I was even born in 1962, let alone before I saw my first *Famous Monsters of Filmland* or attended a fan club meeting. But Geri discovered fandom by encountering author and musician Emma Bull at a mundane party in 1979, They talked for six hours, after which Geri was suddenly a member of Minneapolis fandom.

In truth, she seems like such a quintessential

Minneapolis fan that one assumes she lived in the Bozo Bus Building and was heartbroken when Toronto defeated Minneapolis' hopes for the 1973 Worldcon. But her first Minicon was in 1980. She soon assumed a series of offices in MnStf and responsibilities at Minicons. Her home at 3444 Blaisdell Avenue South in Minneapolis, known to friends as "Toad Hall," soon became the site of many epic fannish parties and hosted traveling fans in fascinated comfort. That house deserved some kind of fannish service award, alongside Courage House, Tendril Towers and the Nunnery,

It's likely that the first fanzines she saw were issues of the MnStf club fanzine *Rune*, then under editors Carol Kennedy and Lee Pelton. But the very air was thick with fanzines then – there were several other fans publishing titles in Minneapolis and each of the

Twin Cities had its own fannish apa. Kennedy and Pelton published 11 issues of *Rune* between the fall of 1977 and late 1980. The title then passed into the hands of a troika including John Bartelt, Garth Danielson and David Stever-Schnoes, and they produced inventive, if erratic issues through the end of 1983. Karen Trego turned the troika into a quartet as of issue #67.

Geri first contributed to issue #75, which was edited by Erik Biever and Mark Digre. Her article, "Indignation and Name Check" described her experiences at the 3rd Corflu in Tysons Corner, Virginia. Her first effort at publishing a fanzine for general consumption was titled *Dare To be Stupid* and gave her

ideas on the many challenges facing Minicon, then going through a huge boom in popularity and population. It was a one-shot fanzine, but was followed by a volume of replies, *Letters To Dare To Be Stupid*. The subject matter was of most interest to the hundreds of fans who regularly attended the convention, but those who noted its appearance agreed that it was a rather impressive-looking fanzine.

My Fingers Seemed to Blur

Three years after attending her first Corflu, Geri put together a committee to bring the convention to Minneapolis in 1989. About the same time the second Progress Report appeared, with a nifty cover by Reed Waller, Geri published the first issue of her general interest fanzine *Idea*. The title came from a piece of intensely local lore, the musical "Midwest Side Story." This was a fannish parody of "West Side Story," written by Susan Ryan, Denny Lien, Jerry Stearns, et al, and performed at Minicon 12 in 1977. The show includes a song called "Idea" – sung to the tune of "Maria" – which expresses the joy of a newly published fanzine.

The first three issues were charming and appeared within the span of one year, with pieces by Dave Clement, Rob Hansen, Elise Matthesen, Jon Singer and Jim Young. They were lavishly decorated with cartoons and fan art and looked **sharp**. By 1988-89, "desk top publishing" had become capable of making a very attractive product and Geri knew how to get the most out of it.

Then, after a gap of 2 & ½ years, IDEA #4 appeared, having undergone a major metamorphosis. The fanzine copy was still generated with a desktop printer, but it was then reproduced on electro stencil and duplicated by mimeograph. The cover featured elements colored by hand and many pages were produced in more than one color. Jaws hit the floor audibly in breakfast nooks across fandom. Mimeographed fanzines were still occasionally seen at the time, but few looked as impressive as *Idea*.

This change in format was attributable in part to Jeff Schalles, who was then Geri's partner and housemate. Jeff had been publishing his own fanzines and contributing to others since the very early 1970s. But I don't know that anything he had produced to that point approached the stunning quality of the 6 mimeographed issues of *Idea*.

Computerized printers produced startlingly clear copy for the stencil and this enabled luxuriously dark reproduction from the mimeo. Both of them turned the mimeo crank several thousand times across the run of *Idea*. I would put the work that Geri and Jeff did on *Idea* alongside the best-looking mimeographed fanzines fandom has done, including Bill Blackbeard's *Queen Anne's Revenge*, Linda Bushyager's *Granfalloon* and Victoria Vayne's *Simulacrum*.

Jeff also wrote an excellent series of outdoor memoirs for *Idea*, titled "Adventures in the Wimpy Zone." His hiking and gardening adventures always stood out from material more directly focused on fandom such as con reports and fanzine reviews.

The other important relationship represented in *Idea*#4 was Geri's mutual affection with British fan Charles Randolph "Chuch" Harris. Chuch

An *Idea* Ahead Of Its Time

had decided that Geri was his mother, during his trip to America for the Minneapolis Corflu in 1989 and she did her best to respond with kindness to the degenerate lad, His article, "The Greening of Fandom," noted that Geri and many other fans had encouraged him into efforts at recycling and composting.

Geri also became close friends with Irish fans Walter and Madeleine Willis, visiting them at their home in Belfast and attending their visits to Florida in 1989 and 1992. It was my pleasure to witness their appearance as Fan Guests of Honor at the World Convention in 1992. Geri was also in charge of the space known as the "evening fanzine lounge" at the Peabody hotel, which was home to the best party in the convention. Geri was an early proponent of the fanzine lounge idea, and her efforts at Orlando n 1992 and Anaheim in 1996 were unforgettable.

Geri was clearly energized in 1992, as two more issues of *Idea* appeared. #5 appeared just two months after #4, and featured Geri's wonderfully bittersweet report on the 1992 Corflu in Hawthorne, California and was accompanied by Linda Bushyager's Guest of Honor Speech. Irish fan and pro James White contributed an original story starring George, the ceramic toad who stood guard at Geri's garden gate.

This Zine'll Cause a Stir!

Issue #6 followed in September, inside a two color cover with art by Stu Shiffman, interpolating Andrew Wyeth,. Alien correspondents like Rob Hansen and Chuch Harris cohabited with Minneapolis locals like Glen Tenhoff, Martin Schaefer and Elise Matthesen to give the impression of a bi-continental barbecue. There was also a well-populated letter-column.

That issue was created as part of the titanic effort which saw Geri in Orlando one weekend and helping to host James White at another convention, Reinconation, in Minneapolis the next. It was an amazing fortnight, but people were asleep on their feet at the end of it. It was little wonder the next issue of *Idea* took 9 months to publish. But it was also a memorable effort.

Issue #7 was printed on a modern telecopier because Geri and Jeff had been unable to secure a large enough stock of good mimeo paper – twiltone – to be able to cover the run. But this was turned into an advantage; Dan Steffan's front cover art looked fantastic, and the interior included several pages of photos which would have been murky at best if stenciled. Much of the issue was about the 1992 World Convention, including Walt Willis in "The Perfect Convention and Other Adventures," Jack Targonski in "Magiconation," Dick Lynch's "What Really Happened" on the mix-up that saw the Best Fanzine Hugo temporarily given to the wrong recipient, and my own piece, "The Wild Geese at the Worldcon." Few world conventions have been documented so thoroughly in a single fanzine.

Another Worldcon had taken place by the time issue #8 appeared in March, 1994, but

the 1993 convention was not quite the love fest as had taken place in Orlando. Ted White's "Nightmare at ConFrancisco" responded to changing ideas and demographics in fandom with a mix of humor and disoriented horror. The rest of the issue's columnists, including Jeff Schalles, R. J. Berlien, Jeanne Gomoll and Luke McGuff, seemed to be taking a break from writing about fandom, with stories about revisiting an old residence, acquiring a new one and getting lost on the prairie.

The letter-column on the enormous 7th issue was substantive and the issue was beautifully reproduced by mimeograph in black, brown and red ink. The lyrics to the song "Idea" from "Midwest Side Story" were reproduced in their entirety on the back cover.

Issue #9 was again too large to reproduce by mimeograph – at 56 pages, it would have taken a huge chunk of out of Jeff and Geri's paper reserve. But it is the nature of all successful fanzines to expand over time – later issues of *Idea* would exceed 70 pages.

Appearing in August, 1995, #9 featured coverage of both the 1994 and 1995 Corflus, Schalles on "Terraforming Toad Hall," and funny pieces from Terry Garey, Kathy Routliffe, Paul Skelton and James White. The issue was also elaborately illustrated with a section of convention photos and a portfolio of art by Tom Foster, Brad Foster, Bill Kunkel, Bill Rotsler and Steve Stiles, among others.

The back cover announced that issue #10 would be a special, entirely illustrated by Steve Stiles. It took 18 months to complete, as much of 1996 was spent in bringing the 10th issue of *Science-*

Fiction Five-Yearly into being. I collaborated with Lee, Jeff and Geri in editing #10; although I didn't contribute much, I was proud of the final product.

When *Idea* #10 appeared, it was indeed entirely illustrated with art by Steve Stiles. Steve also contributed the most singular written piece in the issue, "Passing through Dogpatch," on his adventures in trying to draw a latter-day revival of the comic strip *Lil' Abner*. The letter-column ran for 14 pages and Sullivan still had to omit letters by over a dozen fans. Most of the issue was reproduced by mimeograph on a delicate salmon-colored paper, but an 8-page portfolio of Lil Abner strips were reproduced by laser copier.

Issue #11 appeared in October of 1997 – despite being an immense 74 pages, the entire issue was reproduced brilliantly by mimeograph, with a gorgeous front cover by Glenn Tenhoff. There was a lot of humor in Dave Langford's "Twenty Years of Uproar" and Barb Jensen's travel memoir, "I Yelled at Yanni." But the issue was dominated by Geri's own long examination of her late father through the lens of things he left behind in "Ashes, Dust, 9 Electric Razors." Geri still considers this to have been the most important personal writing she has ever done in fandom and it explained major changes in the author's life and world view.

The 12th and last issue of *Idea* was dated November, 2000. A lot of things had happened in the intervening three years. Geri had become a particularly ardent supporter of the Trans-Atlantic Fan Fund, and this issue featured coverage of the

trips taken by Maureen Speller and Ulrika O'Brien in 1998, the "Year with Two TAFFs." 20 years later, in 2019, Sullivan stood for and won TAFF and is still heavily involved in promoting the fund.

And where early issues often described Geri's trips to fan gatherings in other cities, in #12, everyone seemed to be coming to her. Dave Langford's "Minicon Diary" described a memorable weekend as the convention guest of honor, and the full-color laser-copied cover showed Maureen Speller and sundry other fans at the Minnesota State Fair, enjoying fried delicacies served on a stick. Martin Hoare's "The Art of Roundsmanship" was intimately connected to the consumption of beer, another of Sullivan's enduring passions. And author John M. Ford collaborated with Elise Matthesen on "The Guy Fawkes Songbook," one of the higher expressions of the "filksong" seen in the era.

The fanzine remained a model of Anglo-American cooperation, but some of the most familiar faces were missing. Three fans associated with Irish Fandom of the 1950s, James White, Walt Willis and Geri's beloved "son" Chuch Harris, all died in a four-month period between July and October 1999. Geri noted Chuch's passing by quoting something he had written after losing his closest friend in fandom, Arthur Thomson, in 1990. His words reflected her feelings better than anything she could say.

Toad Away

Still, she gave no indication that #12 would be the last issue. It was produced on a state-of-the-art Ricoh copy-printer, which cut stencils and used them to generate the finished copies in one operation. Future issues were to be produced the same way. She wrote happily of having chaired the most recent Minicon and her intention to take on the hospitality suite in 2001.

In 2001, Geri and Jeff collaborated on another issue of *Science-Fiction Five-Yearly* with Lee Hoffman and *Mota* editor Terry Hughes. Sadly, Hughes died just as the issue was going to press, which cast some shadow over a delicious fanzine. It carried contributions from Greg Benford, Harlan Ellison, Dave Langford, Denny Lien, Stu Shiffman, Ted White and Kip Williams, And it was a fitting coda to Terry Hughes' 40-year career as a fan publisher, which included a 1979 Hugo Award nomination for Best Fanzine.

Years and Minicons rolled by and it gradually became clear that there would be no further issues of *Idea*. We would have to be content with 606 pages of the last great science fiction fanzine of the 20th Century. *Idea* documented people and events that gave fanzine fandom its character in the 1990s. Having attended many of the conventions covered, paging though the fanzine now brings back potent memories for me. The collection of voices in *Idea* was not found anywhere else.

As much fun as it was to read Geri's fanzine, it was even more entertaining to spend time in her company. She set new standards for hospitality suites and fan rooms at conventions in the 1990s and travel in her company held the constant threat of an unexpected feast or pub meet.

I would have loved to see more *Idea*s, especially if Geri would have let me contribute more of my writing. But it was an artifact of the moment in which it was published. Created with the best layout and design software then available, but reproduced on the increasingly archaic mimeograph, it was a unique mix of tradition and innovation. And within a relatively few years, nearly all fanzines would transition to online distribution, rendering everything fan editors endured in the name of quality reproduction suddenly moot. You let the *reader* worry about printing a fanzine, right?

In 2006, Geri and Jeff collaborated with Lee Hoffman and Randy Byers on the 12th and final issue of *Science-Fiction Five-Yearly* Another beautiful work generated by a state-of-the-art mimeo, it had the usual cast of long-time contributors and prolific contemporary fans.

It became certain that this #12 would also be a last issue when Hoffman died in February of 2007. Fandom responded by nominating *SFFY* for the 2007 Hugo Award for Best Fanzine and showed unusually good taste in actually giving it the award! The trophy, presented in Yokohama, featured a statue of "Ultraman" taller than the Hugo rocket.

Geri and Jeff both moved on, and Geri eventually sold Toad Hall and relocated to Massachusetts. She has remained a highly active fan, attending and organizing conventions and working to preserve archival video footage of Worldcons of the 1970s. When she stood for TAFF in 2019, Claire Brialey and Mark Plummer published an anthology, *The TAFF Guide To Beer*, collecting work by numerous writers on one of fandom's deepest and truest passions, including new work by Geri Sullivan, "The Beer That Got Away."

Geri won the race and attended the 2019 world convention in Dublin and she continues to work for the benefit of the fund 4 years later. The only reason anyone hesitated to give her the Lifetime Achievement Award at Corflu Pangloss was that they were reluctant to imply that Geri's career in fandom is somehow "finished." But I prefer to think that honoring someone as young and vibrant as Geri just allows her the time she will need to exceed these superlatives.

Anniversary Portrait Portfolio: A Linoleum Block Print Project
John R. Benson

I have been gafiated for the most part from SF fandom for decades having been distracted by life, the AIDS Crisis, work and the Michigan Renaissance Festival. The latter has absorbed most of my spare time and creativity–especially art-wise. In the 1970's and especially in the 1980's I settled into being a linoleum block print artist hand printing using the brayer and the baren. Then I bought my first printing press–a Kelsey Excelsior 5x8 platen letter press and my first three fonts of type – perfect for printing messages in the greeting cards which have become my main stock-in-trade at the Renaissance Festival. This acquisition also led me into the world of letterpress men and I eventually joined a local club "the Monks and Friars"–a group of old professionals–mostly retired newspaper printers and teachers and a few of their students. There were even a few which had their own public print shops. Over the years the letterpress world has evolved, there are many more women active in the field and few newspapermen and teachers (letterpress is no longer taught in high schools and newspapers are all printed using other technologies). Letterpress is now the domain of the niche printer–wedding invites being our bread and butter, the typographical artist, the hobbyist and the historical re-creator.

So, if you are a letterpress printer, and you've acquired a perforating machine, it has become traditional that you create your own country and start issuing stamps to be traded with other letterpress countries. Therefore, when one of the former Monks and Friars, Phillip Driscoll of Clinton, Michigan, obtained his perforator in 2009 he asked me to create two portraits to celebrate the anniversary of two "immortals"–Charles Darwin and Ludwik Lejzer Zamenhof, the creator of Esperanto – the official language of Phil's country. I have never really done a portrait before so I suggested that maybe my friend Michael Kucharski would be a better artist to ask. Well, Mike said he probably wouldn't have the time so as a backup I created my first linocut anniversary portrait–one of Zamenhof and three different portraits of Darwin through his ages (these three prints have been nicknamed "The Evolution of Male Pattern Baldness"). Two days before I was to deliver my blocks and clean-printed copies of the portraits to Phil, Mike dropped off two perfect little portraits which he found he did have time to produce. Therefore, I now had four blocks of portrait prints to print for the Renaissance Festival and surprise–they were reasonably good and did sell.

Over the next few years I created a few more anniversary portraits and then came retirement and the onset of a new mania. Before my retirement I might have created five to seven anniversary portraits a year. Now I'm creating thirty to sixty portraits–writers, artists, scientists, movers and shakers and a very few politicians–I've finished over 375 so far. Mostly they are dead white men; all my subjects are dead. But I do have a few other notables. This year was the anniversary for Juarez, Paul Laurence Dunbar and Sojourner Truth as well as thirty others. I hope to continue this project for another eight years and then create one big art work with all the cancelled linoleum blocks–there should be 600 to 750 portrait blocks in all.

The portraits in the project and in some ancillary groups, such as my four "Inklings" are generally 4 inches tall by 3 inches wide (well, I did create a 5 inch by 3 inch block for Henri Toulouse-Lautrec, he being such a giant creative genius). They are all hand printed so sometimes one can sense my physical state of the day, some prints show a definite tremor–such are the joys of wabi-sabe. I am using this series to hone my observational and carving skills so some portraits are more successful than others. In linocut I mostly deal with the thick line and mass of ink–I find "shading" to be problematic and I don't really care for these effects. Also, because of registration and ink drying problems, I don't usually do portraits in more than one color. One big problem of course is the source of my images–many photos don't really give enough information and paintings or pre-20th century prints can be really problematic–the image quality can be all over the place. And of course, for earlier notables especially, there may be no image available, e.g. what did Thomas Mallory look like? Sometimes I cobble together a possible image from early portraits but usually I just don't do a portrait when the image doesn't really exist. This work has led to some other larger projects, some of my portraits of Renaissance Festival performers have been quite successful.

[John sent an enormous array of his block-print portraits of mostly authors. If I'd the room I would have published them all. What follows are 60 of my faves. Enjoy! —Wm.]

The Three Stages of Darwin

95

Ambrose Bierce

Aldous Huxley

A.E. Van Vogt

C.L. Moore

Charles Dickins

Chuck Jones

Dashell Hammett

Doris Lessing

D.H Lawrence

Dorothy Sayers

Ernest Hemmingway

Graham Greene

H.G. Wells

Henry David Thoreau

Ezra Pound

Henri Toulouse Lautrec

Herman Melville

Jack Kerouac

Howard Pyle

James Thurber

L. Frank Baum

Jane Austen

Mary Shelley

Owen Barfield

Mervyn Peake

Shirley Jackson

Walt Whitman

Stephen Crane

Rudyard Kipling

William Burroughs

A Pleasure Full Grown

Dale Nelson (left) and Kurt Erichsen long ago and far away...

Dale Nelson

At the end of the 1969-1970 school year, when we ninth graders got our yearbooks, Sue R. of the wavy blonde hair, on whom I had a crush, wrote in my copy, "Dale / To one who slows the world down to human pace."

I quote from memory, though I could get up from my desk and take the staple-bound paperback annual out of storage, with its kid-drawn psychedelic sunflower cover and "Let the Sun Shine In" theme. I hope I've been worthy of what Sue wrote.

Her words link in my mind with another memory, of the *Tinker, Tailor, Soldier, Spy* miniseries with Alec Guinness, the best television drama I've ever seen, in which Peter Guillam is driving spymaster George Smiley at night in rain that is turning into wet snow. Peter is bitter because

he has been sidelined at the Circus, the headquarters of British secret intelligence, and so his foot's heavy on the gas pedal. Smiley admonishes him, "Slow down, Peter, *slow down*."

Our literary heroes may remember the most vital things in the very moment of crisis – just in time -- as the agonized seconds are racing! But does that happen very often in life? Doesn't intense anxiety tend to drive out memory? "I was so upset, I forgot that...." Or just "I was so busy, I forgot to..."

One might even say, "I was so in love with her that I can't remember her face." In Leslie Reid's *The Rector of Maliseet* (1925), the narrator, Leonard Carr, tries to capture something about his experience of first love. Romantic feelings for Miriam Clare have developed:

"…I may yet confidently state that all the inward and outward manifestations of the condition of being in love were there. The girl was constantly in my mind, and *it would perplex me at times when I wished to conjure up her features before me, to find that I was unable to do so.* She persisted on these occasions as a blurred figure, as though viewed through some opacity of misunderstanding …I have laid stress on her femininity, and this, perhaps, is the quality in her that most exercised me."

When I was a senior in college, that's what it was like for me, too.

Occasionally, I involuntarily remember something when I'm relaxed, when I've *slowed down.* The connection between what I was doing and what I remembered might be easy to see. Once, I was boiling an egg, and, looking at the burner on the ranger, I thought of how its pattern would be branded on one's hand if one fell on it; and this made me remember the opening sequence of a two-season television Western from the 1960s, *Branded*: "Branded! Marked with a coward's shame! / What do you do when you're branded, / And you fight for your name?" I might not have thought of the show in years till that moment.

But sometimes there's no obvious connection. Just during the time in which I have been writing this essay, I attended Divine Service on a Sunday morning. The sermon text was that discomposing one of the Pharisee and publican. Without warning, I remembered a two-block alley I used to like to walk when I lived in Ashland, Oregon, many years ago. It's between Liberty Street and Beach Street. Blackberry vines grow up against bare grey fence boards, a sight I love to see -- I took charge of my thoughts and attended again to the sermon.

Forty years ago, I was drowsily reading a history of philosophy when, without warning, I remembered a couple of Signet paperbacks I used to have, a collection of Batman stories and *Greasy Mad Stuff*, reprints from *Mad* magazine. I'd traded one for the other with a kid named Mark, whom I'd known back then, about 14 years before. Then I remembered being at Mark's house one day and watching *The Monolith Monsters* on afternoon TV and how saliva would collect in the corners of Mark's mouth when he talked. I allowed the string of memories to pay out even more, amused by the flow of associations. Another time, also as an adult, I was reading something – was it one of Anthony Trollope's leisurely Victorian novels? -- and abruptly I remembered the Hashimoto-San cartoons about a Japanese mouse that used to be included in NBC's Saturday morning cartoon program *The Hector Heathcote Show*. Why on earth should I remember the cartoon mouse then?

When this sort of thing happens to us, we may begin to perceive that we are mysteries to ourselves; that is, if we are paying attention. If we never pay attention, much of the poetry may go out of our lives. I'm not saying that remembering a cartoon series done with simplistic animation is poetic. But when that moment happened, I was brought into contact with my much younger self, unexpectedly, just a little bit as if I'd heard the doorbell ring and there he was.

A physiological explanation relating to brain chemistry could be hypothesized to account for the popping-up of unsought memories. I'm not going to go into the specialists' debate about the relationship of memory to the physical brain. Incidentally, though -- in *The Science Delusion* (U.S. title *Science Set Free*), I read Rupert Sheldrake's discussion of people with "water on the brain" (hydrocephalus). CT scans have revealed something surprising. A British neurologist studied a certain group of people and found some of them to be "surprisingly normal," and while some were "seriously retarded," others had exceptional intelligence. These were people with extreme hydrocephalus. "One young man who had an IQ of 126 and a first-class degree in mathematics, a student from Sheffield University, had 'virtually no brain'. His skull was lined with a thin layer of brain cells about a millimetre thick, and the rest of the space was filled with fluid. ... his brain *and his memory* were still able to function more or less normally even though he had a brain only five percent of the normal size" (pp. 193-194).

That might sound like something from the most imaginative fiction, not from sober science. Lately, by the way, I've been thinking that the best literary fantasy possesses wisdom as an element in its poetic quality, its "Elvish craft" (Tolkien's term). That wisdom might be put into words or it might not be. When the hobbits are walking through the Shire very early in *The Fellowship of the Ring*, and they're enjoying the rural lanes and the stars, wisdom inhabits the prose because the sentences evoke a kind of happiness that we should never "grow out of." (Note to self: walk under branches today.) But sometimes wisdom is put into words.

So, from a work of fantasy, here's an example of wisdom that relates to the topic of memory. In *Out of the Silent Planet*, C. S. Lewis's Martian book, one of the inhabitants opens the earthman's mind when he says "A pleasure is full grown only when it is remembered. You are speaking as if the pleasure were one thing and the memory another. It is all one thing. When you and I met, the meeting was over very shortly, it was nothing. Now it is growing something as we remember it. But still we know very little about it. What it will be when I remember it as I lie down to die, what it makes in me all my days till then – that is the real meeting. What you call remembering is the last part of the pleasure."

Could that notion be true, of many of the best pleasures of life? Dostoevsky thought so. In *The Brothers Karamazov*, Book 6, we have recorded talks from young Alyosha's *staretz*, the monk Zosima. Here there's the novel's theme of resurrection, of the seed of wheat that must fall into the ground and "die," so that a new life may be raised up. And this relates to the elder's teaching about the great importance of the sowing of good memory-seeds in the child's soul; but even if the family was a bad family, it's "'almost always'" the case that *some* wholesome memories may exist, "'if only one's soul knows how to seek out what is precious.'" The Elder Zosima remembers learning to read from a Bible-story book. "'It is still lying there on my shelf, I keep it as a precious reminder.'"

Sympathy with Dostoevsky's point of view comes from an unexpected source, the author of the Lord Peter Wimsey detective stories. Dorothy L. Sayers wrote an essay called "The Lost Tools of Learning." Very young children, she said, are naturally good at memorization.

"At this age one readily memorises the shapes and appearances of things; one likes to recite the number-plates of cars; one rejoices in the chanting of rhymes and the rumble and thunder of unintelligible polysyllables; one enjoys the mere accumulation of things."

Sayers recommended that little kids begin to learn the basics of Latin grammar. *Amo, amas, amat!* She continued:

"In English, verse and prose can be learned by heart, and the pupil's memory should be stored with stories of every kind—classical myth, European legend, and so forth. ... Recitation aloud should be practiced—individually or in chorus.

"...The grammar of History should consist, I think, of dates, events, anecdotes, and personalities. A set of dates to which one can peg all later historical knowledge is of enormous help later on in establishing the perspective of history. ...

"Geography will similarly be presented in its factual aspect, with maps... flora, fauna, and so on; and I believe myself that the discredited and old-fashioned memorising of a few capital cities, rivers, mountain ranges, etc., does no harm. Stamp-collecting may be encouraged.

"Science... arranges itself naturally and easily round collections—the identifying and naming of specimens ...To know the names and properties of things is, at this age, a satisfaction in itself."

Progressive educators, with their disdain for memorization or "rote learning" would not agree. My heroes include the Grimm brothers, Bishop Jørgen Engebretsen, Moe and Peter Christen Asbjørnsen, Evald Tang Kristensen, Joseph Jacobs, and others who collected and published many hundreds of traditional Northern European tales that were remembered by old folks but that were in danger of being forgotten.

To return to Lewis's Martian – if his teaching is true, that a pleasure is full grown when it's remembered, then it's a countercultural truth. The common assumption is that a pleasure is over as soon as the event has passed, and we need new pleasures, new excitements, new distractions to consume or to be consumed by. What most of us might really need, though, is a slower pace of life and a new attentiveness to worthy but not very assertive inner experiences.

If Lewis's Martian is right, then snide accusations about people who allegedly wallow in nostalgia might often be unfair and obtuse. It could just be the case that many of those people who like to recall particular pleasures are not, in fact, fooling themselves about the good old days. They might know very well that someone's plum examples of social injustice or outdated medical procedures existed back then. But the people thus criticized might be remembering, might be growing, a pleasure that the critic envies or that doesn't fit into his politics. The people remembering those pleasures might affirm the motto of children's author-artist Denys Watkins-Pitchford: "The wonder of the world, the beauty and the power, the shapes of things, their colours, lights, and shades; these *I saw*.

Look also while life lasts" -- and remember.

The Greek word ανάμνησις (*anamnesis*) may be translated "memory," "remembrance." According to something I read many years ago, it literally means something like "to make present." In an earlier issue of *Portable Storage*, I wrote about U. Milo Kaufmann, one of my teachers, and how he kept files of notes about memories that had special energy, special "presence." He said that such memory-notes could be the seed of a poem or a prose meditation. On a windy day, William Wordsworth and his sister Dorothy took a walk along a lakeside. She wrote a note about their outing. Later, Wordsworth wrote "I Wandered Lonely as a Cloud" thanks not just to the walk itself but to Dorothy's note. I'm not sure that I know a greater short "anamnetic" poem than this one.

It helps me to remember my bygone days of Greyhound bus trips, if I write down, not just destinations, but sensory details: I smelled the odor of Diesel fuel and tasted the flavor of my Doublemint chewing gum on those rides, and heard the hiss of air coming through the ventilation openings at the base of the windows. And from my backpack I would take out a book, say de Camp's anthology *The Spell of Seven*, the Pyramid paperback with the Medusa head, or a hardcover copy in black cloth of Colin Wilson's novel *The Philosopher's Stone*, and settle in to read.

I wouldn't want utterly to forget those times. Sometimes, animals must forget, but, when they do, they presumably never realize it. When do children first realize that they can "forget"? My wife and I raised four children, but we don't remember that we ever explained to them what it means to remember, or what it means to forget. Somehow, children just catch on about those rather important matters.

I suppose everyone forgets things and needs a gentle reminder now and then. If I may name-drop: I had a little correspondence with the elderly Inklings philosopher Owen Barfield. In the first letter I sent him, in March 1988, I said I would have liked to hear him lecture at an upcoming Oxford conference. Barfield replied that, no, he wasn't going to be speaking on that occasion. I'd received copies of a handbill about the event, with his name as a speaker, and sent him one. He was amused at his own expense to realize he'd forgotten about the conference to be held that summer.

And then there's misremembering. In a 2006 issue of the *New York Review of Books*, physicist Freeman Dyson remembered:

"When I was a boy in England long ago, people who traveled on trains with dogs had to pay for a dog ticket. The question arose whether I needed to buy a dog ticket when I was traveling with a tortoise. The conductor on the train gave me the answer: 'Cats is dogs and rabbits is dogs but tortoises is insects and travel free according.'"

In fact, as a letter to the magazine pointed out, the conductor's remark came from a cartoon published in an 1869 issue of *Punch*. (Dyson might have seen it reprinted in a book, or maybe the conductor had seen it and quoted it; but it looks like Dyson "remembered" something he'd never actually heard, as if he *had* heard it.)

Julia Shaw's *The Memory Illusion* points out how creative "memory" can be. She is particularly compelling about criminal investigations in which a supposed victim of (say) satanic ritual abuse is encouraged to "remember" things that never really happened, in well-intentioned efforts to bring criminals to justice. The conjured false "memories" may be emotionally powerful. But that doesn't mean that the hypnotized patients were remembering real events.

The late John Mack, head of psychiatry at the Harvard Medical School, astonished me by his reliance on so-called "recovered memories," in his book *Abduction* (1994). Hypnotized people were encouraged in the belief that they were victims of UFO aliens. A few matters that, if they happened at all, would have been of public record, and which should have been easy to check to verify the supposed "memories," apparently were not investigated. For example, in Chapter 12

"The Magic Mountain," the patient called "Dave" tells of driving at night with friends, in New Brunswick, and being passed by a speeding bus. After their alien abduction missing-time experience, they learned of a bus accident in which 65 people had been killed. However, using Google, I found no record of such a horrific crash. Mack should have made an effort, perhaps by calling a provincial department of transportation or a provincial newspaper, to verify that such a spectacular accident had occurred. Mack seemed to think that we should "believe" such "victims" – as if respect for the patients meant that the supposed fact of alien visits to this planet was a matter of secondary importance.

Since I know that misremembering and forgetting are weaknesses flesh is heir to, I sometimes make notes to help me remember a good talk with a friend, a moment of perception and presence with nature, or some detail of the past that came to mind or something that's going on then and that I will want to remember. My handwritten notes on eastern North Dakota's April 1997 blizzard and Grand Forks flood are seven single-spaced pages transcribed into a Word document. On the other hand, just a few sentences sufficed for a ramble to a horse pasture with my five-year-old son. It was early February and the horses had snow on their backs and yellow icicles on their sides.

I save letters. Even in these digitized days, I still get, and write, letters to a first-generation reader and admirer of *The Lord of the Rings*, who was an attendee of Detention, the 17th World Science Fiction Convention, held in Detroit 4-7 Sept. 1959 (that one was only the first of a bunch of Worldcons that he attended), a contributor to noted fanzines such as *Cry of the Nameless*, *I Palantír*, *Niekas*, *Amra*, etc. As I said here in an earlier issue of *Portable Storage*, fan historians should look into the possibility of preserving faanish correspondence, the appropriate permissions having been secured.

So far, the only letters of which I've made copies to donate to an archive are my letters from Owen Barfield. His messages could, of course, have been sent as emails if email had been widely available back then, but I cherish the handwritten letters as tangible artifacts. I began to read the published letters of favorite authors while still a teenager, with the first Arkham House volume of Lovecraft's. Will we one day see editions of the Collected Emails of such and such a writer? More, I wonder about digital natives who sometimes feel a kind of fastidious dislike of "stuff" other than clothes, high-tech devices, sports equipment, and vehicles. Pullman Hotels and Resorts targeted them: "No frontiers, no borders, no limits. You are the beautiful nomads. And our world is your playground." At some point, will the people who responded to that advertisement miss tokens of their pasts such as letters, miss *realia*?

I loved Serge Schmemann's *Echoes of a Distant Land: Two Centuries of a Russian Village* (1997). It reconstructs the way of life of people who became literal exiles: expatriates, or exiles in their own land because of Soviet totalitarianism.

"I discovered information that I never thought still existed – archives filled with documents, records, letters, memoirs, photos, all filed in cardboard folios, tied with little ribbons, sorted in boxes, and tucked away in former churches, institutes, universities, or libraries, maintained through long years of disuse by a loyal caste of archivists. Russians have always had a propensity to squirrel away every piece of paper, but I had never suspected the Communists would bother to maintain so much that so completely contradicted their deliberate suppression and revision of the past. ...With the coming of glasnost, the hidden caches of memory came back to light."

Digital records, however, can be wiped out or altered in ways the Communists could never have imagined in their fondest dreams. One hopes that doesn't happen here. But age has a way of doing something analogous, as we forget or misremember.

It seems my dad, impaired by dementia, "remembered" being a young soldier who got off his ship and hiked overland across Papua New Guinea on his way back from serving in the army of occupation after Japan's surrender. The hike never happened; happily, I'd recorded a lot of Dad's recollections when his wits were sharper. President Biden may "remember" that his son Beau died on a tour of duty in Iraq. The president lies or misremembers; Beau died years after his Iraq tour, at Walter Reed National Military Medical Center in Bethesda.

On the other hand, human beings have been capable of spectacular feats of recollection. Theater critic Kenneth Tynan was a student of C. S. Lewis at Oxford. In an interview, Tynan said:

"Once when I was invited to his rooms after dinner for a glass of beer, he played a game. He directed, "Give me a number from one to forty." I said, "Thirty." He acknowledged, "Right. Go to the thirtieth shelf in my library. Then he said, "Give me another number from one to twenty." I answered, "Fourteen." He continued, "Right. Get the fourteenth book off the shelf. Now let's have another number from one to 100." I said, "Forty-six." "Now turn to page forty-six. Pick a number from one to twenty-five for the line of the page." I said, "Six." "So," he would say, "read me that line." He would always identify it – not only by identifying the book, but he was also usually able to quote the rest of the page. This is a gift. This is something you can't learn. It was remarkable."

Either Lewis could read Tynan's mind and "saw" what he saw, or Lewis possessed an astonishing memory. (That it was the latter is indicated by the accounts of others, who testified to Lewis's ability to burst into a recitation of poetry while on a walk.)

Tynan says that Lewis's power was unlearnable,

and that may be true, but I keep meaning to spend some time with Frances Yates's *Art of Memory*, which deals with the deliberate acquisition and inner organization of remembered things, from Classical to early modern times. In medieval Iceland, a third of the Law was recited every year, in a three-year cycle at the Althing. Ray Bradbury's *Fahrenheit 451* – a book to re-read – gave us the vision of an underground made up of individuals who have taken the responsibility for the perfect mnemonic retention of great literary works. As a last resort under totalitarianism, Aleksandr Solzhenitsyn urged the covert cultivation of memory over against the bogus "reality" promoted by the Soviet state:

"Own only what you can always carry with you: know languages, know countries, know people. Let your memory be your travel bag. Use your memory! Use your memory! ...Look around you - there are people around you. Maybe you will remember one of them all your life and later eat your heart out because you didn't make use of the opportunity to ask him questions. And the less you talk, the more you'll hear."

Solzhenitsyn believed in love as central to a human life. Love and memory go together. On the other hand, the totalitarian will to power wants to replace your memory with its ideology and spurious artifacts.

Milan Kundera wrote, "The struggle of man against power is the struggle of memory against forgetting." That was almost exactly the predicament of Samwise in the orc-tower, separated from Frodo, oppressed by the intense gloom of Mordor and the consciousness of Sauron's probing malice. But Sam's courage revived when he remembered: "above all shadows rides the Sun / and stars for ever dwell; / I will not say the Day is done, / nor bid the Stars farewell." Somewhere Arthur Machen wrote, "Let us not forget in the darkness what we have known in the light." Or maybe it was, "Let us not deny in the darkness what we have known in the light."

Deuteronomy 29:29 could be a household motto for some: "The secret things belong to the Lord our God, but the things that are revealed belong to us and to our children forever, that we may do all the words of this law."

In *The Silmarillion*, Tolkien's description of Rivendell is a motto for a good household: "A refuge for the weary and the oppressed, and a treasury of good counsel and wise lore." I like that word *lore*. It suggests not just something remembered, but things recognized as worth remembering by and among members of a group. Not just orthographically, *love* and *lore* are close to each other.

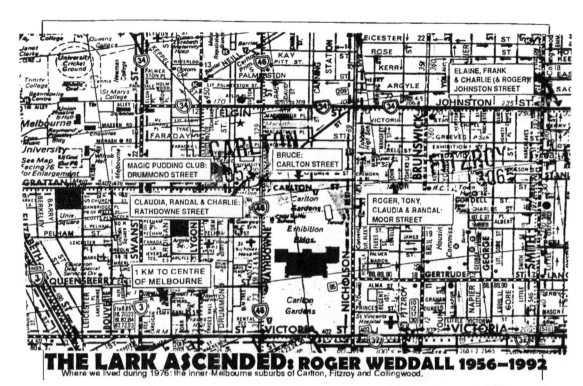

On map:
ELAINE, FRANK & CHARLIE (& ROGER): JOHNSTON STREET

MAGIC PUDDING CLUB: DRUMMOND STREET

BRUCE: CARLTON STREET

CLAUDIA, RANDAL & CHARLIE: RATHDOWNE STREET

ROGER, TONY, CLAUDIA & RANDAL: MOOR STREET

1 KM TO CENTRE OF MELBOURNE

THE LARK ASCENDED: ROGER WEDDALL 1956–1992
Where we lived during 1976: the inner-Melbourne suburbs of Carlton, Fitzroy and Collingwood.

Bruce Gillespie

After Roger Weddall's funeral on 8 December 1992, a large group of his friends gathered at the house where he had been living, ate afternoon tea, and told Roger stories. There are thousands of them, each as varied as the teller. Here are some of my Roger stories. Of course they are also Bruce Gillespie stories.

I

The first time I talked to Roger was in early 1974, after I returned from my only overseas trip. He and Alan Wilson visited the Degraves Tavern, which was once in a basement off Degraves Street in the city, and was the weekly fannish meeting place until it closed in early 1976. When I returned to the Degraves Tavern in February 1974, I found that a new group of people

Bruce and Apple Blossom

had joined Melbourne fandom. The most noticeable newcomers were Don and Derrick Ashby, who had identical midland English accents and black pointy beards. Loquacious and amusing, they held court at the center of a group dominated by Lee Harding and Irene Pagram, and Leigh Edmonds and Valma Brown. Henry, the proprietor of Degraves Tavern, had arranged the tables in a large U shape. Roger and Alan sat way off at the end of one of the U arms. Nobody spoke to them. This was typical. Malcolm Gordon turned up every week for two years at Degraves Tavern before anybody spoke to him. Eventually I said hello, but little else, to Roger and Alan. All I knew about them is that they represented the Melbourne University Science Fiction Association (MUSFA), and that MUSFA people wanted to get involved in general fandom. This did not happen until the late 1970s, and Roger and Alan did not bother turning up to Degraves Tavern again.

During 1975 I was the only person from general fandom who discovered that the MUSFA people were friendlier and less cynical than the Degraves cabal. During 1974 Charles Taylor had introduced me to Elaine Cochrane and Frank Payne, the two people with whom he was sharing a house. The three of them were members of MUSFA. I visited them several times during late 1974. In 1975 Charles invited me to one of the monthly MUSFA Bistro Nights. The first I attended was at the old Jamaica House when it was owned by Monty, a tall black man who was known to everybody in food circles and Carlton bohemia. (After he died, at the age of forty, his wife Stephanie Alexander became Melbourne's most distinguished restaurateur.) Monty served the hottest food I have ever eaten. That night in late 1975, about twenty riotous MUSFAns drank a vast amount, and returned to 10 Johnston Street. Somebody was very ill in the toilet. In the early morning, Dennis Callegari walked home from Collingwood to Templestowe.

Me? I was suddenly stricken by *l-ov-e*.. Not for the first time was I transfixed by the presence of a woman who hardly noticed me. Claudia Mangiamele was the princess of MUSFA, and I suspected all the other males at Jamaica House were equally, hopelessly, in love with her. Not that Claudia meant to be flirtatious. She had (and still has) the rare quality that Roger had: the ability to focus her interest entirely on any person she considered a friend. Because most of her friends in MUSFA were young, single males, her presence created a stronger emotional effect than she intended.

Four weeks later, we held another riotous MUSFA night, this time at a long-defunct Lebanese food restaurant known as Green Cedars. We were placed in a large upstairs room. What better place for a polite riot? Most of these people were under twenty, and not used to alcohol. Yet again, a MUSFAn was very ill. Rigid, he was handed down the stairs of Green Cedars and carried out the door.

I can't remember Roger as being more riotous than any other MUSFAn in those days. He was a lot quieter than the (in)famous David Firman, who needed only the slightest hint of tipsiness to begin singing loud ribald songs. (Whatever happened to David Firman?) But already I recognized that Roger listened to what you were saying while talking to you flat out and carrying on three other conversations around the room. (He also conducted hour-long pun competitions with Dennis Callegari.) Roger included me in the group. That's more than anybody in general fandom bothered to do.

At the beginning of 1976, about thirty of us, mainly MUSFAns, went to Adelaide to join some people from the Adelaide University SF Association at an sf convention at a camp site in the hills. The aim was to repeat the very successful first Advention (held at another hillside camp site) of 1972. The weather was very hot, the chemistry of people not quite right (although meeting Marc Ortlieb for the first time was a highlight of the convention), and a very young, very drunk James Styles caterwauled loudly all one night.

I was glad to escape at the end of that convention, but some Adelaide University people enjoyed it so much that they returned the visit. Anaconda, an entirely impromptu convention held mainly at Claudia Mangiamele's mother's house in Carlton during the Australia Day weekend, 1976, began the most extraordinary year of my life.

People who had been only acquaintances suddenly became friends. Roger decided that I was a person who should be cured of chronic shyness. On the Monday morning after the night of Charles Taylor's twenty-first birthday party, I heard a knock at the door of my flat in Carlton Street. Not only were all those people up, but they had decided to invade my place. After the invasion, they dragged me out to the Carlton Gardens across the street from my place. Never have I met a group of people so glad to be in each other's company! I enjoyed that company, and I was glad that Claudia was there, although it seemed obvious that she was already nuts about Roger. Add to that dynamic several other romances that had begun in Adelaide or during Anaconda, and you have an atmosphere of heady joy that had escaped me during my adolescence but was quite a tonic three weeks before my twenty-ninth birthday.

The events of the next three years turn on a sentence I spoke that morning in January 1976. 'The Magic Pudding Club is only two streets away,' I said. 'Let's invade them.' And we did. The Magic Pudding Club, in Drummond Street, Carlton, was a slanshack that at that time included (at least) Don and Derrick Ashby, Ken Ford and John Ham. (For the story of the Magic Pudding Club, read *The Metaphysical Review* 4; copies are still available.) Staying with them for the weekend was a very young Queenslander named Randal

Flynn. Randal had travelled to Melbourne from Brisbane for the World Convention and Writers' Workshop held in August 1975. He decided that he liked Melbourne and Melbournites so much that he returned. Surely he could stay in Melbourne forever, for free! When we invaded the Magic Pudding Club in Drummond Street, everybody but Randal groaned, rolled over and went back to sleep. Randal invited us into the back yard. In that way Anaconda carried on, while the other Magic Pudding people swore at us and got breakfast.

By the end of that morning, when the Anacondans disappeared out the front door, Randal had become firm friends with Claudia and Roger. Two weeks later, by the time of my birthday party (catered by the Magic Pudding Club, it was also Valma Brown's birthday), the three of them had decided to set up house in Moore Street, Fitzroy, nearly as close to me to the east as the Magic Pudding Club was to the west. My peace of mind was about to disintegrate.

I visited Moore Street often, because Claudia lived there. Claudia didn't notice me, but she certainly noticed Roger. She and Randal agreed that Roger was behaving 'very peculiarly'. Randal had agreed to give a home at Moore Street to two cats, MGM and Gus. Roger had the same magical effect on them as he was to have on Apple Blossom, but at that time he had little idea of how to take care of cats. Claudia and Randal didn't like cats. Suddenly Claudia and Randal were living together, as well as living in the same house. To the outsider, Roger seemed an outcast in his own house. For perhaps the first time in his life, Roger had no idea what to do. Why hadn't he carried off the magic princess? Why had he left her to an cheeky upstart like Randal? And why did magical princesses never notice people like me?

I visited Moore Street when all three of them were there. Roger kept playing records that I had never heard, but which became favorites of mine. If it had not been for Roger, I would never had heard *Crisis! What Crisis?* by Supertramp. That album has never been played on radio, although

Supertramp became popular later in the 1970s. Roger played *American Stars and Bars* by Neil Young. Like many other people, even today, I rather dismissed Neil Young because I had heard only *Harvest*. *American Stars and Bars*, with 'Like a Hurricane', the first of Young's power-guitar anthems, made me a permanent fan. It was because of Roger I discovered Lou Reed — not *Berlin*, Roger's favorite, but *Coney Island Baby*.

Roger, Randal and Claudia agreed that I was somebody who should be rescued from lonely isolation at 72 Carlton Street. Randal made this his crusade. Some days I had to chase him away in order to get some work done. (Unlike Stephen Campbell, another friend of mine, he was not much use for producing fanzines.)

Roger was less insistent than the others about the crusade, but one night he knocked on the door at midnight. 'How'd you like to come around for dinner?' he said. Since I had last eaten at 6 o'clock, and was feeling peckish and lonely, I followed Roger to Moore Street. There I found the main room full of people. I can't remember where they had been or why they hadn't eaten, but Randal and Claudia began preparing food at midnight.

At two o'clock in the morning we sat down to the one of the grandest feasts I've ever been to. It was the first time I really saw Roger in action as the Great Celebrator. He was able to draw the best out of everybody in that room. From then on, I took it as an axiom that even a social troglodyte like me would always enjoy a social occasion organized by Roger.

Roger's dinner parties become art events. Not that he cooked home dinners, or paid for restaurant meals. All he had to do was ring you. You dropped everything to make sure you attended these events. If you sat down between two people you didn't know, Roger made sure you got to know them. If you didn't, he changed seats to sit next to you. If the whole dinner party failed to sparkle, he managed to get everybody to change chairs. This was hell on the waiters.

Randal and Claudia moved to a large two-story terrace house in Rathdowne Street, Carlton, leaving Roger by himself at Moore Street. Tony Sullivan, the almost invisible fourth member of the Moore Street household, had already moved. Charles Taylor moved into the new Rathdowne Street slanshack. Roger could not afford the rent, so he gave up the Moore Street house and moved in with Elaine and Frank.

Meanwhile, Elaine had picked up Apple Blossom on a building site at 1 a.m. while walking home from the Easter 1976 Convention held at Ormond College, Melbourne University. (All the action of this saga takes place within walking distance.) Roger and Apple Blossom fell in love.

II

In the end, 'Roger's cat' Apple Blossom out-lived him by two weeks. Roger died on 3 December 1992, and Apple Blossom on 18 December. Not that Roger ever owned Apple Blossom; she owned him. So did every cat that Roger ever patted.

When Roger shared the house at 10 Johnston Street, Collingwood, with Elaine and two other people in 1976, he was already a person who slept during the day and lived by night. When he arrived home at some late hour, he listened to records on headphones. Sitting in the bean bag, he fell asleep. Apple Blossom fell asleep on top of him. When they were both awake and in the same house, Roger teased Apple Blossom. She spat and howled and clawed, having a wonderful time. She had the world's second-best vocabulary of cat swear words. Apple Blossom lived in the same house as Roger for only about four months. He ran out of money, and returned to his parents' place. Elaine and Frank asked the other person to leave, and I joined the household.

After Elaine and I got together, each time that Roger visited he called first to Apple Blossom, who always expected to be picked up and teased. Howl, spit, claw. What fun! In 1982, when Roger returned from overseas, and had been away from our house for about a year, Apple Blossom remembered him immediately. After Roger died, when his father visited us, Apple Blossom tottered towards him because for a moment it seemed that Brandon Weddall's voice was that of his son.

III

In October 1976 I was still in love, to the amusement, annoyance and embarrassment of everybody I knew. Instead of Worshipping From Afar, my usual approach to falling in love, I had Declared Myself. And got nowhere. But I still lived within a hundred yards of the Beloved. No, I was not ordered from the door. Claudia and Randal always welcomed me whenever I

visited, as they welcomed everybody else in Melbourne fandom. It was quite common for a nightbird such as Don Ashby to call in at Rathdowne Street at midnight because he saw an upstairs light. Rathdowne Street became host to some of the most spectacular parties I've ever staggered away from.

For the first and only time in my life, I began to hold parties at my eyrie in Carlton Street. I went as close as I've ever been to madness. I needed people desperately. If I couldn't entice them around for a beer or a yarn, I would find any available excuse to visit them. Carlton Street became the epicenter of one instant party after another. Roger and I began to demolish bottles of Southern Comfort as if they were mineral water. During one

party at my place, Roger succumbed to alcohol early in the night. He locked himself in the toilet and wouldn't emerge. Fortunately, long-suffering Martin, who lived in the flat below, was away for the night, so the rest of us could use the downstairs loo. When everybody else had left, Roger was still in the loo. I hauled the spare mattress down to the kitchen. Next morning, he was lying on it. He was lying so still that Flodnap, my cat who was so shy that nobody but me had set eyes on him for months, was circling him unafraid. For a few moments I thought Roger had died. He got up, said 'Good morning; I'm fine', staggered up to divan in the living room, and fell asleep there for another four hours.

One night in late October, one of my parties finished with Roger, Claudia and I sitting together on my living-room floor. Fuelled by Southern Comfort and coffee, we talked all night. It was bizarre magic. At dawn, Roger and I walked Claudia back to Rathdowne Street. We all said goodbye, and I floated home.

I slept for a few hours, and woke to the strangest weather I have ever witnessed in Melbourne. A seamless shroud of luminous orange cloud glowed across the sky. The weather was early-summer warm, but not yet hot. There was no wind. We all waited for the total eclipse of the sun. Roger had gone with a group of MUSFANs to the hills to observe the eclipse. I had been invited to Claudia's mother's place to join the eclipse-watchers there. The air became quite still. It became nearly dark, and the air glowed. I glowed, and knew I would never again feel such a stranger to myself.

Leigh Edmonds called the events of my life during

October and November 1976 my 'crushing blows'. For years afterward ignorant fans believed that my entire function in life was to fall under crushing blows of ever more devastating strength. Within twenty-four hours, (a) Claudia told me very clearly of what she thought of the ragged idiot (me) who kept claiming her affections without having the slightest reason for doing so; (b) the estate agent sent a letter saying that the house at Carlton Street would be sold, and that I should leave the flat as soon as possible; and (c) it became obvious that my regular free-lance employer had dispensed with my services for the time being.

Within a month I found a job of sorts (half-time assistant editor of *The Secondary Teacher* for the Victorian Secondary Teachers Association, at a miserable pro rata salary), but not until I had nearly run out of money. I survived only because Bruce Barnes, a kindly soul who is constantly in the background of all this action, lent me a large amount of money in order to set up *SF Commentary* as a commercially run magazine. Business success, as ever, evaded me, but the loan gave me an improbably provident cushion of money during those difficult months. During my enforced holiday I published some of the best issues of *SF Commentary*, but they produced few new subscriptions.

I decided to become a sensible person again, but this proved impossible. After spending most of my life trying to keep human beings at arm's length, I found I needed them very badly. Or was it simply that visits from friendly people gave me an excuse to drink too much?

I visited Elaine and Frank and Roger several times at Johnston Street, Collingwood. This old bluestone house had always been a gathering place for MUSFA people. However, Frank was often at Melbourne University, studying for fifth year Medicine exams, and Roger was rarely home. He returned very late at night, and woke up sometime during the day. Already Elaine and I were enjoying each other's company.

Soon my worries had narrowed to one problem: where would I live? Upstairs at 72 Carlton Street was the first place that was really *mine*. It was my home; I could not face the thought of living anywhere else. I was offered a few rooms in a vacant house, but I could tell from the description that my books and records and duplicating equipment could not fit there. The Final Notice to Quit arrived in January 1977.

In January Chris Priest and Vonda McIntyre arrived in town to conduct, with George Turner, the second large SF Writers' Workshop. (Ursula Le Guin had conducted the first in 1975.) Vonda visited a fan gathering at my place. People dropped in from everywhere to say hello to Vonda. Elaine and Frank visited as well. On that night, only about a week before I had to leave Carlton Street, they offered to accommodate me at Johnston Street. Roger had run out of money, and was returning to his parents' place. Elaine and Frank wanted to get rid of the other bloke. And I needed two entire rooms, plus a lot of the store room, to fit in my junk. And it was decided that night. I had always said that I would not share a house with other people — but I had grown desperate for company, and I needed the accommodation.

This story has become more about me than about Roger. Roger had separate groups of friends, entire worlds of people who did not know each other, but knew Roger well. He would disappear for weeks at a time, then visit every night for a week. Yet we never had a sense that he was slighting us. Of course he would always return. He would be drawn back by Apple Blossom as well as the other cats. The household now included Solomon and Ishtar, Elaine's cats from 1973/74, my cat Flodnap (inadvertently named by Randal in 1976), and Julius, a half-wild black kitten who was, strictly speaking, Flodnap's cat. I suspect the real reason why Elaine asked me to move to Johnston Street was because one day at Carlton Street Julius fell at her feet and declared his unending devotion to her. And thus it was until Julius disappeared in 1980.

IV

1977 was a difficult year. I had little money, and I was living a household in which Frank and I whinged at each other whenever we saw each other. I was sharing space with Elaine. We discovered that we ran the household together rather well. As far as I knew, she and Frank were a permanent couple, so I didn't allow myself to think libidinous thoughts. I published some magazines, wrote a bit, and generally wished I could find a way back to 72 Carlton Street. (The house sold for $50,000 at the beginning of 1977, was renovated and sold for $100,000 two years later, never occupied before it was sold again two years after that for $150,000, and would be worth at least $350,000 these days. This property-speculative process explains why none of us lives in Carlton these days.) The VSTA job seemed designed to make me feel incompetent — the lowest of the low. I gained some extra money by typing (including the first draft of what eventually became Gerald Murnane's *The Plains*) or editing occasional monographs for the company that had dumped me in late 1976.

1977 was also a healing year. I saw Randal and Claudia very little, so I regained a sense of perspective. I reduced my drinking, sobered by the rapidly rising price of alcohol during the mid-1970s. Roger turned to tequila from Southern Comfort; I was content to go back to beer or Coca Cola. Except for typing *Yggdrasil*, MUSFA's magazine, during that year, I was out of much of its activity.

The more I was sure that my life had stopped altogether, the more it moved towards great change.

Frank finished sixth year Medicine, and in December 1977 was offered a residency at Hobart Hospital. Elaine and I were left in the house together. Things did not seem well at Rathdowne Street. On the day when Roger introduced me to Patti Smith's *Easter* album, Claudia and Randal seemed hardly to be talking to each other. Roger, Alan, Dennis and the other MUSFA members were attempting to organize their first national convention for Easter 1978. Within twenty-four hours, both Roger Zelazny and Brian Aldiss accepted Roger's invitation to be *the* guest of honor at the convention. Roger moved house to Nicholson Street, Abbotsford, to live next door to Don Ashby, who had moved after the Magic Pudding Club broke up.

After a month of growing desperation, I asked Elaine if she would live with me. She said maybe, but flew to Hobart to work out with Frank if their relationship was actually over. It was, and I was deliriously happy. Elaine seemed pleased about the new arrangement, although she probably would have liked a bit more freedom from stress to decide the direction of her life.

Roger asked Don for a Tarot card reading about the rapidly approaching Easter convention. After giving his reading, Don threw away his cards. Is disaster, he reasoned, in the prediction or the expectation? And can the person who tells the cards escape the upcoming catastrophe?

Roger was merely one of a committee who ran Unicon IV, the notorious 1978 Easter Convention, but somehow he copped all the blame for its failures. His crime was to be the most visible to a group of upstarts who were trying to put on conventions without the help of the 'real fans'. The convention events were quite enjoyable, and I had a good time.

But my position was supposed to be *the* Ditmar Awards Committee. My decisions should have been absolute, so that the committee could not be accused of self interest. But the committee had allowed on the ballot (and allowed to win) MUSFA's own magazine. Worse, the committee changed my casting vote in one category. A rebel meeting during the convention declared several winners void. The recounted results pleased no one. When the awards had been given out, I received a non-Ditmar committee award for my work with Norstrilia Press. At the end of the day, the committee gathered all the attractive green lucite trophies for engraving. I kept mine. The other trophies disappeared into the Geology Building of Melbourne University, never to be seen again. Mine is still on the mantel.

The 1978 Convention had two Guests of Honor stalking the corridors glaring at each other. Roger Zelazny and Brian Aldiss each put on good shows for the crowd, and Elaine and I had several wonderful long chats with Brian. But Roger Weddall was blamed for the situation. Some years later, he visited Brian in England and they made friends again.

Roger's crime? Oh, he was young and naive in 1978. All through January, February and March 1978 he would insist on saying: 'Everything will turn out all right at the convention, you'll see.'

Then as now, I never trust anyone who says everything will turn out all right on the night.

Roger has rarely been under greater pressure than during those months. We knew his personal life was in tatters, but he could not tell us how or why. The convention was *not* all right on the night, but it was more memorable than any dozen perfectly run conventions held since.

Roger took everything right on the chest. So did

Alan, Dennis and a few others who remained members of the convention committee. Nothing annoyed his critics more than Roger's relentless cheerfulness. In the end, that cheerfulness saved the convention and made Roger quite a few lifelong enemies.

A few days after the Convention, Claudia rang. She had split up with Randal. Could she bunk down at our place for a fortnight until she could find somewhere else to live? She arrived, but we hardly saw her. Soon she departed to join a strangely mixed household in northern Carlton (including Henry Gasko, Keith Taylor and Carey Handfield, as I remember it), and set out to make up for lost time. Roger and she were now, we were told, 'an item'. Okay, I thought, that settles that. That's how things should have been all along.

And Roger? Not for the first or last time, Roger disappeared. When Claudia visited his place, he was never there. Distraught, she would go next door. Don and whoever else was semi-living in the house at the time welcomed Claudia. A few months later, Claudia and Don began living together, and did so for five years.

V

From 1978 onwards, Roger appears less frequently in my story, yet becomes more and more a mainstay of it.

Roger made grand appearances. He disappeared for months at a time. Then a phone call. 'Why don't we go out somewhere?' And it would be the best night out for months. We went with Roger, Charlie and Gerald and Catherine Murnane to the Mermaid Restaurant before it burned down. One night when we felt rich we took Roger and Charlie to Two Faces, by reputation the most expensive restaurant in Melbourne. $100 for the four of us? Yes, that was expensive in 1979. The food came in tiny portions, and did not seem remarkable. The wine cellar *was* remarkable. The bottle of 1972 Wynn's Coonawarra Cabernet Sauvignon we had that night is the best bottle of wine I've ever tasted.

Roger and Charlie were sharing a house in Whitby Street, Brunswick. At the same time, Roger had gone back to university to do one subject a year. He joined what was called the Part Timers' Association, which connected him with a completely new group of friends. Some of them were also in MUSFA, but many were not involved in science fiction. Charlie got a job teaching at Monivae College in Hamilton, in the Western District of Victoria. We saw him once or twice a year. Roger moved house many times.

In 1980, Roger set out on his first overseas trip. He worked out a way to extend the life of his Eurail pass.

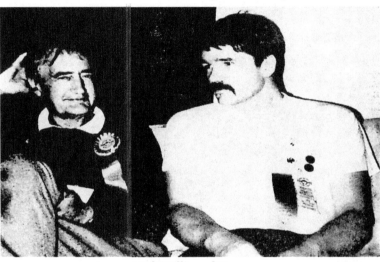
Walt Willis and Roger

He often slept on the train to save on expenses. In a letter that he sent to Phil and Mandy, he drew a map of his European rail travels. The crisscrossing lines blacken the middle of the continent. He visited almost every country, and went to some, such as Finland and Hungary, whose languages were too difficult even for him. He walked along the coast of Cornwall to Lands End, and visited Bergen, the northernmost railway station in the world. He sent vast letters written in mountains of tiny writing. His photos, particularly of Norway in winter, were magical. On the way home, he visited Sri Lanka. A few weeks later, when we took him to Phantom India restaurant, he asked for the hottest curry in the house. He ate it, too.

There were odd elisions in his account of the journey. What really did happen during that glorious Christmas Eve at Innsbruck? Roger would never tell us, although he told a few people. He did tell us about the girl he spent some time with. They arranged to meet a few months later in Paris, but Roger said that he simply could not bring himself to turn up to meet the appointment. The lady obviously had marriage on her mind, and Roger (it always seemed to me) was determined to avoid permanent relationships of any kind.

Roger was always master of the information brick wall. I remembered a night at Enri's Restaurant about a year before Roger went overseas. We had dinner with a friend of mine who counted himself as a bit of a psychologist. Roger managed to get Rick's life story out of him without any trouble. When Rick began to ask questions of Roger, he gained nothing.

The head of the Lifeline telephone counselling service, speaking at Roger's funeral, said that although he had worked with Roger for six years, he had learned about his connection with science fiction only the day before!

I still wonder what Roger really discovered about himself during his first overseas trip.

When he returned, he seemed to be the same Roger. He still regarded the company of other people as the only valid focus of his life. He visited his friends regularly, offering gossip, humor and even advice and comfort when needed.

When he returned, he was *not* still the same Roger. During the early 1980s he began to shrug off many of his butterfly tendencies. For the first time, he would commit himself to a time and date, and *actually turn up at the right time on the right date*. For the first time he committed himself to regular publication of a fanzine. He and Peter Burns took over *Thyme* magazine from Irwin Hirsh and Andrew Brown. In that magazine Roger showed journalistic skills and powers of wit and sarcasm that nobody had suspected. Some people were determined to be annoyed by Roger's repartee; others realized that he had an unerring eye for the true pattern of events. As someone once said of Jane Austen — he might have been protected from the truth, but precious little of the truth was protected from him.

Elaine and I remember Roger best because he helped us so often. In 1982 and 1984 he allowed us to take trips to Mount Buffalo because he minded the house and took care of the cats while we were away. After we returned from our first Mount Buffalo trip in 1982, the woman who lived next door said: 'What has that man been doing to your cats? They've gone completely *mad!*' Of course, Roger knew exactly the right way to entertain cats.

Roger's 1985 overseas trip was quite a different journey from the 1980–81 lark. We received almost no letters. Several long letters from Egypt went astray. On the way overseas, he lost his luggage. (It stayed in an airline office in Manila for six months until he returned for it.) In Egypt, he suffered a near-fatal road accident. Or rather, it would have been fatal if the bloke he was travelling with hadn't been an American. Transferred

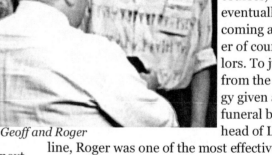
Geoff and Roger

to the American hospital, his body completely wrapped in plaster, Roger gradually improved. Eventually he reached Britain, then home.

After he returned from the 1985 trip, Roger began to acquire an unexpected quality — purpose. Roger had always lived every moment as it came, usually successfully, but often to not much effect. Again he took up the reins of *Thyme* (from Peter Burns, who had successfully pretended to be Roger the whole time he was away). *Thyme* won a Fanzine Ditmar in 1987.

Roger became a volunteer of the telephone counselling service known as Lifeline. He took this activity very seriously, often going away for weekend training courses, and eventually becoming a trainer of counsellors. To judge from the eulogy given at the funeral by the head of Lifeline, Roger was one of the most effective counselors they ever had.

Roger got a job. A real job. He became a social worker with Bridge House, a halfway house to train intellectually handicapped people to join the general community. As far as I know, he was very good at that job.

Roger disappeared again. Spectacularly. The people with whom he was sharing a flat did not see him. They woke up in the morning to find attached to the refrigerator a brief note and enough money to pay the rent and expenses. They guessed that he had, after all these years, become involved with somebody.

They did not know how far he was taking the experiment.

After a yum cha lunch at King Wah Restaurant in the city, Roger took the tram home with us. This was unusual, as we thought he had been avoiding us. As we were clumping along Keele Street, I overheard him telling Elaine that he had just broken up with a particular bloke. His first attempt at a serious relationship had been a perplexing disaster.

I don't think we were surprised to be told, in the most offhand way, that Roger had decided he was gay. Or rather, that for him sexual relationships with men had become more satisfactory than his many relationships with women had been. Many bits of the Roger pattern began to fall into place.

Later we surmised that for many years Roger had been deeply puzzled about his sexual identity, probably beginning with the failure of his relationship with Claudia. Some event during his 1985 overseas trip had made him decide that a satisfying homosexual relationship might have been what he was seeking.

As I said, only during the 1980s did Roger gain a sense of purpose. Soon after his first relationship failed, he introduced us to a bloke named Geoff Roderick. They set up house together. Geoff is a very quiet bloke when you first meet him, but Elaine and I felt from the first that he was exactly the person Roger had been looking for all his life. (Yet for many years Roger did not know he was looking for anything, let alone anyone.)

Roger and Geoff's good luck ran deep for about four years. And then . . .

VI

In an issue of *The Metaphysical Review* that's appearing right now, you can read about our Garden Party. Right there at the beginning of May 1992, it was one of the few highlights of a dismal year. It wouldn't have been a great celebration without Roger's at-tendance. Roger sparkled. Everybody sparkled, especially Monty our cat. Roger introduced Geoff to Claudia.

A few weeks later Theodore, our ginger cat, couldn't pee again. (I've told the story of Theodore's ghastly 1992 in my reply to Mae Strelkov in *TMR* 19/20/21.) Roger rang. 'Geoff and I want to visit. We have some pretty bad news to tell you.' 'Even worse than a cat who can't pee?' I said. 'Yes,' said Roger, 'it's even worse news than that.'

On 30 May 1992 Roger and Geoff arrived at our place. The place had been full of visitors all day. It took awhile before Roger could begin his story. He had suffered a lump under the arm about six months before. It had been diagnosed as 'cat scratch fever'. The lump returned. It had been tested a couple of days before our Garden Party. In late May it had been diagnosed as lymphoma, but doctor said that it could be treated successfully.

Roger swore us to secrecy. He knew that the lymphoma was very dangerous, but all the medical personnel assured him that he should be optimistic. A Chinese doctor in Richmond said: 'I can cure you!' but put Roger on an unexciting 'treatment' of meditation and macrobiotic food. The important thing was optimism. We weren't allowed to be anything but optimistic. We would rather not have known the secret at all, especially as we could not say what we really felt. We could not even say: 'Roger, if your life is nearing the end, why not end it properly? Let's talk about all the good and bad times. Roger, have you made your will?' (He hadn't.) 'Roger, let's say goodbye.' But we could never allow ourselves to say goodbye.

Roger won the DUFF trip to America. He was greatly pleased at the honor given to him, and he and Geoff had made elaborate plans to travel through America and Europe for six months or more. However, he had to tell some people about his condition because he had to cut short his August–September trip to America in order to return to Australia for chemotherapy. When Roger returned, it was found that the cancer had travelled to a section of his spine, giving him dreadful pain. Treatment actually removed the growth in his spine, but not until he had been placed on heavy pain-killers. Also, no treatment could stop the growth and eventual spread of the original tumor.

We knew, as few people did, that he was ill and in great pain during the last two public events he attended — the farewell party for Mark Loney, and Mark and Vanessa's wedding. But Roger sparkled during Mark's party. Nobody could have suspected he was ill. I'm told that it was obvious he was in pain during the wedding, but in photos taken then he looks no different than most people remember him.

For Elaine and me, Roger *appeared* ill only about a fortnight before he died. Very few people ever saw him other than the exemplar of amiable energy photographed so well by Dick and Nicki Lynch in the latest issue of *Mimosa*.

On 3 December, Geoff phoned us late in the afternoon to tell us Roger had died. He invited us to the hospital to make our own farewells. There we met Beryl and Brandon, Roger's mother and father, Deb, his sister, and Dai, who lives with Deb. In 1979 Roger's father had built the renovations for our Keele Street house before we moved there from Johnston Street, but I had never met Roger's mother before. I had also never met Deb or Dai. It was a bit startling to meet Deb, since she resembles her brother very much. Within a few minutes we felt we knew her and Dai.

We went to say goodbye to Roger. As when my father died, I felt that the unmoving shape on the bed had very little to do with the person we had known. After all, hadn't Roger always represented the Spirit of Life Itself? And if that life disappears, cannot it reappear?

Roger's funeral at the Springvale Necropolis on 8 December was the saddest event I've ever attended. Many of the several hundred people who were there had not known Roger was ill until after he died. His co-workers at Lifeline and Bridge House were as afflicted as his family and the hundred or so fans who attended. The service included a brief section from Vaughan Williams' 'The Lark Ascending', Roger's favorite piece of music, and a eulogy. The celebrant spoke some paragraphs that Elaine and I had written. The head of Lifeline spoke about Roger's work with that organization. And Deb, courageous, said: 'Roger was no saint; he was unique.'

Roger was unique because he was the only person I have ever met whose central interest was other people. Not just selected individuals or groups, but all people. Roger was equally available to all his friends. He paid absolute attention to our concerns, and remembered what was important to us. He made patterns from people, seeing unexpected connections between them or healing emotional wounds. There were only a few people he gave up on, usually egocentric people who could not stand slights or prickings of their pomposity.

Roger became angry with friends who sold themselves short. A few weeks before he told us about the cancer results, he listened to me wondering whether I would ever make a success of anything non-fannish. 'Let's face it, Bruce,' he said. 'You're a failure! Enjoy it.' What he was trying to say but couldn't was: there are much worse things than petty abstractions like 'failure'. His impatience and his words seemed strangely liberating at the time, but gained extra meaning when I learned of his illness.

Roger's great strength was also a weakness. He never finished his degree in Psychology because the university course made it into an abstract study. Because he did not finish his degree, Roger could never get the jobs for which he was really suited until he gained the position at Bridge House.

In times of trouble, I trust the dream machine in my head to tell me what is really happening.

In one dream, I was sitting in the next room while Roger and Elaine were talking. I wanted to go in there and say, 'Why are you talking like this as if nothing is wrong? Roger will be dead tomorrow.' When I woke up, it took me some minutes to realize that it had been a dream. I dreamt it on the night after the funeral, but my main feeling remains disbelief that Roger is no longer a central part of my own story.

Another dream was surrealistic, but just as vivid. I was on an train travelling around a curved valley. The carriages of the train had running boards on the side, as in Western movies. Rocky Lawson appeared as a train-napper. He was climbing along the running boards outside the carriages, attempting to stop the train. He reached the engine, and I'm not sure what happened. The train stopped suddenly. Carriages spilled off the rails into the valley. The engine was balanced on its back end. People wandered around hurt and dazed, but nobody was killed. I was unhurt, but had no idea how to help the others. Suddenly Roger was there. I stared at him in disbelief. He shrugged. 'Sure, I'm back,' he said, as if I should never have doubted otherwise. 'I'll be leaving in a tran-scendental ascent into heaven next time, but you won't be there to see it. Now let's help these people.'

In another dream, Melbourne University's Union building was a giant glass palace featuring a double-story restaurant. I was at one huge table of diners, and went to get some extra wine for the table. As I looked down the sweeping staircase between the two floors, I saw the other group of diners I had promised to be with that night. I went down to talk to them, and they begged me to stay. But I still had to fetch the wine for the table upstairs! I had no idea how to resolve the situation. At the end of the dream, dressed in nothing but shirt and shorts, I was running in the driving rain away from the Union building.

I suspect my dream showed me what life was often like for Roger. He promised so much to everybody that often he was caught in the middle of all us, unable entirely to enjoy the celebration.

But Roger enjoyed most of his life. What I'm really mourning is life for all of us who are left. We're all stuck for someone to talk to in an emergency. We don't know to whom we can tell all those secrets and jokes we could only tell Roger. We don't really believe what's happened. And maybe we never will.

I have written you 500 letters in my head.

I think of you more often than that.

Sometimes time rushes fast past us all.

—Billy Ray Wolfenbarger
March 28th, 2022 (to G. Sutton Breiding)

The War to Make War of the Worlds: Goliath

Joe Pearson

Sit right down and I'll tell you a tale. It's a classic story, one featuring nostalgia, hubris, friendship, innovation, H.G. Wells, betrayal, big dreams, Teddy Roosevelt, near and actual bankruptcies, all night sing-alongs, Martians, con-men, artists, financiers, Teddy Roosevelt, Ninja Turtles, Heat Rays and more. And it's all true.

It began back in 1962 when young Jody Pearson was laid up at his Grandmother's apartment for much of that hot Van Nuys summer with massive second-degree burns all over his back. I'm talking blisters the size of golf balls and full body Vaseline soaked wrappings, not unlike Karloff's Mummy. Constrained to Grandmother's small apartment I was left with little to do except draw, read comics, watch old black and white movies on TV and delve into my grandmother's large book collection.

This was a surprisingly varied library with volumes ranging from H.G. Wells' *Outline of History* to Kipling's *Jungle Book* and *Just So Stories*.

Having recently learned to read pretty well our young protagonist devoured them all, but one book really gobsmacked me and that was Wells' seminal *The War of the Worlds*. It was the first real fully "adult" book for me and it was a monstrous and compelling beauty, filled with an absolutely relentless and savage recounting of an invasion of our planet by an utterly ruthless alien species. Man was reduced to a hapless victim and food source in the matter of weeks by the advanced Martians and driven like cattle from the 100 foot tall Tripods of the Invaders.

I had never read anything like that in my life. It was horrifying. It was enthralling. It was my first encounter with science fiction and it remains to this day one of the best of the thousands of books I've read in that genre. Adding to the freaky mind bomb of this book on my nine year old brain was that my gentle and loving grandmother, "Sweetiepie", had a rather unique pamphlet on her bookshelves; a little gem of psychotronic religious horror and prediction titled *1975 in Prophecy*.

Created by the religious cult of the Radio Church of God and penned by its founder Herbert Armstrong, this 31-page tome, reproduced on a weirdly slick, almost oily, white glossy paper, was a gruesomely detailed warning and "prophecy" of the impending End of the World in 1975. Armstrong shoehorned the hallucinatory visions of the Book of Revelations into the modern history of the Western world, with the rise of the New Roman Empire (the European Common Market and Germany in particular), the appearance of The Beast and the seven years of Trials and Tribulations, ending in the Battle of Armageddon and the destruction of the planet.

Scary shit, eh? Well, it was made more intense by seven, full page illustrations from the pen of the great cartoonist/illustrator Basil Wolverton showing in gruesome black and white ink detail the Tribulations; tidal waves, plagues, boils, giant rocks falling from heaven, nuclear planes saturation bombing cities and ending with giant bulldozers scooping thousands of mangled and disfigured bodies into mass graves. And it was all going to hit the fan in 1975! Only 13 years in the future!

To say that this was unnerving would be an understatement and combined with my contemporaneous reading of *The War of the Worlds* made a deep impact on my developing brain. Wolverton's horrific illustrations merged into the mayhem and slaughter of Wells' Martian Invasion scaring the living crap out of me. But youth is nothing if not resilient and I soldiered on and eventually healed in body and mind and was able to enjoy the last month of that Van Nuys summer with the neighborhood kids; playing army, climbing trees and watching 25 cent double bills at the Fox and Capri theaters.

But the memory lingered and *The War of the Worlds* never completely left my psyche and came into full flower 44 years later.

In 1997 I was living the dream, running my own independent animation studio, Epoch Ink Animation, in Santa Monica. We had just finished twenty-six episodes of the "Captain Simian and the Space Monkeys" series and, after downsizing to a core group of about twelve artists and crew, were doing preproduction for a number of other L.A. studios like DIC, Dreamworks, MGM and Film Roman. To keep the team working on the downtime I decided to go into a heavy development on

Art: Basil Wolverton

our own Intellectual Properties (IP's). As you may know it's extremely difficult to sell original content in Hollywood. Everyone wants to hedge their bets and dollars by investing in an IP with pre-existing audience recognition and market performance.

So I was casting about for something like that and *The War of the Worlds* came immediately to mind. It was a well-known and received book and movie and about to go into Public Domain in a large number of territories. But what to do? An animated adaptation of the novel seemed unmarketable as it was so extremely adult in content and the essence of the story was a brutal beat down of a hapless Mankind by a more advanced Invader, it struck me as being a hard sell. Of course eight years later Spielberg proved me fully wrong on that idea when he made his own powerful *The War of the Worlds* movie, using that original story, but updating it into the '90's.

Well, what about a sequel? I'd always wondered what would have happened after the first failed Invasion. You knew that the Martians would return; they had no choice as their planet was dying. So what would Man do? It seems obvious; we'd bury our dead, pick ourselves up by the bootstraps and rebuild. Rebuild as fast as possible using whatever retro-engineered Martian tech we could salvage from the abandoned Mar-

tian war machines. And we'd do it and arm up fast because you knew the space bastard's would be coming at us again.

That was the genesis of the IP. And setting it in 1914, a pivotal year in our own "real" timeline seemed like a good choice. We had all the Great Power rivalries ramping up to a global war with each other. We had colorful historical figures like Theodore Roosevelt, Tesla and the Red Baron that could be dropped into our storyline, and it was a perfect time period to create a visual fusion of a steam/diesel punk aesthetic. And it would be written as a series proposal, which would give us the opportunity to really explore all of this unique alternative history and world.

I settled on the main story of a crew of young soldiers training under the command of Roosevelt in an international rapid reaction army (ARES) in Southern Manhattan Island. They would be equipped with their own battle Tripods and super zeppelins and battle trains, designed in-house by Tesla. On the eve of WWI the Martians would return and then it would be "Michael Bay" time.

I wrote an initial show "bible" with a twenty-page story treatment and a set of character bios for the series 8 principal characters, while my crew produced some killer character

THE WAR OF THE WORLDS.

Designer Lee's original character line-up

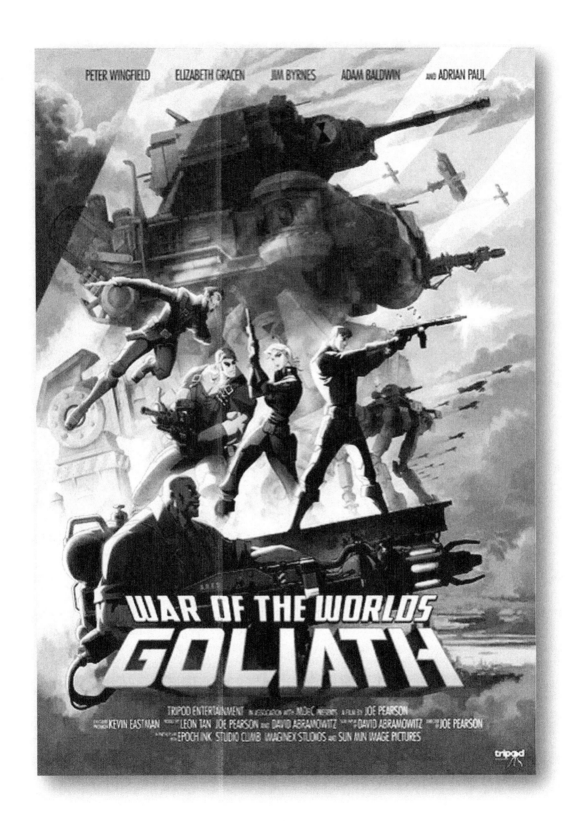

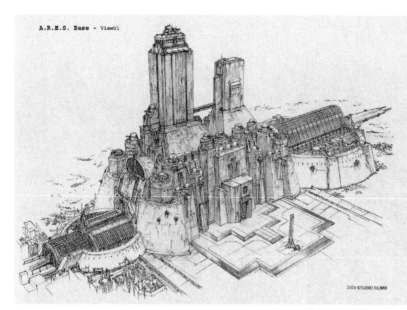

A.R.E.S. Base - View01

2000 STUDIO CLIMB

and mecha designs for the ARES and Martian Tripods.

And then began a short round of pitching. We showed it to a friendly animation exec at Fox who was currently developing the *Titan A E.* movie. He passed, but did casually ask if I'd be interested in directing *Titan A.E.* I was stunned at the generosity of the offer, but didn't feel like shutting my own independent studio to take the gig. Which seemed like a good idea at the time, but occasionally I wonder what would have happened if I had said yes. Well maybe there's a quantum universe/timeline where I took that path for better or worse.

We pitched *War of the Worlds: ARES* to a few other possible execs and groups, but no-go. The most infuriating response was one studio genius who opined that the design of the characters and world looked "too old-fashioned" and would not click with the Network audience for an animated kid's series. If I had thought faster I could have responded that yeah, it would look "old-fashioned", just like the uniforms and design did in *Star Wars*, but sadly I'm not that quick on my feet.

Anyhow after a month or two, it looked like the IP was not going to get a pick-up so I tabled it

and moved on. And when Spielberg's massively budgeted and generally excellent version of *The War of the Worlds* came out in 2006 that felt like the last straw. I mean how you top that? But that turned out not to be the case.

Around the end of 2000 I was just finishing a two year run as the Creative Director at the Bohbot Kids Network (BKN), working on a number of their shows and show running the animated SF series *Roswell Conspiracies; Aliens, Myths and Legends. Roswell* was a real joy as I had near complete creative freedom to produce and t run the show the way I wanted, from budget to crew and casting, to writing and animation. After the fourth episode I never received any editorial notes from the higher powers at BKN. That's a real "Unicorn" for Network kid's animation at that time as show's ALWAYS had multiple overseers from the Network, the investor, the toy company and others. Miraculously, I didn't have that monkey on my back on *Roswell* and aside from a tight budget and schedule it was a wonderful experience in creative freedom. 'And a damned good SF series.

But when I left BKN in late 2000, I knew one thing for certain; that kind of freedom almost never occurs unless you own or control all the pieces on the table: financing, creation, production and especially DISTRIBUTION. 'But how to get ahold of all of those pieces?

Enter Kevin Eastman. Kevin is one of the two young artists that set out to make their own homage to Marvel comics by creating and self-publishing the *Teenage Mutant Ninja Turtles* comics in 1984. The rest, as they say, was

126

history. Both Kevin and his co-creator became very wealthy and Kevin used some of his money to purchase the venerable teen/adult graphic story magazine, *Heavy Metal* in the early 90's.

I had become acquainted with Kevin after he was shown a copy of my Heavy Metalesque animated short, *Collet .45,* and came over to Epoch to talk animation and comics. We soon partnered with Jim Lee at Wildstorm to develop "Heavy Metal TV", a proposed animated series that would be hosted by Kevin's wife Julie Strain and showcase animated series based on *Heavy Metal*'s, Epoch's and Wildstorm's IPs. We pitched it to Showtime and got interest, but no pickup and that was pretty much it for *Heavy Metal* TV. However Kevin and I started up a professional relationship that carried on for a long time.

So in my search for a distribution engine a few years later, *Heavy Metal* Magazine and Kevin came immediately to my mind. I approached Kevin with a plan to form *Heavy Metal* Video (HMV) and fundraise for a slate of 6 direct-to-DVD/video, teen/adult animated features that would be created, produced AND promoted/distributed through *Heavy Metal* Magazine and their vast in-house distribution system.

Kevin jumped onboard, and I spent a number of months working out what came to be a near 200 page, in-depth business plan for potential investors.

War of the Worlds: ARES and our old femme fatale *Collet .45* were all a part of the initial slate of 6. At one point, both *The Crow* and *Conan: Red Nails* were also attached as proposed films. We took HMV on the road for about five years and fifteen serious rounds of discussions and even serious contract negotiations with a

score of interested investors from L.A. to New York, to Tokyo and Seoul. We got extremely close a number of times, but ultimately money never made it into our bank account. I could write a book about the highs and lows and absolute freaky coincidences weirdness of that adventure. If you've ever have the chance to catch the brilliant *The Offer* series on the wild ride to get *The Godfather* made into a feature, you can get a bit of the feel for what Kevin and I went through.

One short example was our pitch to the head of Fox Home Video in December of 2003 in her penthouse office on the top of the Fox Tower (the *Die Hard* building) in Century City. We were introduced by a middle man, Eugene, who was a big fan of our plan. The pitch went well. The exec loved our idea of edgy "American Anime", the IP's, and our production model and enthusiastically committed to doing a deal with HMV and Fox Home Video. Kevin and I floated out on a high, but a few weeks later heard through the grapevine that she was leaving Fox and that she and Eugene were forming their own entertainment company to produce "American Anime". Holy frak?

But then Kevin and I received a call from Eugene on Christmas Eve telling us that we would be included as partners in their extremely ambitious plan to become a "mini major" entertainment group and run their animation division. As Kevin would say, "cool beans". This was followed by a near year of writing up yet more proposals and company and IP descriptions on my part, but in

the end the proposed newco's fundraising never came through. The ex-Fox exec moved to New York to lick her wounds and Eugene apparently left the country as the last I heard from him was a post card from Ireland. And so it goes, and goes, and goes.

At one point a Korean animation studio that I had worked extensively with on previous animated series bought fully into our dream and created a major *Heavy Metal* Video pitch event at the prestigious "63" business office building in Seoul, taking over an entire floor and ballroom to create a kind of "*Heavy Metal* world" for potential investors, and packing a huge ballroom with more than 300 invited guests to hear Kevin and I pitch our plan. That night Kevin, Simon Bisley and I dined with a number of Korean *haut monde*, including the head of the Korean National Assembly. Ultimately we couldn't bring in matching monies and the Korean investors lost interest. Still, Kevin, Simon and I had some truly epic and surreal adventures during our stay.

To add to the frustration of this money hunt was the fact that two years after we initially went out into the industry with our HMV business model, both Marvel and DC/Warner's launched their first slates of direct-to-DVD/video animated features, pretty much using the exact model I had brainstormed for HMV. Most likely it was just one of those ideas whose time had come and not a rip-off of my concept, but we'll never know.

One ray of sunshine in these long fruitless years happened when our pitching led Kevin to recon-

nect with Tom Gray the ex-Golden Harvest exec who's efforts got the first *Ninja Turtle* movie greenlit. Tom had just joined the newly formed and funded Imagi Entertainment group and asked us to pitch the *Heavy Metal* plan to them. They didn't buy in, but did bring us on to help produce the *Highlander: the Search for Vengeance* anime feature with the renowned Madhouse Studios and anime superstar director, Yoshioki Kawajiri.

Aside from being able to work with a visionary like Kawajiri Kevin and I also got to work with the esteemed *Highlander* TV series showrunner/key writer, David Abramowitz. We spent a long brunch with David getting acquainted and brainstorming the basic concept/plot of *Vengeance*. That process went so smoothly and easily, and David was such a talented and genial person to work with, that two years later when I needed a writer for *War of the Worlds: ARES* it was a no brainer to bring him onto that project.

2006 came around and after six years of these ups and downs, Kevin and I were about to throw in the towel as. Working nearly full time on HMV had nearly exhausted Epoch's bank account and it wasn't easy for Kevin either as *Heavy Metal* Magazine took a major hit when one of our ventures with a potential fund source collapsed. It was time for one last hurrah and I took one of the HMV IP's out with me as an invited guest to the Tokyo International Film Fest (TIFF) held every Fall in the city's Roppongi District. The project was called *Lost Angeles* and it was a three-way creative concept and development between myself, Kevin, and Simon Bisley. The movie was basically *The Warriors* meets *Romeo and Juliet* in a post-apocalyptic Los Angeles fought over by rival gangs and neo-kingdoms.

I put together a promo short which featured

Metal Magazine well. He said that he thought that with the right project he might be able to find production funding out of Malaysia.

We started a correspondence and a few months later he came out to LA for more in-depth discussions. He really liked the *War of the Worlds: ARES* IP and we agreed that along with Kevin Eastman's marquee it could be a good piece to pitch to a Venture Capital Group in Kuala Lum-

Kevin and I talking about the project and lots of concept art and flew to Tokyo to make the presentation. It was well received and a couple of the reps from major U.S. studios expressed interest, but later passed on the project. The Market looked like a bust then something happened on the morning of the last day of the TIFF that changed everything.

I was catching the last bus of the morning from my hotel to the Festival and found myself alone on the bus save for one young Asian man in a suit and tie. We struck a conversation and I found out that his name was Leon Tan and he was a Chinese Malaysian representing his audio studio in Kuala Lumpur at the TIFF. Leon had seen the *Lost Angeles* presentation and opined that he was a major SF and fantasy fan and knew *Heavy*

pur, MAVCAP. This group had funded Leon and his partner, Mike, in their audio house, Imaginex Studios, which was now doing quite well producing world class music and voice and sound EFX design for the Southeast Asian marketplace. Leon would pitch the film and partnership as a way for the Malaysian government to continue to expand and nurture their country's animation talent pool and studios.

I liked this approach and agreed to partner with Leon and Mike in a new company, Tripod Entertainment SDBN, to produce *War of the Worlds: ARES* (now renamed *War of the Worlds: Goliath*) as a low budget, animated, direct to video/ DVD feature.

As the funding was all from the Malaysian government with the intent of growing Malaysia's

129

animation industry it was incumbent upon Tripod to do as much in-country in Malaysia as we could.

The plan evolved to house the production with established Malaysian animation house Silver Ant with me co-directing and producing with the owner of that studio, Goh Aun Ho, and with Leon, Mike and Kevin on board as fellow producers.

The budget was not large for such an ambitious project, running about 1.6 million USD or much less than a minute of Disney or Pixar's animated feature budgets. It was closer to the Warner/Marvel direct to DVD animated features although still budgeted 50% lower than those films. The movie was to run 75 minutes and take about 2 years for the whole production once a final script was approved.

After some back and forth with MAVCAP and a visit to L.A. from an executive team from MAVCAP, a deal was struck and we had our money!

It seemed like a dream come true at the time; after many long years my homage to H.G. Wells and his seminal novel was finally going to see the light of day. In retrospect it didn't all pan out as we expected and going full tilt on an independent, low budget, animated war movie using a new production team and without a firm distribution agreement in place, was perhaps not the wisest decision on my part. Still, with heads high and hearts open we plunged into production.

Kevin and I traveled to Kuala Lumpur (KL) for the agreement signings and to speak to a huge audience at a government sponsored international media conference in KL City Center. It was my first time on the ground in Malaysia and I was anxious to meet my new production partners and teams and get a feeling for the animation talent pool in that country. The audience at the speaking event would be indicative of the people I was partnered with and would be working with; young, educated, English speaking, enthusiastic and fully connected to the rest of the world and all of its news, trends and media.

Most unique about Malaysia was its multi-ethnic and multi-cultural society with a national population comprised of 63% native Malays, 20% ethnic Chinese, and 7% East Indians. Rounding up this mix was a large group of local mixed Asians and Europeans and expats and immigrants from neighboring countries and the West. Each of these groups lived and interacted relatively harmoniously despite their ethnic, religious and cultural differences. I was always struck by the way native Malays (who were all Muslim by religion and culture) mixed and mingled tolerantly with their Chinese compatriots in KL's many malls and public spaces. You would often see Malaysian girls and women with head scarfs and loose body concealing clothing mingling comfortably with Chinese girls who were wearing very little in the hot SE Asian climate.

For decades the government had nurtured a strong Malaysian middle class and spent billions in roads, housing and education and as a result, Malaysia, out of all of its fellow SE Asian countries and societies (excluding Singapore), had the least stratified society and income inequality in the region. In fact, Malaysia was a work/living destination for hundreds of thousands of immigrants from Indonesia, the Philippines and Thailand.

It was not a perfect society, but one head and shoulders above its near neighbors in terms of stability and quality of life. Thanks to dedicated government investment, the nation had developed a world class IT infrastructure and connected population. This translated into Malaysia having a huge and growing pool of savvy digital artists and animators. And it was a country where near everyone spoke English and fully understood Western culture and media which would be a massive help during production.

So it was a good start and looked very promising for the kind of production that WOTWG would require. But problems did raise their heads. Malaysia's government and animation industry was heavily centered around digital production; I.E. computer generated (CG) animation. While there was a small talent pool of accomplished 2D animators most of them had focused and trained on the classic "stretch and squash" style of animation and not the rigorous "realistic" character animation that *WOTWG* would require.

This was going to present some serious production problems. Silver Ant (SA) was the only available KL production house at the time that had the history and potential of making a film like, *WOTWG* as they had been producing very strong, highly realistic game animatics and movies for the video game industry, primarily for Konami. When Kevin and I toured their studio in KL we were extremely impressed by Goh and his all-Chinese Malaysian team, particularly his two key designers, Spencer Ooi and Wei Siong. They were good as any of the best design talent that I had worked with in my previous 30 years in the LA animation industry.

But SA was an entirely CG based studio and at the very modest budget allocated for the 75 minute film the character CG animation would be very limited; an *Uncanny Valley* writ large. At best we would have been able to produce character animation close to the level of the first *Star Wars* animated *Clone Wars* series which was very stiff and unemotive. At worst we ran the risk of CG characters that acted and moved like near human "zombies".

To resolve this I proposed that all design, layout and background environments, CG vehicle modeling and animation and final camera be done at SA with Goh co-directing with me. The storyboards would be done by my LA studio, Epoch Ink, and would be a fusion of LA based artists and the in-house team at SA. Character animation would be done in Seoul at Sun Min Image Pictures; a strong Korean 2D animation House that I

had worked with extensively over the previous two decades. Voice acting would be directed by Imaginex's voice director's (Mike along with Gavin Yap) and use a combined LA and KL cast. The film's score would be done at at Imagainex by a talented Croatian composer, Luka Kuncevic. It was a somewhat awkward mix, but seemed like a good solution and a way to keep a large part of the animation in Malaysia.

Allow me to pull back a minute and preface the rest of this piece by laying out the production's schedule, budgets and general creative approach which right from the beginning became heavily challenged and strained by various production issues, decisions and constraints and led to the film taking much more time and money.

WOTWG was planned to be a 75-minute, direct to DVD film, taking two years to produce at a budget of $1.6 million. By the end of the production *WOTWG* had evolved into a much more ambitious 98 minute, limited theatrical release film which would be followed by direct to DVD and broadcast, offering full stereoscopic 3D theatrical and 3D DVD/Blu-ray versions. The production grew to four plus years and a total budget of $2.2 million. That's a huge change across the board and in the end even the budget increase was inadequate to the expanded scale of the film. That was to put a real strain on many aspects of the movie and added to the doubling of the production time.

I'll detail how this happened as we go along. Some stuff came at us out of the blue or as the result of working with new creative partners, but we also took some hits because of some bad initial decisions and assumptions that I made. From the beginning, I had underestimated the cost of the final film. Add to that the potential issues of producing a low budget film with big aspirations with a country and studios that I had never worked in or with before.

After a couple of weeks in KL Kevin and I headed back to LA in late October of 2007 to start production in earnest. I immediately reached out to David Abramowitz to see if he'd be interested and available to write the film's script and forwarded a copy of my initial story treatment and series bible to bring him up to date. David loved the project and story and enthusiastically jumped on board, taking on a producer role as well.

While he worked on the script I began a hunt for a designer and look for the film's characters. I sent initial funds and directions to a half dozen selected artists (along with the initial character models from the 1998 development) to see what they could come up with. We got some good work back, particularly from Malaysia based artist, Sandra Khoo, who had a very strong, Disney adventure influenced design style. But the initial set off characters from Seoul based Lee Seong Gyu really nailed the look I was hoping for. They were very "anime" influenced, but still kept a mix of Western animation elements. So he got the gig and started producing final models beginning with the film's core team of characters.

Simultaneously I began to receive images of SA's design teams initial concept art for the movie and it was stunning to say the least. Without any initial input from me and based only on the original character and vehicle designs they produced close to thirty evocative concept paintings. Clearly they had the chops and drive, but missed the boat at times because I wasn't there on a daily basis to give them hands-on guidance.

We resolved that by bringing Spencer Ooi out to LA that December to spend a couple of weeks working with me daily at my Venice Beach studio on designs and some initial storyboard sequences. Spencer and I got a huge amount of work done in those weeks.

Working with an artist at the level of Spencer in LA was a fantastic experience and excellent collaboration. Along with his fellow concept artist at Silver Ant, Wei Siong, he ended up doing all of the film's highly detailed design for props, backgrounds, layouts, including all thirteen of our fully designed, blueprinted and modeled CG models for our seven different tripods, four aircraft and one megazeppelin The only issue I ever had with them was that using just two (and later three) designers on *WOTWG* meant the initial 6 months design process we planned on ended up taking more than three years. And that wasn't because they were slow designers as Spencer and Wei were lighting fast, but the film required an immense amount of design and they were only two guys.

Spencer and I quickly locked down the ultimate design look for the film's human defenders' home base on the southern tip of Manhattan and the tech and aesthetic approach to their vehicles, weaponry as well as the architecture of our alternative history New York City. Set in a 1914 world, fifteen years after the failed first Martian Invasion, the technology would be a variation on the tech of that time in our history, but also modified and accelerated by Man's retro-engineering of the abandoned Martian technology scattered around the planet. So not full-on "steampunk", or the early WW1 tech, but more of a fusion of that with mid-30's

designs and technology; "1914 meets 1933 meets Mars". 'Essentially full-on "dieselpunk". This translated to all of the movie's clothing, weaponry, vehicles and architecture, the later which I pictured as an early Deco look mixed with extruded steam piping and the remnants of late 19th century buildings.

By that point, David's script had come in and except for a few very minor items, I very happy with it and so was the core creative team. He had adapted and expanded and improved my original short treatment in very dramatic and theatrical ways and added in a strong sequence in a Martian controlled power plant that Leon had conceptualized. It was everything I wanted and more, but it was clearly going to be long; significantly longer than the initially planned 75 minutes.

One key issue for the film's limited budget was its massive scale, with sequences set extensively in our new, New York City and the ARES base, around the Southwest and Upstate New York and featuring massive battles between armies of human and Martian tripods and mecha. Again, this was a frankly hubristic decision on my part. All of my animation training and producing experience had taught me that in regards to modest budgets in animation, less is better, but caught up in the zeitgeist of actually getting to make this movie I pressed on and went for the gusto. In the end, we generally pulled it all off, but at a price.

A big worry of mine in terms of design and scale was an early sequence in the movie in which our main hero, Eric Wells, travels on an elevated train through our alternative history NYC and down to the ARES citadel and base at the southern tip of Manhattan Island. A bigger budgeted film would have simply designed and built NYC in CG allowing us to camera move freely and fully in and around the buildings and streets. But our budget would really only allow us to build CG models for our dozen Tripods and aircraft (and that was really pushing the envelope). So we had to design and conceptualize a thriving metropolis carefully and within our budget constraints.

I decided that the best way to show scale and give the viewer a glimpse of this post-invasion and rebuilt NYC would to identify a street and route for Eric to take the elevated train from just below Central Park to the ARES base at the island's southern tip. It needed to be a street/route that showcased as many iconic NY buildings and locations as possible on its journey. Looking at maps of the city with Spencer it came down to a choice between Broadway and 5th Ave. In the end I chose 5th as it featured a plethora of the city's great buildings including St. Patrick's Cathedral, the NY Library with its monumental lion statues, the Triangle Building and the Arch at Washington Square. At the Square I decided that the train would make a hard left and then a right and continue down through the lower West side of Manhattan to the base.

Ideally we should have gone to NYC itself for a research trip in order to really walk the streets and get a deep feel for the layout and spaces involved (much like Kawajiri did with his Madhouse design team when they were designing their dystopian NYC for the *Highlander* anime). But we didn't have that kind of budget luxury so Spencer and I loaded up on a number of architecture books of the city, particularly the ones featuring photos from 1899 through the mid-'30's. And Spencer set up a Google Earth "camera run" down the center of 5th Ave. at about the height of the elevated train Eric would be riding which confirmed our choice in routes. I will admit to being an Old Dog that was simply blown away by this kind of new research technology.

We also spent a few days with me driving him around LA in my beat-up Pontiac Sunfire convertible taking in all of the city's wonderful art deco architecture. LA easily has one of the largest collections of gorgeous, large scale art deco buildings and interiors in the world and I wanted Spencer to get an on the ground look at actual structures built in this unique style. And I confess we may have hit a couple of LA's vintage Irish/English pubs as well; all to give him a good "inside" feel for the design coming up for the "Greenman Pub" where several sequences of the film were to take place.

Spencer also spent a couple of days drawing a masterful storyboard for Eric's train ride sequence down to ARES Base and it really brought home to me just how wonderful it would have been to have him on as a co-director on the whole film with me. But he (and Wei Siong) were essential to the design and direction of the film and I couldn't spare him. If only clone technology was a bit more advanced!

While in LA Spencer confided to me his grave concern that Silver Ant was going to have huge problems providing all of the background layout and color for the movie's more 800 scenes, as they did not have an in-house team that could do that many scenes under the current schedule and budget.

For a static background the simplest and quickest way is to draw it hand drawn and then paint the background as one single image, not building out the entire image as a full CG model that can be viewed from any angle. As an all-CG based and trained studio, SA's crew never actually hand drew or painted the final backgrounds for their film's scenes. They were trained to design and then "build", and then render all of the backgrounds in full CG, whether it was for a static non-moving background or a background where the camera moved extensively.

This meant that all of the film's 800 or more separate backgrounds would have to be produced in full 360 CG, a task impossible in the two year production schedule and the cost of the labor alone would push SA out of its budget limit. This was clearly worrisome and it would come to a head less than a month later when Goh let my co-producer's and I know that he had read and broken down David's script and it was too ambitious for the budget and time we had planned for SA's work on the film. We needed to talk.

In late January I flew to Kuala Lumpur to meet with my fellow producers and Goh and the audio team at Imaginex Studios (where Tripod had an office). Worries and all it was just good to be back on the ground in an Asian city where the super advanced collides with the ancient and exotic. And it was in the middle of the Chinese New Year celebrations, which added to the sense of being in a foreign culture and had the bonus of an absolutely insane all-night fireworks shows mounted from Chinese neighborhoods all over the city. These shows actually topped any of the many wild July 4th shows which I've experienced in the States.

I arrived to find that SA was going to drop out of the production, which wasn't a surprise at that point and was frankly, completely understandable. I would have done the same in Goh's shoes. The surprise was that Spencer and Wei Siong wanted to stay working on the movie and were jumping ship from SA and forming their own company, "Studio Climb". Well, that was good news for us, but the problem of where to host the body of the production remained. I cut that Gordian Knot by shifting the layout, animation, ink and paint, EXF and final camera all to Sun Min studios in Seoul. As a part of their ink and paint process Sun Min would also set up and train a digital ink and paint team in KL that would be housed at Studio Climb.

Problem resolved, but what I didn't really grok at the time was that now with Goh and SA off the movie, I was de facto the sole director AND line producer on the film. This was going to add heavily to my own workload and inevitably add a lot of time to the production schedule, and added financial risk to me personally as my already minimal producing/directing salary was going to be cut massively by doubling or tripling my hours on the movie without an increase in fees.

And my lack of revenue meant that I had to continue to work on outside jobs at the same time as the film and during the production on *WOTWG* I produced and directed on the side an animated short for Microsoft's Zune initiative and a fashion animated cartoon for Filmmaster in Italy as well as producing the game cinematic storyboard for an upcoming Marvel Civil War game. I was also the lead producer and co-director on a separate animated 22-minute pilot Tripod was producing for a potential Saturday morning kids series and producing and directing the design package and two three-minute trailers for a proposed animated Arabian horses series for Al Jazeera Children's Network. As they say, it never rains, but it pours.

Then you add in the fact that as fast as Spencer and Wei Siong were, they were still only two guys so the design schedule was going to

triple as well. They did add another good designer to their team in the following months, but it wasn't enough to seriously impact the inevitable lengthening of their time on the production.

It was clear that the film was not going to get done in the initial two year timeframe, but in January, 2008, no one thought it would more than double. In retrospect, I should have really brought in another director and fulltime line producer/production manager, but it wasn't in the budget. Fortunately, I had no health issues or breakdowns during the four years of production or the film would have stopped dead in its tracks.

I settled into a production routine for that initial year; breaking down the script and handing out storyboards to mostly L.A. based artists, and guiding Studio Climb's team and Lee in Seoul on their designs so that the design and storyboard teams were in full synch. My plan was to focus heavily on the designs and boards needed for the first half of the film and then get that combined package out to Sun Min to begin layout and animation. Then when the first half of the film was in full animation, focus on the second half of preproduction. This breakdown works well for accelerating production, but it also means that you never have a full finished animatic of the entire film to review before going to animation.

With the script in, Leon and I also focused on casting. That's where David Abramowitz stepped up. He could have simply thanked us for the script money then kicked back and said something like, "Thanks kids, I'll see you at the wrap party", but he went the extra mile.

David had been the showrunner on the long running *Highlander* TV series developing a strong friendship with the show's principal's and he asked us if we thought that some of the key actors might be a good fit for some of *WOTWG*'s characters.

It was a surprisingly natural and easy fit, casting Adrian Paul, Peter Wingfield, Elizabeth Gracen and Jim Brynes as major characters in the film. They were all consummate professionals and just

really looked forward to these trips and spending time with good artists and friends in fascinating locales.

And I did make good friends in both countries. I grew particularly close to Leon and Mike and got to know much of the accomplished team at Imaginex. They were a fully professional and talented crew and well supervised by Mike and his key in-house production manager, Jazzlyn. They worked hard and played hard. One night during the production, Leon, Mike, Gavin, Leon's brother Alex and I stayed up the entire night drinking and singing along with a really great cover band in the city's Bangsar District, something I hadn't done in many years. At another time, when they were all in L.A. for some of the film's voice recordings we rented a dome house up in Joshua Tree for a few days of hiking and bonding in that iconic locale.

wonderful people on a personal level. And their involvement added a whole other promotional boost to our film as the large and friendly *Highlander* fan base embraced both the film and the team as part of their big *Highlander* "family".

Leon and I then reached out to a number of popular SF genre talents including Adam Baldwin, Beau Billingslea, Mark Sheppard, Matt Letscher, James Arnold Taylor, and Joey D'Auria, all of whom jumped on board. We filled out the cast with some excellent actors out Kuala Lumpur, including Rob Middleton and Tony Eusoff.

My third partner in Tripod, Mike Bloemendal, and Imaginex's in-house voice director, Gavin Yap, handily supervised the voice direction and incumbent audio, both out of their Imaginex home base in KL and then in LA at Vitello Post. In the end, casting and voicing proved to be one of the easiest and most seamless aspects of the production.

While I was able to produce and direct much of the production from out of my Venice Beach studio, there is nothing like being able to collaborate and troubleshot face-to-face. This was particularly true in the pre-Zoom world when we were producing the film. So I would make an average of four, two week long trips a year to Malaysia, and then as Sun Min kicked off their part of the production, I would spend a week in Seoul and then go south to KL for another week. Tiring as they were with the long flight and inevitable jet lag, I

My time with the team and crew at Sun Min and Seoul was also a good mix of work and time spent socializing with the crew and my many friends in the Korean animation industry. I'd been working with Sun Min since the mid-90's on various animated series and shorts for Epoch Ink and had developed a long friendship with Young Sang and much of his core team. I had other colleagues in Seoul as well and enjoyed exploring parts of that always fascinating city and culture with them.

This production process continued for three more years with my making periodic trips overseas to Seoul and Kuala Lumpur. An interesting part of my production trips to Asia was the vast difference in weather I would often encounter. During my Winter trips I'd leave relatively balmy L.A. and drop full-on into a snow bound Seoul and then after a week of working in very cold weather there I'd fly the 3,000 miles south into a full-on tropical KL.

The mix of American, Korean and Malaysian talent created some interesting fusions of culture and style as well. During a trip to KL with Sun Min's owner, Young Sang and his head of layout, we joined Leon and Mike and their families in a

trip down to the port city of Klang for a large dinner with Leon's parents, and his brother and wife. At one point around the table someone mentioned the classic American TV series *Combat!* and spontaneously ALL of the men at the table began humming that series' iconic theme song. After we rolled out the last few bars of the *Combat!* Theme we tried to figure out how all of these three different generations of guys, based in three different countries knew this show and song so well that they had imbedded it deep in their memories.

It turns out that this was because *Combat!* apparently aired in all three countries at different times to different generations. In the States it came onto TV in the early '60's, which hit me at the age of nine or ten. In South Korea it aired about a decade later which would have been at the time Young Sang was that age and it hit Malaysia a decade after that when Leon and his brother were young kids. Vic Morrow would be proud.

The third year of production continued in much the same vein as the other two. Sun Min was well into the final animation and camera on a good portion of the film after a rocky start and some emergency team meetings in Seoul. Kwang Seouk Yang was brought onto the Korean team as the new director of animation and the jump in animation quality was dramatic. Layout also improved as the production went into its second full year in Seoul. As did the studio's CG unit's animation which I spent a lot of time with in Seoul guiding and finessing with their animation.

It was now clear that we were not going to be able to finish the film in the original timeframe as all of the delays I mentioned above regarding design and direction were coming to fruition. It also became apparent that the direct-to-DVD/video model we had been producing the film around was a rapidly declining marketplace as one by one, major distributors like Tower Records were going under and the new streaming services like Netflix and Amazon grew in importance. A 75-minute direct-to-DVD/video was not looking like a viable commercial option.

As some of the early footage on the film looked surprisingly rich and "big" and looked like it could hold up on the big screen we decided to go for it, doubling down and expanding the length of the film to a full 90+ minutes and enhancing the scope of some of the sequences to accommodate a full theatrical release.

This added an additional 300K to our budget, which Leon managed to raise from different Malaysian investment groups and film funds. This was arguably pretty risky as even with the extra money we were still attempting to release a theatrical animated feature at a budget of about 1/100 of a Pixar or Dreamworks animated film and about 1/10 of the budget of a Japanese animated feature. And of course adding more footage and enhancements added more time to the production as well. It did make for some nice improvements like the addition of falling snow into what became the opening sequence of the film, set in Leeds, England.

Actually, the Leeds Sequence was never intended to be the opening sequence of *War of the Worlds: Goliath*. From the moment I conceptualized the initial treatment I had envisioned a sequence set on the plains outside of St. Petersburg during the first Martian Invasion in 1899. It was to feature an entrenched Russian battalion being annihilated by three Martian tripods and end with a doomed Cossack cavalry charge led by the man who would, fifteen years later, become the lead General in ARES; General Serguai Kushnirov. I had Lee design all the models and characters for this sequence and had about half the storyboard prepped when I decided to abandon this bravura opening because of the cost and the difficulty of animating a thousand charging Cossack horsemen.

We were able to portray this sequence in comics form when the story ran as a fully painted sixteen page tour de force by the brilliant "Puppeteer Lee" in the all *War of the Worlds* issues of *Heavy Metal* Magazine. All in all we produced over a 150 pages of outstanding comics stories based on *War of the Worlds: Goliath* using top talent from around Malaysia. We were able to fund these comics stories by a generous grant that Leon pulled in from MDEC, the Malaysian Digital Economy Corporation. The stories ran in various issues of *Heavy Metal* Magazine.

Kevin was very supportive of the film in both his magazine and at the San Diego Comic Con where he allowed the *Goliath* production crew to share space with him at the Heavy Metal booth for the full four years of the film's production to promote the film to the fans at the mammoth convention. We ran screeners and promo trailers at the booth and handed out a LOT of swag including multiple posters, t-shirts and mini-design booklets. We also made friends with a lot of great people who were early and loyal fans of the film (many of them initially drawn to *WOTWG* from its *Highlander* connection).

Kevin allowed us use the booth for multiple autograph sessions with Adrian Paul and Peter Wingfield, David Abramowitz and myself. I always looked forward to the fun "madness" of the Con and the gang at the *Heavy Metal* booth.

One benefit of showing clips at the SDCC was that we could get early audience feedback and that helped in some ways to enhance the film. At the 2009 con we had enough footage to assemble a pretty strong promo trailer and ran that near continuously at the *Heavy Metal* booth. One sequence in the trailer shows our hero's father in close-up as he literally "skeletonizes" and disintegrates from a Martian heat ray and every time this scene came on it produced a deep, collective gasp/grunt from the appreciative fans around the booth; clearly they liked the strong, graphic impact and animation of death by heat ray. I wasn't surprised as Sun Min's animators and EFX team really stepped up to create an extremely visceral piece of animation. So I decided to add in a number of similar shots throughout the films many battle scenes and personally storyboarded them myself.

In our final year of production in 2011, 3D was becoming a new trend in the release of films so once again we doubled (or should I say tripled) down and raised the extra $$ to convert the finished film into full stereoscopic 3D. Our post-production house in KL, Base Camp (BC), smoothly supervised the entire 3D conversion process.

Converting the film to 3D was not cheap, but it was far less expensive then it might have been as many of the film's scenes were already being animated and produced in multiple separate layers and levels before being locked down in final camera, so we were able to get a lot of the layers direct from Sun Min. Non-layered scenes were converted to CG by the laborious process of creating matts and hand separating flat images by hand. This was largely done in India, under BC's supervision.

A note here about the raising of extra funds for the movie; by the end of production in 2012 the film's budget had gone up over 30% above the initial raise and Leon deserves all the credit for actually shaking the trees in Malaysia and raising that extra funding. It was no easy task and at the end he personally put a lot on the line to get the final funding in place for the 3D.

Were we right to keep doubling down on the film, adding length and detail and the stereoscopic 3D conversion? In one sense we were much like the classic parable of the "Monkey Trap" in which food is placed in a narrow necked glass jar (or coconut) and a hungry monkey reaches in and grabs the bait, but then is trapped because he can't get his clenched fist/hand out of the jar without releasing the food. We knew the film had potential and had put too much sweat and $$$ into it to abandon and cut our losses, so we kept doubling down and upping the ante.

Did it payoff? Sadly, I think the answer is *no* as the film never reached a big enough audience to make its money back. But it did make it a hell of lot more interesting for those who did see it.

As the production continued into 2011, we began to feel pressure from our now multiple investors to finish the production and bring in some serious revenue. That was completely understandable, but there wasn't much that we could do to accelerate the production train at that point. If there was more in budget we could have brought in more designers and animators, but there was simply no more money available. We were running into the classic production triangle. Good. Cheap. And Fast. You can have any two of those, but not all three. We were striving for Good and Cheap, but Fast just went out the window.

The team in Korea was having trouble finishing up the final shots so I flew to Seoul and camped out at Sun Min for close to three weeks in late 2011 to personally trouble shoot and supervise the final push on animation. That helped to cut a month or two off the process. I was helped by having a terrific layout artist, Park Min on board along with Lee's independent studio to help finalize and conform all of the complex background layouts with me for the film's final battle with the Martians and ARES in New York City.

I also spent a good part of 2011 editing the footage with two different editors from KL. Both had worked extensively with Basecamp, mostly on commercials. Both were quite good, but editing a long form animated feature was a new experience for them and frankly, for me as well as all of my prior experience was in shorts or 22 minute series. Also, editing in animation is generally very different from live action. In live action film the director generally shoots hours and hours of extra footage, often shooting the same scene from different angles and then winnowing it down to the final film length. *Apocalypse Now* had over 230 hours of footage that was edited down to the final 2½ hour theatrical cut.

In animation, you don't have a lot of extra footage to cut because everything is animated from storyboards and the timed animatic shot from them so your film's animatic is generally the place where most of your changes and edits are done and new scenes added or revised if necessary. Basically you go to animation with the film essentially preedited. Not so with *Goliath*. A number of the sequences worked fine in final animation as planned, but a few needed some creative editing and occasionally some bridge animation to make them work.

The Fight in the Green Man pub was a good example. Originally it was written and boarded to show much more of a rollicking fight among the troops and Roosevelt before General Kushnirov shows up and brings it to an abrupt end. Unfortunately it became clear from the final animation that the actual "fight" footage and staging just wasn't strong and aggressive enough and would need major revision and reanimation to pump it up. However, making it more violent would also make it a lot more brutal and that would undercut the "band of brothers" feeling among the combatants that the end of the sequence would require. I decided to cut out most of the actual fight footage and instead I storyboarded and expanded the build-up to the fight with various characters taking preliminary fight stances and preparing to punch it out; a solution that I think worked much better in the final film.

Another large area of editing involved cutting out about ten minutes of finished footage, including some early shots that were removed to keep momentum moving forward to the first big battle about thirty minutes into the movie. If I had been able to animate the big battle outside of St. Petersberg as planned at the beginning of the film,

those cuts could have been kept in the film. Oh well, that's just some of the painful choices you have to make on a low budget film. Or as David Abramowitz put it, "Sometimes you have to be willing to kill your baby."

Other cuts include a fully animated battle scene that takes place about mid-way through the film that felt extraneous and editing out about thirty seconds of very explicit animation of our two leads, Eric and Jennifer, making passionate love in the control room of the Goliath battle tripod. Yes, we actually had "sex in the cockpit" which would have garnered us a full-on "R" rating. But censors in Malysia would not allow us to portray even a passionate kiss, much less actual lovemaking. Not surprising considering that Malaysia is a Muslim majority country. I'm still bemused (and grateful) that they actually stepped up to fund a

violent, SF war movie.

The editing process went on up until the final picture lock in KL at Basecamp in early 2012. Truthfully, I regret not holding a screening at that point for the key creative crew to get their final feedback and more critical eyes looking at the final cut, but again the pressure from our investors on all of us to finish the picture and put it to bed was immense and there was no remaining budget for retakes at that point. So we locked it and moved on to color correcting and final audio post and the final 3D stereoscopic conversion. By the beginning of summer the film was fully finished and wrapped and ready for the world.

The timing was good, because we had planned to do a preview screening of the film at a theater in the Gas Lamp District adjacent to the San Diego Comic Con. The screening went well and the audience was very enthusiastic. Many had been waiting for years for the film to release. Peter Wingfield and Adrian Paul attended as did most the film's key creative from LA and KL. We had an unexpected surprise guest as Ann Robinson, the lead actress from George Pal's classic adaptation of "War of the Worlds", attended the screening and really seemed to enjoy the movie. Or at least said she did. Ann was, and still is, a very classy and gracious lady.

A few months later in September, we entered the film in the 3D Film Festival held at the Regal Theater in the heart of the LA Live complex in Downtown. Again, the audience response was enthusiastic and *WOTWG* actually got a first place award for Best Animated 3D movie beating out a lot of much more expensive fare from studios like Dreamworks, Disney and Laika.

By the end of 2012, I flew out to KL for the movie's premiere and opening in the city. It was a surreal experience being in a huge cinema complex in the heart of this tropical metropolis. A light rain was drifting down and from the balconies of the theater complex/mall you could see the glowing KL Towers looming through the misty air a few blocks away. It felt very *Blade Runner* to me. A huge crowd, including many government officials and their families, attended the movie. I was a bit distressed by the presence of a few young children scattered throughout the film as it was definitely NOT a kids film and if rated it would receive a PG13 rating.

Again, the movie seemed to be well received, although between the massive jet lag and the heady experience of

KeyBG Seq25 Sc 36 -info-

actually being a director at his own film screening, I was pretty dazed. It was that rare feeling of celebrity and being a center of attention and good wishes that was overwhelming, not unlike what I felt decades earlier at my wedding to Lisa. There were even what seemed to be very friendly groupies, but I was in no condition or state of mind to take advantage of that. Also, I was experiencing a low level of anxiety during much of the viewing as I knew all too well where we had to cut corners or do work-arounds and was all too aware that the audience might see that too.

All in all, the only negative side to the event and my week in KL was a growing and perceptible distance towards me that was coming from Leon. He and I had grown very close over the many years of partnership and

production, but both earlier that year in LA and then at the premiere week in Malaysia it was clear that something was deeply amiss at his end. I did not understand why, but a year later it would become clear.

And that brings to a head the final "war" scenario; the distribution war to get *WOTWG* out to a wide audience and market; a war, which in many ways, we failed to win. Right from the beginning a very low budget, animated teen/adult war movie was never going to be an easy sell, even one with the worldwide pedigree of HG Wells' famous novel. A careful print and ad campaign and a thoughtful rollout directed to the film's teen and young adult audience was needed. We attempted the later via promotion online, in *Heavy Metal* Magazine and at the *Heavy Metal* booth at the SDCC, but it was to prove to not be enough.

Leon was responsible for marketing and merchandising the film and he went through three different distributors during the last two years of production before he settled on the final one; a small company run by an East Indian gentlemen. To be honest I was not particularly impressed with Leon's final choice. Part of that was because the distributor and his company had never handled any animated films, much less a teen/adult animated film like *WOTWG*. My other issue aside from his inexperience at distributing animation was his histrionic personality, which swung from the obsequious to the weirdly arrogant and aggressive to the point where he literally unloaded a screaming shit fit directed at me during a dinner where we were discussing distribution. We had met him years earlier at the Heavy Metal booth at the SDCC and he had pretty much attached himself to Leon to make his case for representing the movie. Leon was sold on him and the guy was very enthused about the movie and his ability to get it to market so I reluctantly went along with the plan.

To his credit, the distributor was responsible for getting WOTWG into the 3D film fest in LA and he negotiated a DVD/Blu-ray release deal with Wal-Mart's primary film/DVD distributor, Anderson Digital to produce a total of a 100,000 DVD's and Blu-ray for distribution at Walmart, Target, Best Buy and similar street level vendors as well as online distribution at sites like Amazon. That was actually pretty good for an independent film in the days of distribution shifting heavily to streaming.

Speaking of streaming, he also negotiated a two-year release of the film on Netflix, but for a relatively low amount. Leon trumped that by negotiating a deal for all rights in China for an even lower amount. That turned out to be pretty ironic as WOTWG ran daily on Chinese broadcast TV for yeas and received over 25 million views online in that country.

As part of his deal with Anderson Digital, the distributor had to get some kind of limited theatrical release for the film. He did this by essentially renting out screens on a limited number of venues around the country for a two week long release. This was not a bad plan in theory, but most of screens were in southern, rural, areas, which were perhaps not the best audience base for a teen/adult, animated war movie. Ideally, the movie should have been heavily marketed and released in high urban, college and university adjacent locale's as that really is where the target audience was. This film was also released with zero print and ad buys in any media, so aside from Tripod's online marketing campaign there was relatively no marketing for the film anywhere. It's not a surprise that the theatrical revenue numbers for the movie were low.

Despite this, the distributor could have been credited with making a good faith effort, save for the facts that he initially missed three contracted quarterly revenue reports that were mandated in his contract with Tripod and then when pushed by me, he finally did release a report, it was filled with inconsistent numbers and many dubvious expense claims, including a failure to account for the spend on a $100,000 distribution grant/fund that Leon obtained for him from a Malaysian film fund. When I wrote a calm, detailed response requesting more accountability, he went ballistic and essentially said, "Fuck you. Sue me."

Well, what do you say to that? Tripod could have/should have sued, but at that point we were deep in debt and in battle with our investors over the low returns on the film. The investors were threatening to shutter Tripod and both Mike and Leon were concerned that Imaginex could also go under so they asked me to not rock the boat and back off on any legal action.

The final blow came when it was revealed that for more than a year, Leon had been setting up a new entertainment company behind my and Mike's back. He had met an accomplished film/media mogul in LA who had already set up an entertainment group centered on China and Asia, so Leon clandestinely partnered with him to form a new LA/KL based entertainment group. He had done this in secret over the previous year, a time when he should have been focused on marketing and merchandising WOTWG. And he had raised money from Tripod's initial investors for his new company, falsely telling them that Mike and I were okay with this and in the loop, when actually we were fully in the dark.

To say I was surprised when it all came to light would be an understatement. As I've mentioned previously, Leon and I had become extremely close and I considered him a dear friend. And vice versa. But I had noticed a change in his attitude towards me and a distancing beginning in late 2011, which in retrospect was a result of his clandestine activities. Ironically his new company with the Hollywood bigwig collapsed when that individual had a heart attack and died less then a year after he and Leon went public with their new film group.

In some ways, I fully understand the pressure Leon was under and why he decided that he had to step sideways to stay in the game and to recoup what was looking to be a major loss in revenue. Tripod needed a "9" or "10" level film and what it looked like I had delivered was more of a "7" or even a "6" in the end. So he did what he felt he had to do. What was hard to forgive was that he did it behind my and Mike's back's and that he did it on Tripod's dime and at a time when he should have been focusing like a bat out of hell on getting *WOTWG* into profitability. And that he did it while professing that I was his closest friend. Well, live and learn, right?

By the end of 2014, Tripod was a company out of money and with a broken partnership. The film ended up being seized by the bank that had funded the 3D conversion and is now off the shelves and off the air in most places, although it has been running for a few years now on Netflix Asia.

On a creative level it was a devastating conclusion to a long 5-year process and on a personal financial level, even more so. I had borrowed heavily on my Venice Beach home to cover my expenses for the extra two years plus of production on *WOTWG*. It seemed like a good gamble as I had negotiated an incredible backend deal on the film which would have given me a 25% cut of all net profit on the film. That was now up in smoke and I was stuck with a massive mortgage from the refinancing. Tripod was belly up and the hope/dream of future production was finito as was my very real friendship with Leon. Fortunately, my friendship with my other Tripod partner, Mike, survived and remains strong to this day.

As the wag says, "That's entertainment".

So, what's the moral of this story you may well ask? Truthfully, it's a mixed bag. I had the experience of actually getting to make a feature SF film that I conceptualized and directed and make it largely on my own terms. A movie that I'm proud of.

I had the opportunity to work with some truly amazing and talented people and had that rare "band of brothers" experience you only get when striving together for a long time on a production like this. And I would not have traded in the many, many, many friendships I developed over the long years of production. My friends in Malaysia: Imaginex, Studio Climb, Basecamp and elsewhere. My friends in Seoul at Sun Min and around the city. The simply terrific actors from the *Highlander* series and SF community. The many wonderful individuals in the big family of the *Highlander* fan community and the many steadfast fans that I got to know in the vortex of working the *Heavy Metal* booth at the SDCC. These are friends that I will cherish and respect forever.

And I got to know and live in a truly fantastic and exotic country like Malaysia, a place completely off my radar before starting *WOTWG*.

But it is human nature to look back and think about that road not taken; the "what ifs" that might have occurred if different choices were made. For myself, there's a lot that I would change or redo if I could.

If I could do it over I would not have taken the golden funding opportunity offered by Leon and Malaysia and used it to make an independent, low budget animated war film, without a lot more money and a guaranteed mainstream distributor with skin in the game. Actually, I probably would not have attempted a full feature at all, but would have instead pushed for MAVCAP to fund Tripod in much the same way it funded Imaginex; provide enough money to fund offices in LA and in KL, along with a small team of producers and salesmen, for at least three years to develop IP's, look for coproduction partners on those IP's and look for work for hire jobs for the company. In that scenario, *WOTWG* and *Zoorocco* and a score of other IP's of mine and Kevin's would have had development dollars to produce the three minute animated proof of concept promos and full series bibles that we could take on the road to find coproduction and distribution partners.

I would also have invited Kevin Eastman on board as a full partner in Tripod, perhaps branding the company, "Kevin Eastman Entertainment"; an idea that seems obvious now, but did not occur to me back in 2007. I think that we could have built this new entertainment group into a solvent and long running business.

But if making a full *War of the Worlds: Goliath* feature was the only option in the end, then I would go back and consider making the following changes:

Animation Director Young Hwan Sang, Designers Lee Seung Gyu and Spencer Ooi with Joe.

Leon Tan, David Abramowitz, Kevin Eastman and Joe Pearson

rah, rah, Man Against the Martians, old school war movie.

Simplify the character designs to have less detail on their uniforms and to be less "broad shouldered". Lee's designs really gave the animation team at Sun Min a lot of trouble with their small heads and huge shoulders, especially on Patrick and Abe. Early own the Director Sang asked me to have them redesigned, but that ship had sailed. This was not Lee's fault. As the director and art director I approved and ran with his initial design take. On some post *WOTWG* projects with Lee, I've had him design some really strong characters in his style, but longer and leaner and more graceful then the *WOTWG* team design overall. And they look and animate great.

Make it much edgier, concentrating more on the crew and their internal dynamics and conflicts and delve more into the "war is hell" vibe like the excellent and very dark tank warfare movie, *Fury*. Or even *Apocalypse Now*. As it stands, *WOTWG* remains teetered on an uneasy balance between its PG 13 violence and a

Fought from the beginning for a higher budget and a second director and line producer. We could have done this by not producing a full pilot of the proposed *Zoorocco* kids series and simply done a trailer instead. Even better we could have not have attempted *Zoorocco* at all. That would have shifted $330,000 over into *Goliath*'s budget which could have paid for a second director, a line producer and a lot more.

Delay sending any animation and design to Sun Min until we had a full animatic of the film with an audio track to review and nuance with the key creative team. That's the only way to preview an animated film before going into full production and to identify story and pacing issues. That's what is normally done with the bigger animated productions, but was a luxury we didn't have.

Finally, here's a wild "what if". Back when we were just funded up for *WOTWG*, I met an individual at my gym in Marina Del Rey who was very tight with John Milius, the notorious director/writer of *Conan, Red Dawn, The Wind and the Lion, Big Wednesday* and other movies (including co-writing on *Apocalypse Now*). I don't agree with a lot of his philosophy and politics, but at his best, his screenplay writing and directing is brilliant, edgy and powerful. To this day, *The Wind and the Lion* remains my favorite epic film of all time.

I toyed with the idea of approaching John and asking him if he'd up for writing the script for my little movie: and even co-directing. It seemed like a long reach. John was a major Player and I doubt he would have been interested or affordable, but who knows? His career had been stonewalled for a while and he might have jumped on the opportunity to do something "fun" and keep his chops in the game. And if he was interested, I think I could have reached out for more money for him and the

film; a LOT more money.

So a John Milius *WOTWG*...it boggles the mind and certainly would have put it/us on the map for a bigger impact and audience then we received. But I didn't step up to make the ask and maybe that's the thing I regret the most. Famous B-Movie director/mentor, Roger Corman, had two axioms for any would-be director. First, always sit when you have the chance. And second, never be afraid to ask. I didn't heed this last point so I'll never know what might have happened with Mr. Milius.

Well, as they say, "Hindsight is 20/20" and we'd all like to go back and revisit our past decisions to make improvements, but we can't (unless you're a main character in the *Peripheral* universe). So *War of the Worlds: Goliath* is what it is. And in the end I'm absolutely content with that.

And I got to experience the rare satisfaction of actually getting a movie made and making it for the most part without any censorship or mandates from above. For better or worse (and I'll leave that up to you to decide) *War of the Worlds: Goliath* is a Joe Pearson film. That is a very rare beast in the entertainment industry. I did get to make a film my way and with many of my favorite things like diesel punk SF, battle zeppelins, Martian tripods and of course, Teddy Roosevelt standing on top of a battle tripod and firing a handheld heat ray cannon. Even its limited distribution garnered millions of audience eyes (if not dollars) and as a creative that's what it's really all about, right?

As Teddy Roosevelt would put it, "Bully!" Bully indeed.

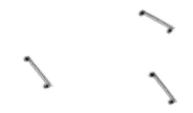

THE CRACKED EYE

Gary Hubbard

I never graduated from high school. Well, actually I did, but not in the official, cap 'n' gown way. What I mean is, I got my diploma, but had to attend a session of summer school to get it. I wasn't a dullard by any means; I did pretty well academically with a minimum of effort. No, being widely read, I hardly had to study at all. But what I didn't understand was that I was expected to participate in the social side of school at well.

But fuck that. School was just a job for me. I put in my hours and left at the end of the day. But I didn't join clubs or go to dances or football games. That *Happy Days* crap just didn't interest me. In retrospect, however. Because at the end of four years I was missing ten activity credits. Activity credits? No one told me I needed activity credits to graduate. Why wasn't my academic performance enough? I suppose my counselor could have clued me in, but I have no recollection of ever having talked with her.

So there I was, at the end of my senior year without enough green stamps in my book to graduate. I had to take a class where my missing activity credits were converted to academic ones and I was finally let go. Naturally, this failure to launch resulted in a certain amount of acrimony at home, but I don't want to go into that.

So...out of school; money spent; saw no future, and the Old Man wanted me to start paying rent. He used his influence at the auto plant where he worked to get me a job, but I wasn't suited for factory work. I kept destroying the machinery and messing up the assembly line. I guess I should have taken shop.

So as an alternative to honest labor, I joined the Army.

This was in 1964, and I know what you're thinking: You *joined the Army during the Viet Nam era? Didn't you read Catch 22?* Well, back in '64 Nam wasn't that big a deal yet, you know; no one thought it would last. In fact, during basic training I came across this cartoon book called *The Lighter Side of Viet Nam*; probably the most ironic title of the twentieth century. Nobody in those dear old days thought we would lose, and that idea persisted throughout the time I was in the Service. I remember this one time when I was in Germany and the XO (Executive Officer) held a sort of pep rally to point out to us that victory was inevitable. Following a script handed down from some propaganda office, he informed us that the average Viet Cong soldier was sickly, undisciplined and had poor morale. I was pressed into service as a visual aid while he talked, because typecasting.

But I'm getting ahead of myself (and probably will again).

At the Recruiter's office, they gave me an I.Q. test and declared I was of above average intelligence. I don't remember what 'average' was supposed to be, but it must have been pretty modest if I was able to rise above it. Upon reflection, I bet he said that to everyone who came through the door. He was, after all, just a salesman.

In my case, he said I'd do well in Army Security. I didn't know what that was, but it sounded pretty cool and he won me over. The only catch was that I'd have to sign up for four years, instead of the usual three. Well, what was one extra year, after all, I reasoned. It just meant one more year I didn't have to find an honest job. But what I didn't realize was that this was in Army years, and it turned out to be the longest four years of my life.

As mentioned above, you're going to have to expect a lot of gaps in this narrative from here on in, because this all happened so long ago and it's getting harder and harder to patch all the memories together.

I can, for example, no longer recall if my mother and sister cried when I left or if the Old Man took me aside to give me a word of sage advice. (God I hope not. If it was anything like that sex talk he gave me when I was fourteen, *yeesh*!). All I can recall from that long ago was a midnight train ride to Missouri. The only things significant about that ride was packing a copy of *Gulliver of Mars* by Edwin Lester Arnold and sharing a compartment with a guy headed for the same destination. When the porter came in to turn the couches into beds, we were both too excited to sleep and stayed up all night talking. I'd just read *All in Color for a Dime* by Richard A. Lupoff and regaled him with the parts of it I remembered.

Fort Leonard Wood, Missouri, was named after a Lt. Leonard Wood, from the Spanish-American War. He, along with his troops, were pinned down by Spanish gunfire, but he stood up and said: "Those who are brave follow me!" Those were his last words, I think; that's why they named an army camp after him. But ever after, the phrase became an in-joke among the crowd of malingerers I eventually fell in with whenever we were about to do something stupid.

The first days of Basic remain a blur and there are only two things I remember clearly.

The first was when a Chaplin gave us newbies a lecture on comportment: Basically, what to salute and when and how to properly conduct oneself. By way of illustration, he had a picture I'll call "Goofus and Gallant". It depicted two soldiers walking along side by side. Gallant was the perfect picture of a soldier. His uniform is starched and without a single crease. His arms are close to his sides at he strides along with confidence and his face bears a neutral expression. Goofus, of course, is the complete opposite: His uniform is wrinkled, he has one hand in his pocket, his hat is pulled back at a jaunty angle and he has a silly grin on his face. Personally, I liked him a lot better than that stiff, Gallant, but I wasn't supposed to, and my affinity for Goofus would cast a shadow over my military career.

The other thing I remember was this guy who was freaking out about the army food, because he'd heard they put saltpeter in it to quell the raging beast. Well, he was right sort of, but not for that reason. When I was sent to Korea, I was in a unit that had a mess hall called the Company Four, because it serviced four companies and had four entrances. About a month before I arrived, there'd been a massive outbreak of food poisoning and they were carrying guys out on buses. Thereafter, we referred to the mess hall as Four Doors to Ptomaine.

On another occasion I had KP, so I got to see how army food was prepared and saw this cook who'd been outside working on his car come in and, with oil-stained hands, blithely take up some dough and make biscuits. After that, I avoided eating in the mess hall unless I had to, like at the end of the month and I'd run out of money.

Basic was eight weeks of hell characterized by early morning calisthenics, then long marches out to the rifle range or hand-to-hand combat practice. Or bayonet drill, which I actually kind of liked. But mostly it was the pits. If this had been a movie, there would have been a training montage at the end of which I would have emerged as Conan or Mulan (something like that). But this was before the invention of montages and at the end of the eight weeks I was hardly any stronger than when I started. The most embarrassing part of Basic for me was the obstacle course where you had to crawl under barb wire with your rifle cradled in your arms. I've seen this in movies where the soldiers have nice soft sand to crawl over, but this was Missouri. No sand, you had to crawl over gravel, and it hurt. I always took forever to crawl the course, long after everyone else had finished, to invariably be greeted with a dressing down by a Drill Sergeant. "You're pathetic," they would kindly say. Most of them were sorry that they were no longer allowed to hit you and made their displeasure abundantly clear. Of course, they could make you go over and do it again.

Another thing that gave me trouble was grenade practice.

You had to throw this dummy grenade at a ring on the ground several feet away, kind of like pitching horse shoes. You could throw it under handed or sideways, but never overhead, a style called 'John Wayne'. Drill Instructors didn't much like John Wayne—said he set a bad example.

My problem was range. I never could quite get a grenade to land within that ring, but I didn't get time to improve before they marched us out to the live practice range. This was a place where a low wall had been built on the top of a gully. They took us up, one by one, to the side of the wall and handed us a *real* grenade. You were told to pull the pin out , toss the grenade and duck down behind the wall before it exploded. When it was my turn, the instructor handed me the grenade and asked me a question: "Are you afraid?' I shook my head - and I wasn't afraid, not really. Actually, I was a little disappointed, because it didn't look like the grenades in the movies. It didn't look like a John Wayne grenade. It looked more like a Mattel toy – such an innocent little object.

Anyway, I stood behind the wall, pulled the pin and tossed the grenade. It sailed over the wall, landed on the ground a short distance away and started rolling down the side of the gully. I was already on my way down behind the wall when the instructor yelled, "short one!" and flattened me with his body as the grenade exploded, sprinkling us with little bits of hot metal. "The hell you aren't," he said on top of me. If I wasn't afraid, it was plain that he was. You see, this guy was a Reservist, a Weekend Warrior, putting in his time and probably looking forward to getting back to his regular job alive.

The rifle range was another area where my performance lacked luster.

In my defense, the M-14 rifle was kind of

hard to operate. Unlike these AR-15 rifles or whatever death sprayers you read about these days, the M-14 was a heavy single shot gun that had to be fired in a prone position and kicked like a mule when you pressed the trigger. I never could figure out how the gunsight worked and invariably flinched when I fired it and threw off my aim.

By now, though, the Army stopped expecting much from me, because I was such a Goofus, but there was this guy in our unit whose name was – no kidding - Virgil Earp, who was a descendant of the famous Earps (Virgil or Wyatt, I'm not sure), so there was a lot of expectation on him to do well. Trouble was, Virgil had the famous Earp chin (a lot of people out west seem to have large chins), which got in the way and poor Virgil always came off the range with a bloody chin.

After Basic, fortunately, I never had to look at a gun again, (except to occasionally re-[dis]qualfy), because my MOS didn't require it.

Now, I don't know how many of my readers are familiar with military jargon, (although I hope many of you had the good sense to avoid service), so I'll explain. MOS meant Military Occupational Specialty and upon getting out of Basic, I was now a Specialist 4. That sounds grandiose, but it merely linked my rank with my job. Spec 4, I think, was equivalent to Private. Above that in the hierarchy of army ranks was Spec 5, which was probably equivalent to Corporal. Spec 5s (sometimes E-5s) could boss E-4s around, but were still human. Above that were the Girbs: the various species of sergeants from Staff to Sergeant Majors. We in the lower ranks referred to them as Girbs, because G.I.R.B. stood for G.I. Rotten Bastard. Above the Girbs were the Officers, guys with brass on their shoulders. You didn't want to have anything to do with them and they didn't want to have anything to do with you.

But here I am, getting ahead of myself again.

After Basic I was sent to a base out east to learn my MOS, Communications Monitor, about which up to this point I had been pretty much in the dark. I soon found out it had to do with code – in this case it was Morse code, not what you're thinking. Back in the day all the military organizations in the world used Morse code to send secret messages - maybe they still do for all I know. So I had to learn Morse well enough to listen and translate all those dot and dashes into ABCs and transcribe them on a typewriter. In other words, I (along with a bunch of other guys) was being trained to be a sort of secret stenographer.

Every morning the Girbs would rouse us from our beds and march us up to the school, where we would listen to recordings of Morse code being played and copy what we heard on the tapes. At first it was easy, but then they started cranking up the speed and distorting the sound to the point where it got to be nearly impossible to figure out what was a *drit* compared to what was a *dra*, and I started having trouble keeping up. Eventually, I was sent to Remedial where we had to start all over again at a lower level. In Remedial, the Girb there gave us a stern lecture about malingering and implied we could end up in the stockade if we didn't shape up.

It was in Remedial where I met my best friends: Guzman, Siglia and, notably, Sam Weaver; collectively we proudly owned the title Malingerers.

Guzman was Hispanic, and the hairiest man I've ever seen – really! His chest, from his shoulders down was covered by a thick mat of fur, enough to make a decent throw rug out of. He regularly got care packages from his mom that he shared with us, usually tacos and burritos, which was pretty exotic stuff to me. Back in the Sixties, Mexican food was pretty rare where I came from. She also sometimes included a Waldorf cake, which was all red and kind of velvety. Guzman said she got the recipe for it exclusively from a chief at the Waldorf Astoria hotel and nobody else had it. It was pretty good.

Siglia was Italian. He was short, wide and had a head shaped like a bullet. I know I'm making these guys sound like comic book characters, but in Siglia's case that was pretty close to the truth. He was immensely strong. I once saw him pick up an office safe that none of us could lift and carry it out of the room. He used to boast that once he got a grip on you, it would be impossible for you to escape.

I took him up on it and, sure as shootin', it was true. I squirmed and kicked, but couldn't break free, so, finally, I resorted to kissing him on the head and that did the trick. You see, it isn't always about strength; sometimes it's about embarrassment. He let go of me like I was a hot potato.

Sam and I shared a common sense of humor. We both liked making fun of old movies and called it 'camp.' In wasn't true camp, of course. It was just the kind of camp we'd gotten from Playboy and Mad magazine. You know, making fun of clichés like "Those who are brave, follow me", "Surely Professor, you don't believe this superstitious nonsense" and tried to make up entire conversations based around them.

Once we went to see this movie at the base theater called *John Goldfarb, Please Come Home*. I don't remember much about it (it was some kind of political farce), but it starred the lovely Shirley MacLaine, and we were both quite taken with her. Sam more than I and all you had to do was mention her name and he would go weak at the knees and pretend to have an orgasm.

One time I came upon Sam, who was looking out a window of our barracks and the following exchange took place.

"One day this will all belong to you, my son," he said.

"Aw, say it ain't so," I replied.

"You dirty rat! You killed my brother."

"He ain't heavy, Father, He's *my* brother."

"Many year Red Man live in peace. Then White man come with his steaming Iron Horse."

"Shirley MacLaine."

After the second time I landed in Remedial, the Army decided I was never going to master Morse code, so they found something else for me to do. At the end of our training, we were all given overseas assignments and scattered to the wind. I never saw any of those guys again, although I heard later that Guzman had been injured in Viet Nam. As the years progressed, the specter of Nam loomed larger and larger in our collective consciousness. There was always the chance that one might end up there, like Guzman did. I was sort of lucky, because I did a tour in Korea, which was considered a hardship duty, even though the Korean War was long over. I guess that was because it had ended in an armistice, so technically we were still at war with the North Koreans (and still are, I suppose). I was off the hook because I had a brother serving in Nam and there was a thing called the Sullivan law which prohibits members of the same family from having to serve on the same front. This came out of an incident in WW II when five brothers named Sullivan had all joined the Navy out of patriot zeal and ended up getting sunk on the same ship. Hollywood made a movie about it that caused an uproar and hence the Sullivan Law. Mom saw the movie on TV in the Fifties and was charmed by it, because it was about five brothers who stuck together and came to each other's aid when the need arose, unlike my brothers and myself, who were always engaged in internecine warfare. Mom thought we should try to be more like them.

"But Mom, they all died!"

Speaking of internecine wars, in Germany I found myself in the middle of a power struggle between the CO of our company and the XO.

The CO was the unfortunately named Captain Tinkle. He was a short, fussy man lacking in a commanding presence. None of us in the lower ranks (and maybe some of the Girbs) respected him and there were stories nosed about how he was a forty year old man who still lived with his mother. Most of us, most of the time, skirted pretty close to insubordination. There was a thing we did: pretending to march off to our jobs chanting, "Him, him! Fuck him!" The XO wanted his job so he winked at our bad attitude. Things finally came to a head when someone drew a mustache on the portrait of Captain Tinkle that hung outside his office. He gathered us all together and raged ineffectually at us, demanding the culprit show himself, but that never happened. Instead, someone at a higher level promoted him to major and booted him upstairs to an administrative position in Frankfort.

Having ridden himself of Captain Tinkle and assuming the mantle of CO, the former XO (I wish I could remember his name, but it hardly matters after all these years), rounded up everyone he considered a ringleader and a disciplinary risk and had them transferred. I ended up in Vincenza, Italy, which wasn't such a great place in itself, but it was a short train ride away from Venice, where I used to hang out on the weekends with two of my friends: Alvy and King.

At first, I didn't much like Alvy. He was opinionated and anal retentive. He used to complain a lot about how it wasn't dark enough in his room, because there was always some outside light seeping in around the window shades. Like I said, I didn't much care for him until one night when we were both sitting at the same table at Rick's American Café in Venice (Yes, there really was such a place) and it somehow turned out that we both liked Edgar Rice Burroughs and, after that we bonded over the exploits of John Carter and Tarzan.

King was from California and a babe magnet. Girls were attracted to his blond good looks and it was annoying sometimes. For instance, we would go to a restaurant and he and the waitress would start flirting with each, leaving me out of the picture. Eventually though, she would turn her head and seem startled to see me sitting there, as if I'd showed up out of nowhere. Another time, we were in Venice and encountered two vacationing American nurses and offered to show them around. King and the one girl were chatting and carrying on like they'd come from the same town. I, on the other hand, was having trouble getting a rise out of the other girl. The four of us were walking along a street in Venice (the most romantic city in Europe), it was dark and the moon was out. I was blathering some nonsense when I suddenly realized that I was all alone. The others had vanished into thin air. I had to take the train back to Vincenza all by myself. Later on, in the barracks, King ribbed me good-naturedly. He never revealed what else had happened that night and I didn't care to find out. However, this incident didn't prevent us from going on furlough to England together, which is a story for another day.

I was only in Italy for a short while. By 1968, Viet Nam was getting pretty bad. One of our stations there was overrun by those very Viet Cong I'd impersonated for the XO, and people were being drawn out of the other stations *en masse*. In fact, by the time I got back to Germany they were closing that station. Everybody who had time enough left was being transferred to Nam, but, here again, I lucked out, because I only had a couple of months left on my service. As it was, they gave me an early out, and I suspect that by this time they had no use for me, anyway (remember, Goofus).

In the day, the war was so unpopular that people looked down on you if you were in the military whether you were in Nam or not, while at the same time, hippies started wearing fatigue jackets. Nowadays, when someone finds out I was in the Army (especially around Veteran's Day) they come up to me and thank me for my service. In turn, I graciously thank them back, but have to smile at myself. (If you only knew. I fucked up, goldbricked and drank my way across three continents.)

A Mixtape

Alva Svoboda

Dream Sentence

The sentences appeared to me in a dream on the verge of waking: "I was born1 over there in that realm of light and magic. A wave has carried me here to this other shore, and that wave was music." I had been mulling over writing this piece for Breiding, knowing that I wanted to write about music and not knowing how to start, and as my insomnia gave way to a profound doze, my situation in the dream was exactly the same, but in the dream I knew what to do and what to write. And so the sentence came to me, and sensing that it offered a lead, I propelled myself back into the waking world and wrote it down.

I wouldn't have thought much of the dream sentences if I'd been awake when they were composed. But the words having been whipped up in the semi-darkness of sleep, I felt respect for the unknown beings within me who brought the words to me, and so I could convey them without hesitation and without shame, despite the cliched elements they seemed to be built of.

A friend of a friend recommended the poetry of Saint-John Perse to me a couple of weeks ago, and on the first page of the New Directions *Selected Poems*, like a message direct from the gods, I found it expressed more eloquently in "Pictures for Crusoe":

"You wept to remember the surf in the moonlight; the whistlings of the more distant shores; the strange music that is born and is muffled under the folded wing of the night, like the linked circles that are the waves of a conch, or the amplifications of the clamors under the sea . . ."

Earworms

On a biographical level, music offers a metonymy, independent of any attachments or achievements. Meanwhile, the stew of music has operated sub rosa, on a neurological level, the associations not to events in a life but, like dreams, to supporting structures in the brain. The earworms wake just before I do every day. One morning I wake with the theme for the children's television show *H.R. Pufnstuf* playing, just a bar, and the word "*H.R. Pufnstuf/H.R. Pufnstuf/Can't do a little cuz he can't do enough*" sung along, no idea what those words mean... Another morning it's "Beautiful morning" at the tempo of a funeral march, another "Good King Wenceslas," another morning a snippet of Neil Young. None of these are associated with any particular memories, not even of the moment when a particular earworm was acquired and embedded in whatever overarching repository it is that carries them indefinitely.

I think it would be additionally accurate to describe earworms as mouthworms, because they're the source of subvocalizations as uncontrollable as the fragments of tunes I seem to hear on infinite repeat in the morning. It's even possible that what I hear as an earworm is the tenuous whistling or humming that is carried in my first breaths of the day. These tunes are the product of a "person" who is not my waking self, who insists on having its way for no reason apparent in this world, but apparently compelling in another.

Is it possible that earworms utilize the pre-human structures that make phenomena like instinctual birdsong possible? Unlike birdsong, my earworms are not shared with others, but perhaps that's only because the linguistic capabilities that supplant them have pushed the helpless making of sounds back into the rear of the voice box, where it might serve as a kind of metronome or just a background hum, but contributes nothing to social expression. Or maybe it's a substrate of memory, a compost, out of which connected recollection can emerge. I may just be, to borrow the title of Steven Mithen's book on the subject of music and language, a Singing Neanderthal, expressing my genomic roots without regard for composition or grammar.

There's a far shore reaching back hundreds of thousands of years, though the view seems clearer of the nearer lost shores in my own life.

Late Pandemic Entertainment

"This other shore" might plausibly be interpreted as this other shore of the pandemic, the voyage being the one we've taken through to where we are now from being marooned, like Crusoe, for however long we locked down (more than a year in my case, and in some ways, it continues). But the metaphor would be equally apt to describe other historical fissures, the election of Reagan or the rise of Homeland Security, which made the worlds that came before equally inaccessible in definitive ways. Days the music died. And across each of those fissures, or lakes, or whatever the metaphor might be, fragments of music, bits of songs drift across and indicate that the far shores are still in some sense present and available.

Until my punk rapture in 1979, I remember music as a thing other people, or movies, brought to my attention, not a subject of personal obsession. My mother's records, movie matinees, and other kids acquainting me with their enthusiasms all overwhelmed me with musical associations, but there was little sense of my being the driver, or even one of the drivers, of my own tastes.

At college I was lucky enough to have my musical purview widened with the help of a couple of friends, one of whom took me through a crash course on blues and jazz that included my own attempts to improvise wailing on a harmonica, and the other of whom made me aware of avant-garde currents in "free jazz" and avant-garde classical music that matched the attraction I already felt to abstract, nonsensical poetry and painting.

So even though the music didn't spring from within, and even though I didn't possess anything like "knowledge" of music, I felt free to pretend. I even contributed a "libretto" to a short opera based on the story "The Juniper Tree" from the Brothers Grimm (which I think of as being from Maurice Sendak because I discovered it in his illustrated edition of fairy tales).

Punk rock (a category that for me included a lot of pop music that at least temporarily gave a nod to punk in 1979) did activate something within me rather than impinging from without. For the first time I identified *my* music as something different from other people's music. I had dropped out of college, tested my pacifist radicalism and decided I didn't have the stones to continue after spending a couple of weeks in jail, and finally wound up in Santa Barbara with a job at Ross Perot's data-entry company entering meaningless numbers at a tremendous rate for eight hours a day. All of that went well with the cynical but still somehow idealistic sensibilities of the punk communities I hung around the fringes of, or simply imagined, listening to vinyl singles in my Isla Vista apartment.

I opened myself to the music I was listening to in ways I hadn't before, and in so doing felt I was opening myself to *life*. Invited to guest DJ on the college radio station in Redlands where I had done a show called "Poem Air" that was about reading poetry live, I played Talking Heads "Don't Worry About the Government" over and over until the station manager (a very open-minded dude, I should make clear) told me to stop. I guess the secret to opening myself to *life* was not worrying about whether I was taking on the role of boorish twit in other people's lives, but letting the music fill me to the point of becoming intolerable.

For the most part, though, I did better to sit or stand gaping at live performances that I went to some pains to get to, negotiating Greyhound from Santa Barbara to Los Angeles and then bussing along Sunset Boulevard to the Roxy or Whiskey A-Go-Go. I heard Television play at the Roxy, and the Avengers (with the Weirdos and the Screamers) at the Whiskey A-Go-Go. The music stayed with me; it filled my head, satisfying desires I either hadn't known previously, or had thought could only be addressed partially in other ways.

I may have had no musical ability per se, but with the help of a friend who did, Tim Van Schmidt,

we created an acoustic folk-punk group called the Bag Ladies. The song I remember best was one that played off the drought conditions that existed in California around that time; the repeated lines of the song were "If it's mellow let it yellow/If it's brown flush it down/My head feels like jello/Seeing you in your evening gown." Two copies of our duo's cassette were made, one for myself and one for Tim, and they are lost in the waters of time.

As the punk era crested, a club in downtown Santa Barbara called George's opened itself to regular local shows, far cruder and less original, but more essential to the social formation entailed by the music. The movie "Twentieth Century Women" captures the atmosphere of that club so perfectly I feel sure the makers of the film were trying to re-create their own memories of the same place. But the crest corresponded to the very months in which the presidency of Ronald Reagan began to seem fearsomely possible. Graduating from the university, which I attended while mostly continuing to work for Perot's company, I determined to get out of the country to avoid the dark impending clouds of History and joined the Peace Corps. I went to Swaziland with nothing but a radio that could get South African Top 40 and occasional tinny transmissions from Mozambique. And unable to take most of the music with me, and most importantly unable to transport the scene, punk and my musical life subsided.

By the time I got back to the U.S. and into graduate school, punk seemed as remote to me as it does now. My daily musical tastes meandered through new country (Nanci Griffith) and world music (especially African music, King Sunny Ade, Philemon Zulu, Ladysmith Black Mambazo, that resonated with my Peace Corps memories). Easy listening, in other words.

I did continue to have an interest in experiments and sheer noise, especially as recommended by my artist pal Randy Greif. Along with a few intermittent projects, we even made a cassette collaboration, "Easy Green Proof," combining poetry, portentously intoned by me, in Randy's musical compositions. My heavily manipulated words and voice were at once inspiration, vocal accompaniment, and grist for the musical mill. It's not an easy cassette to find anymore, but it did exist in an edition of more than two, so it does serve as a shout across the waters to whatever shores are yet to show.

It wasn't until nearly the end of my graduate studenthood that I became engaged with live music again. That next wave of musical enthusiasm began, or this is how I remember it, with a cousin living in the California desert playing "Smells Like Teen Spirit" on his car radio. That wave was strongly driven, at least initially, by listening to a radio station that played grunge and indie while driving my car wherever I drove it to. But it was moved in wider directions by my sister and her husband in Paris, who got me listening to My Bloody Valentine and Lisa Germano when I stayed in their flat for most of a February, and took me to Throwing Muses and House of Love shows.

The possibility of rock shows as quasi-religious events was never realer to me than at a My Bloody Valentine show at the Warfield in San Francisco, early '90's. It was the loudest concert I'd ever been to, by far. The group simultaneously channeled the simplest, most melodic pop sensibility and sentiment, and an abstract wall of sound that painted my insides with warnings of impending dissolution.

And then sieur William Breiding directed me to a whole little mini-fandom briefly existing around the female groups and performers, like Germano and P.J. Harvey (as well as around actors like Drew Barrymore), who flourished then. I didn't include myself in the identity part of that flourishing, but the spirit of its waves of generous noise exalted me.

I took joy in the loud music throughout the Nineties. Naturally I blame History and mass counter-terrorist shutdown for ending that interlude in paradise. Turn of the century followed, and everything of the previous century became tinged with age instantly. I turned into a dad, a socially approved form of total self-involvement that also left me ignorant of anything happening outside the house for years.

When I woke up again, it was due to a combination of my younger daughter Charla becoming interested in old-time music (meaning shoegaze and punk) and Covid turning our household into a sedate version of the Mosquito Coast, confined to a nuclear family configuration for six months in which listening to streaming music seemed to be one of the least soporific forms of diversion available.

Musical discovery was facilitated by e-zines like Pitchfork, certainly, but the real instigator of new enthusiasms was Charla, who played me her Spotify playlist on a long drive from southern to northern California. It turned out there were a lot of new groups hearkening back to the fuzz and buzz of My Bloody Valentine in 2020, and a lot of similarly psychedelic, electronic or otherwise experimental music that had been exploding for a couple of decades that I had not encountered.

After getting vaccinated, I hesitantly explored the idea of leaving the house for something other than a bit of fresh air or picking up groceries. I thought about spending time in public places, masked, as limiting my exposure to viral load without eliminating it altogether; so I had a budget of time/risk I could use for diversions, time I would certainly not waste as I would have in the past on work, "conferences," face to face meetings with strangers, or plane flights (am I not lucky to be forced into any of those?) My first expenditure was an exhilarating techno show by Kelly Jean Owen at Oakland's Starline Social Club, and I've continued to go to shows regularly, often with Charla, in the two years since – always masked, and as time has passed more and more notably in a masked minority, even in the Bay Area.

As in some Hieronymus Bosch painting, the music was sometimes shadowed by the dark presence of disease: I walked out on a show by Savage Republic, which had been one of my favorite tribal punk bands around 1980, because the lead singer intimidated the percussionist into removing his mask on stage. Purity Ring insisted on everyone in the Fox Theater being masked, handing out custom masks at the theater entrance, and powerfully described the sense of danger at least some musicians have felt in performing before audiences willing to be infected or infect others. And Santigold cancelled a performance I had tickets to because she realized she wouldn't be able to afford the measures required to afford her a measure of safety while on tour, being a middling sort of celebrity and having to absorb a lot of the costs and risks on her own (unlike the big stars with their machineries of protection, and unlike the impoverished musicians who tour to travel or just work and can't afford even such considerations).

But in spite of the darkness, the effect of a multitude of musical performers wanting to connect with their audiences again after the lockdown resulted in a span of a couple of years that felt almost literally like an artistic renaissance, with pretty much everybody I would want to see coming through Oakland or San Fran during that period, at an almost frantic pace. Beyond that cultural moment, rock bands give me at least as much belief in a future beyond my own mortal horizon as reading *Science* magazine or watching soccer or getting texts from my gallivanting daughters. The frenzy seems to have calmed down some as of early 2023, or maybe it's been moved to the realm of music festivals, which I have no interest in. The music of the 2020's seems to have collated all of the music I've ever liked and put it together into a rich strew of punk, shoegaze, indie grrl, and psychedelia.

Having arrived at the shore I rest on today, the question has to be asked whether my musical memories are anything more than a tincture of nostalgia. In trying to justify the importance of what are not really personal memories, I return to the idea that music in its remembered form (whether the memories are almost autonomic, as with earworms, or richly detailed flashbacks) might be a fundamental structure of reality in a human brain such as mine, and that it serves this purpose with or without the past being missed or longed for. The tincture may therefore be neither the flavor nor the meal yet to be digested, though it points to the truth that all of these memories found are also irretrievably lost.

Alva at Uni

The Writing Cure

I gather that *Portable Storage* may be ending with this issue (though I've seen "last concerts" by groups like the B-52s and Roxy Music that I'm not sure I fully believe in either), and with that in mind look back not only at the shores of memory but at the writing William has inspired me to contribute over the short lifetime of his fanzine's magnificence. It occurs to me that by encouraging me to write, almost always in some form of memoir, William has got me to go over my life repeatedly, trying to make sense of it in some pretty disparate modes. It hasn't pointed me toward any underlying unity of self, but the effort has served as a kind of compulsory therapy: a writing cure rather than a talking cure. Thanks to William's magisterial editorial talents, I find myself more ready for whatever it is that is to come, and for that I send my sincerest thanks, both to him and to all readers.

Hidden Machines

Jeanne N. Bowman

Resting Twig Space

Out back by our quiet summer boudoir the long dead oak, stripped of bark, arches over the clothesline, no longer an upright traverse for the gnarly old gray day time roaming racoon boar. The deadwood drifted to earth over a few rainy days and is now a scenic bowed arc that frames the ravine. The multi stemmed pasture oak has busted again, the busted branch split, the twiglets, and branches in the dirt at right angles to the torn off leader. It is a tori gate, without, yet, the hanging circle to complete that imagery. There must be a wine barrel hoop around here somewhere. The stand of gully guarding oaks along the west fence line is tilting, laying gently down. One has set twigs and branchlets that once reached and now walk, resting, fingering into the earth while the central bole leans against it's neighbor with its angled trunk pulling into the daylight and limbs knotting into an understory with the upper branches of another dying oak, all three slowly giving in to gravity, roots released soundlessly from the slurry that the

soil has become. That third tree looks to be dehydrating as it stands, with parallels splits and cracks from the ground to each crotch on up the trunk, like yarn untwisting with strands about to separate, like the cartilage in an alter cockers knees. Jaime and I check the much smaller cracks of another stalwart live oak with similar separations in the bark. Jaime says, no, no, those are growth cracks. But look, the original small hollow has expanded from a bird nest size knothole to full pirate hide out. All the way through the center of the tree is open shady space. With a generous hold of bilgy stump water at the bottom. Where years ago, a single branch fell off there are now three more windows joined into a cavern. Okay, fourty years ago it was a single branch, a bad cut or two and a worse crotch. Jaime says, hey, healthy and growing does not mean it is structurally sound. This hidden bog is a quarter the size of the empty stump by the driveway that now grows gigantic glow in the dark mushrooms (if not the actual glow in the dark jack o lantern, Omphalotus olearius, a very close relation) This has been the season for them, dozens, each bigger than the last.

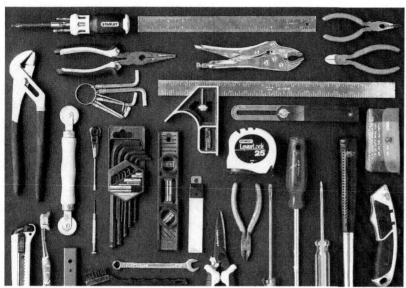

(and all those other straight line mid-century Moderne loons, just to color my opinion into it), who designed furniture for the Knoll factory came into play.) Do you know about knolling? Is this like the *belfie*, a neologism that has been around for a while but not where I've been hanging out? The evanescent article touts knolling as an alternative to avoid the yeet of Marie Kondo (take yeet, right? When was the first time you heard that? And who explained it to you? I am attempting to understand "clutch" outside of driving a stick, too.) That ghost write up I skimmed by claimed the knolling neologism happened in 1987 with janitor Andrew Kromelow and at the Knoll furniture plant, but further unchecked random internet search credits Florence Knoll as the designer and architect who owned the plant and that the photographic flat lay design style has origins in the 1930's. Florence Knoll was a big name in corporate office design in the 1950's, her furniture line whose designs you would recognize (Angular! Modern! Concise!) as Mid Century Modern, sharp with a perpendicular square chromed leg, few angles other than hard right (except for the back of the signature tufted couches) (made to make deals, not to rest!). Except that another source says that Kromelow called the arrangement of tools knolling because the way he straightened up the place (and took photos of it) reminded him of the furniture being made for Knoll. But wait, Jacob Osborn writing ManofMany in 2019 says that Kromelow worked in Gehry's studio, in the manufacturing plant he owned, making Knoll's line of chairs. Hold on now, in this other place Tyler Watamanuk at Dwell

Always Be *What?*

I made a fanzine for the amateur press association I have joined, given that this will be the final issue of Portable Storage and I wish to fully embrace such a venue to encourage my writing in the future. Why not have a tidy captive audience of two dozen, with perhaps a higher rate of commentary (as a percentage) than evinced by the glorious random editorial whims of Wm. Brieding and our motely entourage? Here I go on to explore yet another way urban lore is stranger than fiction expecting to exercise my inner art critic and knee-jerk social cynic. Were I an accurate reporter or have serious journalist leanings or technical know how I'd have linked to the aspirational article as it scrolled by. A write up that I did not bookmark or save or make a note of nor have I been able to find again, not being erudite with finger ticking tech.

Yes, I learned about "knolling". A process where things that are being used, but not yet put away, at the end of the workday are categorized and lined up (one story says by the janitor Andrew Kromelow at the Knoll furniture manufacturing plant.) Or an array of useful things is made in a flat lay (straight from above, the bird's eye, perspective) so photos can document it (wherein I surmise the ascetic of Frank Gehry, architect, https://www.dwell.com/article/the-life-changing-magic-of-knolling-5efe3c96 which also talks trash about Kondo style minimalism and might have been the door to this rabbit hole, says Sculptor Andrew Kromelow coined the name in 1987 while working as a janitor in Frank Gehry's studio; artist Tom Sachs, who also worked in Gehry's studio at the time, popularized the organizational concept. Gehry may or may not have been designing those chairs. Or Gehry's furniture store sold the Knoll brand. Or Knolls made and sold Gehry's chair designs. Gehry designed bentwood (and super uncomfortable looking) chairs and such for Knoll's furniture line in 1992.

Meanwhile Tom Sachs, artist, was working as a 'fabricator' in Gehry's Santa Monica studio, with Kromelow, and coined the phrase "Always be Knolling". He took inspiration from Kromelow's photos, made an art piece of his own that 'popularized' the style in 1987 (except I can't find it) and thus the date of origin. In 2009 the now bricolage sculptor Tom Sachs wrote in "Ten Bullets", one of his fanzines, this guidance for how to knoll:

1.   Scan your environment for materials, tools, books, music, etc. which are not in use.

2.   Put away everything not in use. If you aren't sure, leave it out.

3.   Group all 'like' objects.

4.   Align or square all objects to either the surface they rest on, or the studio itself.

I will need a great quantity of museum putty or stay tack, but not cyan acrylic glue, to fully explore this new to me organizational process, not having much horizontal flat studio space. I pretty quickly dumped out my pencil case and realigned the contents on the kitchen table. Great way to inventory – I need a sharpie and another eraser. Back into the bag it all went. Oh, my pens and stuff weren't too colorful. So I reached for my

knitting catch all and rolled out the sox project. Vibrant color everywhere. Lots of ways for little tools to be tangled up in the yarn. (Also, the knitting of socks does not lend itself to right angles and uses from two to six needles at a time for each sock, so number 2 is important.) It helped to see all the small things oriented toward the work in progress and tidied together in like ways. Now my extra needles are all zipped into one place and the pastel foam keepers, bitsy marking rings, darning needles, tape measure, shiny snaggled stitch holders are behind the clear window of a new, bright, notions wallet. I can see them. I can find them. I do not aspire to align further within that small, curated space.

Ah, wasn't that restful? I like trying out this new to me motto "always be knolling". I went to the websites that came up with the names of the major characters of this whimsy. I found that the Florence Knoll legacy company tm's her signature pieces of furniture. I worried that she was being in some way being made sport of in the verbing of the knoll. There is no direct mention therein of the flat lay, nor of Kromelow nor Sachs. Gehry, yes, of course. Sachs on Sachs, who enjoys current renown, backhandedly says.

"I don't want to call it brand collaborations, because the only real brand collaboration I've done has been with Nike, the sort of, only brand I have an ongoing, collaborative relationship with. I kind of like it that way. There are other brands that I've had longstanding relationships with, like Knoll." https://huckberry.com/special-projects/artists/tom-sachs   Uh Huh. I will buy the quoted Ten Bullets fanzine anyway. I like his stuff.

While former janitor Kromelow, like Knoll herself, unacknowledged as an artist in many of the short shrift bits of algorithmically attention deficit search results, met my expectations about the world of art. I like his sculpture a lot too. Inspired by Knoll to coin knolling, about tidying up and taking pics be aware that he has since taught at Columbia and says on his website http://www.andrewkromelow.com/ "Any attempts to rip off the artist will result in death."

A Few Moments...
Chris Sherman

Just when you think things never end, they do. A parent dies. A crucial skeletal joint suddenly and inexplicably fails and needs to be replaced with metal. Hundreds of homes in your community are totally destroyed by fire sashaying with gale-force winds through neighborhoods you still need to navigate through every day afterward. Two close relatives are told to "get their affairs" in order. Bah. Even Christmas past has passed.

Then the good stuff intervenes.

I've been both lucky and fortunate to transverse a large expanse of this world, mostly with others paying for the experiences. Also lucky and fortunate to recall these moments for Wm's various zines. But now, with all of the right reasons, he's changing things up for a new phase of life. Another way of saying all good things end.

on the steering wheel, or possibly even lose grip on everything before we emerged from this seemingly endless wormhole we were navigating in the far-northern depths of the earth.

I live in Colorado. Between regularly driving atop some of the tallest mountains in the country and flying millions of miles around the world (always in a window seat) I'm well adapted to altitude change. But this was different: I was willing my way through an impossibly narrow tunnel driving a seven-gear manual-stick shift Skoda Superb Estate. A vehicle not as huge as a Chevrolet Subdivision but still gutrenchingly large for making your way through tunnels that had surely been hewn by Norse Vikings or possibly even Middle-Earth trolls.

Rural Norway, late 2010s

It was dark. And despite the car's admirable driving-assist features I was motoring far more slowly through the tunnel than the speed limit permitted. And growing concerned that my tightly clenched sweat-drenched hands would lose grip

Norway is astonishing. I freely admit to genetic bias (ya, my surname derives from "Shoreman" you betcha), but I still assert that the country is one of the most spectacular places on the planet.

To start: the western coastline is more than 1,500 miles long. Mercator's projection doesn't do justice to the actual size of our earth's polar regions, but hey, most of the planet's northern and southern reaches were Terra incognito when Merc was creating his maps without benefit of GPS affirmation. Perspective: Norway's 1,500 mile coastline rivals the length of the entire west coast of America.

If you factor in all of the twisty inlets gnawed into the country by the glaciers that created Norway's spectacular fjords, the actual length of the country's coastline expands to nearly 18,000 miles - nearly two-thirds of the earth's circumference. The super/protocontinentient Pangea's tectonic machinations were astonishingly efficient in accomplishing what our favorite SF writers used to describe as terraforming. Many fjords are actually deeper than the adjacent Atlantic ocean.

This means that the land sloping up from (or down to) a fjord is usually incredibly steep. So while Norway lacks significant peaks - Galdhøpiggen is tallest at about 8,100 feet (less than a half-mile above the elevation where I live in Colorado today) it's entirely possible to experience Hitchcockian vertigo while spiraling up or down some of the country's remarkably efficient roadways.

Norwegians, being Norwegians, decided vertigo was a problem that needed solving. Today you can fully and frequently experience their solution: Tunnels. Lots of 'em. Norway modernized its transport network by blasting tunnels between fjords so you don't have to shimmy up and down or around the ancient cow-paths turned-roads that used to add all kinds of time to your journey.

Back to darkness. There are more than 1,000 roadway tunnels throughout Norway's primary highway system, and many of them are long. Most are not illuminated and offer a scant foot or so of median on either side of the invariably rugged passageway.

Back to the moment: Approaching Vallavik Tunnel. It's not the longest in the country but was predictably narrow. Before entering I caught a quick glimpse of the obligatory entrance sign that informs you of length and probable (hopeful?) time of passage:

Length: 7.5 kilometers. Time: 13 minutes.

OK. Clenched harder on the wheel and the stick shift. Willed my pupils to dilate to adjust to the impending darkness.

Ingress.

Maybe midway through, but with no sign of light at the end of the tunnel, the GPS (what? underground?) startled me with one of the most bizarre guidance directives I've ever heard.

"At the roundabout, take the first exit," it calmly instructed.

What!? We were driving in murky darkness under a mountain! Roundabout?

That the GPS was even functioning under millions of tons of rock and dirt was astonishing, but now it was instructing me to maneuver on an immanently upcoming roundabout? Seriously?

Then, just like that, we were circling through the roundabout. I had no time to marvel at the engineering feat that had conjoined two major roadways beneath thousands of feet of rock or the fact that the GPS even knew it was there. No alternative. As instructed, I took the first "exit."

Then abruptly emerged into brilliant light on a mile long suspension bridge nearly a half-kilometer above the Hardangerfjorden. Turns out its main span is one of the longest bridges in the world. It is also the longest tunnel-to-tunnel suspension bridge on the planet. Oh, did I mention that as soon as we successfully crossed to the other side we immediately plunged back into another frickin' tunnel? Had Pythagoras been alive and fully vaxxed, he would surely have been proud that I hadn't lost my grip.

As we sailed over the fjord at altitude, I breathed

a sigh of relief that years earlier I had been trained and certified to operate formula race cars at the Skip Barber Racing School on various tracks throughout the USA. Which brought back a moment in Florida gasping in horror as a fellow-trainee (who had just published a bestseller about eagles learning to fly) spun-out, his car inexorably sliding into an everglade swamp filled with hungry alligators.

My fellow trainees and I garbed in flame-resistant racecar suits despite the hot and sultry weather raced out and pulled David from his car and back to safety, averting tragedy but sadly depriving the reptiles of what they surely considered well-deserved compensation for our obnoxiously loud vehicles roaring around their idyllic wetlands. But that's a tale for another moment. (And no, I'm not making any of this stuff up. Really. I'd have to run for political office otherwise.)

Castaneda moment I had not brought a flashlight (nor food or water for that matter. Fucking fool). Then multiple BOOMS! sent me flopping to my belly, be dammed the potentially lethal encounters with scorpions or rattlesnakes who might have been lying passively on the desert floor beneath me.

Backstory: I was a teenager living north of San Diego in Del Mar at the time. Open to adventure but not particularly savvy about how the world worked at that point (More "relevant" backstory: I had founded Apa-50 four years earlier, and many of you know how that all worked out). When my housemate mentioned he was driving to Tucson for the weekend I puppishly asked if I could hitch a ride. He grinned and said if I would fill the tank he'd be happy to drop me wherever I wanted.

Tucson, Arizona, late 70s

The first gunshot shattered the silence in the canyon and blew shards of rock everywhere. Percussive echoes ricocheted and cascaded across what Lovecraft might have called the blasted heath of the Santa Catalina mountains. I couldn't see the shooters, nor could they see me because in my foolish determination to have a Carlos

So I headed East. My mother was born in Tuscon and my family had deep roots there, but I arrived without a map or a clue or anything else other than flimsily inadequate clothing. After circumventing the gate to the state park, I strolled up the arroyo - easy to do in those days, when there was little water flowing in the canyon and long before I had to heel to the demands of a titanium hip. Af-

162

ter a spectacular sunset found myself on a ledge that had a pleasant overlook of the city. Plopped down and settled in and soaked up the view of the city lights below, reminiscing about the acid-enhanced vistas over San Francisco bay at Wm's friend Gene's apartment in Delores Heights. When I first visited Wm. in the early 70s, he arranged the best deadhead experience for a Minnesota teenager you could imagine, altering both my life and brain forever (in the best possible ways, at least as I recall).

Then the lightning started. No rain, just spectacular displays of fractals shattering the deep blackness of the sky. And after a respectful pause, thunder resoundingly booming through the mountains.

A moment later, without drugs or any other sort of mind-altering substance, I found myself going full Castaneda. Totally absorbed into that unique mindspace - that's what attracted me to science fiction in the first place. It frequently distorts time, space and reality, and sometimes the effects spill over into real life.

Flash: Whoa! There's Wm. laboring over a mimeograph, pulping out pages of Starfire. Flash crack! which improbably looked like it was unfolding backward: Wm. gut spilling in Apa-50, with immediate responses from Larry, Leah and Ken urging restraint and then all sorts of teenage weirdness at MidAmericon and likely elsewhere.

Final flash: Again, with time distortion, just a few days ago yet decades later in my post-Tucson future, Wm. gently but patiently reminding us of all of the final Portable Storage deadline, thankfully with just a single ALL CAPS exhortation and a single exclamation point! (he's definitely not MAGA yet...)

Winding up, winding loose, then finally winding down.

So now it's time to end. No more Conrad-slash-Bryson wannabe tales I was planning to spin (watching the drunk guy flee the *Policie* in Prague; nearly getting shot at the Wailing Wall in Jerusalem; wine-tasting in south Australia; narrowly avoiding getting swept into the sea atop a tall cliff in western Ireland; yada yada) and simply wish Wm. and Gail all the best as they transition to Albuquerque.

LETTERS
OF
COMMENT

[Greg Benford urged me not to mention that this is the last issue, fearing no one would write locs. But I thought I owed it to everyone to be clear about it. I do urge you to write locs on this issue. If enough come in I will edit them and create a PDF and post them to eFanzine.com as Portable Storage 9.5. *Get crackin':* **portablezine@gmail.com** *–Wm.]*

JIM MEADOWS
waltham3@gmail.com
Urbana, Illinois

I am sorry for being so late in sending in comments for ***Portable Storage Seven***, Sercon Issue Pt 2. This tendency to delay my locs played a role in my gafiation from fanzines 40 years ago. Nowadays, it seems I often have the letter written in my head, but I do poorly at actually getting it written out in the physical world.

One thing that caught my attention was the one page that I failed to find a credit for --- the parody mail order ads on the back cover. I would love to know who wrote and designed these. The "Free Seeds" ad referencing "Invasion of the Body Snatchers" was of particular interest. Despite strong memories of that movie (ever since first seeing it around the age of seven, on TV while visiting my grandparents in Louisiana), I had forgotten the "love desire ambition faith" quote that summed up what the pod people were offering. Now, I think I will remember it always.

*[Apparently I created some confusion about **Alan White's** brilliant back cover to* Portable Storage Seven *by not displaying it in B&W on the first page of the issue with the front cover. Sorry Alan!]*

As I looked through the rest of the issue, putting it together with the previous sercon issue, I had a strong sense of reconnection. Many of your contributors were writing (and drawing) for the fanzines I read in the 1970s and '80s. Reading them now, after being largely away from fanzines for several years, felt like coming back to a long conversation that had never stopped, despite my absence. When I was first reading fanzines, the writers were mostly young, and the topics and authors they wrote about were the ones that won their youthful enthusiasm. Now it's 40 to 50 years later, and your contributors are writing about topics they've been interested in for a long time. I guess this could be tiresome, but it's not. Your contributors' enthusiasms seem tempered by maturity.

Just to pick an article at random, it was interesting to read Joe Pearson's "A Fanzine Changed My Life", and for him to discuss fandom -- indeed his whole career --- in terms of the past, instead of the present and future. "I still keep in touch with a number of fans", and "I've had a good 35-year long career" are lines I don't remember reading in the 1970s, even though some of the writers (Harry Warner Jr. comes to mind) were not young. Maybe it's just because I'm older myself that I focus on these references to being older and of time passing. And the fact that Pearson used part of that career to make an animated feature, which I can now view on Youtube is a little mind-boggling --- partly because the sf speculations I read about electronic media half a century ago did not really figure on the internet, which has changed our access to media content dramatically.

Cy Chauvin's "Would They Have Changed Science Fiction?" is another article that I think would not have been written when young. Chauvin writes about writers who died before their time --- Cordwainer Smith, James Blish, Roger Zelazny, C.M. Kornbluth. Some of these authors had already passed away when Chauvin was writing in the fanzines I read in the 1970s, so I guess he could have written about them then. But I think it takes the passage of one's own lifetime to gain the perspective that allowed him to ask the questions he posed about these writers' unfulfilled potential.

[There were many Old Fans, and Tired, when you and I were crass neos, back in the seventies, but I think you are right. Very few of them were backward-looking in the sense that you are talking about. There was always "timebinding", but that's not what you are trying to peel open. I think Boomers tend to verbally note their aging process: they were the ones that were changing the world, revolutionizing it, they were the rock'n'roll generation! And now they are old—and dying.]

TOM JACKSON

tomjackson@fastmail.com

Berea, Ohio

During a point in my life when I was a member of both FAPA and APA-50, I once photocopied a *Spirochete* zine by Redd Boggs I particularly admired, included in one of the FAPA mailings, and franked it in one of the APA-50 mailings, simply because I loved Boggs' prose so much I wanted to share it and give other APA-50 members a chance to discover it. And I mentioned my interest in Boggs in my bio when I contributed to *Portable Storage* a couple of issues ago.

So I was very pleased to get my copy of the new issue in the mail and read Andy Hooper's article on Boggs and the reprint of the Boggs piece. Andy's comment, "The best way I can communicate the virtues of Redd Boggs' fan writing is to share some of it with you," exactly captures my impulse when I reproduced an issue of *Spirochete* in APA-50. And I was pleased that Andy defended the worth of fanzine writing and Boggs' concentration on writing for fanzines.

Boggs' fannish friend Dave Rike, mentioned in Andy's article, published a fanzine in 1997 called *Redd Boggs, Selected Works, Volume One,* that cost me $28.61 when I bought it from Amazon earlier this year. It's a good collection; Andy Hooper reviewed it for issue 79 of *Apparatchik,* available at efanzines.com. Copies of the fanthology don't seem to be easy to find; it would be good for a digital version to be made available.

But if any of your readers become interested in Boggs because of Andy's article, quite a few PDFs of some of Boggs' zines are available. Many issues of *Sky Hook,* Boggs' 1940s and 1950s fanzine, are available at fanac.org. The same website also has issues of Boggs' zine *Retrograde,* which later became *Discord.* A few issues of the later perzine *Spirochete,* which is how I got interested in Boggs, also are available at fanac.org. It's pretty cool that efforts are being made to make Boggs' work available to more readers.

I want to read the history of the first Worldcon that Andy Hooper is writing, according to the bio in your zine, and I hope I somehow find out about it when it becomes available. I've CC'd Mr. Hooper with this email.

I hope that I succeed in writing a follow-up LOC, but I never completed the one I started for your last issue, and so I want to hit "send" and get this to you. I always liked your writing, but what a great job you are doing, late in life, of being a fanzine publisher and editor.

DARRELL SCHWEITZER

darrells@comcast.net

Philadelphia, PA

By the way, in response to a comment made by someone in the lettercol last issue (I think it was Cy Chauvin), no, I did not interpret WATCH THE NORTH WIND RISE as fantasy because I am a fantasy reader or writer. (Bias implied). I am also a *science fiction* reader and writer, I hasten to add. As I write this my most recently published story is clearly science fiction, and in the current issue of STARTLING STORIES. I interpreted the Graves book as fantasy because it has an on-stage, active supernatural being, a goddess, moving the plot along. That, to me at least, makes it fantasy, despite the futuristic setting.

HOPE LEIBOWITZ

tiki@interlog.com

Toronto, Ontario

The major thing on which I wanted to comment on is Phil Paine's bit about Gord Downie. Wow. I saw a movie about Gord Downie's last days, probably with Charles, at Dundas Square, a place that used to show movies for free in the summer. It was just horrific, as he got less and less able to function. Then sometime after I played all seven of The Tragically Hip CDs that I have. I've known way too many people who died of brain cancer and I can't think of any more horrific way to die. And yup, cannot hear "38 Years Old" without sobbing. Tearing up now, oops. Such a horrible/horrific thing to go through. Anyway, thanks for the beautiful zine, and someday I hope I can manage to LoC it properly!

LYNN KUEHL

lynn@berkshire-books.com

Concord, California

Read and enjoyed the latest *PS*. Glad the slow delivery is getting resolved. Just FYI, I have questioned a postal clerk about how tracking works and found out (according to him) that it works by the tracking number being attached (if that's the right word) to the employee at the post office who is responsible for it. Found this out when a tax bill I was sending to Sacramento was showing thru the tracking system to be somewhere in Southern California. Apparently, the postal employee who was handling it was recently transferred from SoCal but that hadn't been registered with the Post Office database, so it showed my mail (among others I suppose) as being in the employee's old home area. Very confusing, to say the least. Anyway, latest *Portable Storage* is another triumph. Like the *New Yorker*-style layout. Much easier to read. Altho I keep expecting to read an article by James Thurber or A. J. Leibling. Your contributors are worthy however, so worth the extra effort I think. Especially enjoyed Gary Casey's piece about his SciFi book club criminality. Hilarious!

KENNEDY GAMMAGE

gammage.kennedy@gmail.com

San Diego, California

Another fabulous issue; is *Portable Storage Eight* really next-to-last ish, just when you're getting so good at it? I mean, this wraparound cover by Joe Pearson and Sung Woo Hong is so beautiful. Wanted to immediately comment on *The New Yorker* design and formatting – so spot-on and well done. I'm a big fan of *TNY*, submitting Shouts & Murmurs pieces to zero response, but also critical letters ("You haven't published an important poem in years - Rae Armantrout is phoning it in.") Ha ha – I'm not going to kiss their ass when Sutton's "A Letter from Gertrude Stein's Left Breast" is ten times better than anything the magazine has published in the past decade. Roger D. Sween's "Best of Days" also! Wm, you are publishing better poems than *The New Yorker* does! I was going to say that, following the Sercon two-hander, this issue seemed to be a meeting place of ideas, but Pauline Palmer described it better as a party for old friends. Certainly I was honored to share the lettercol with Robert Silverberg! One of the greats, I own and have enjoyed so many of his novels and anthologies. In fact I quoted him on the Senior Pipedreams page of my high school yearbook, from *Up The Line*: "You haven't lived until you've laid one of your own ancestors" – Metaxas. That raised a few eyebrows! #RIP to Robert Lichtman and Billy Ray Wolfenbarger! So many great articles in this issue. Bruce Gillespie on Alice Sheldon. I liked the name of Jeff Smith's pers-zine: *Kyben*. Those were the space aliens infesting LA's Bradbury Building in Harlan's "Demon with a Glass Hand" *Outer Limits* episode with Robert Culp. Phil Paine on Gord Downie. (I still think Gordon Lightfoot is the Greatest Canadian.) Dale Nelson on Samuel Palmer. (He's not in my English Romantic Writers anthology, probably because he's a painter!) Have to pick a friendly bone with Alva about his paean to PG&E (AKA the Evil Empire) – yes the grid is taken for granted, but what about the revolution in Rooftop Solar? Andy Hooper on Redd Boggs. Loved the Donn Brazier mention re: Redd's *Chronoscope*. Sandra Bond on the song "Daisy Bell." I had a technical question for Jeanne Bowman about "Crack," which documented a series of 11 trees falling on her property over a period of 5 years. Were you keeping a journal during that time that you were able to refer back to when you wrote the article? Seems like the slow motion train wreck of climate change (or at least drought) at work. Loved Kurt Erichsen's "In Sound" about the Cyrkle and other bands of the time. I love that kind of music! Still listen to it – YouTube is a great source for wild hair instant musical gratification. "Red Rubber Ball" still sounds fresh. Pretty sure for most readers Joe Pearson's memoir of Kyiv 30 years ago was the highlight of *Eight*. There was so much detail – it was like being there! Slava Ukraine! Jon Sommer's article about atheism left me wanting more: if Richard Dawkins is failing to make the case, I'd like to hear Jon explicitly make the argument for atheism himself. I would be highly receptive to it. Cheryl Cline's "Burrs Under the Saddle" continues her investigation of the Western genre brilliantly. I went back to *Seven* to confirm she cited the first volume of Stephen King's *Dark Tower* series – but for my money the fourth volume, *Wizard and Glass*, is the Best Western of the series, where the young Roland and his ka-tet Cuthbert and Alain, ride horses in Mejis (a mid-world version of Mexico) scouting the rising fortunes of the sinister John Farson, the Good Man. Recommended. Wm thanks for introducing me to M. John Harrison's *Light*. That's what I was talking about: *Portable Storage* as a meeting place for ideas. We are all like individual cells in the *PS* brain, firing wildly! On to *PS9*. Ultima Thule!

STEVE JEFFERY

srjeffery@aol.com

Kidlington, Oxon

Lying in bed listening to the radio this morning I caught a report by a female gamer about the level of toxic misogyny and hate comments prevalent in her industry against female gamers, some of it from boys as young as 14, which reminded me of Ulrika's eye-opening "Talk of the Town" comment piece in this issue of *Portable Storage*.

Gaming is obviously a very different (and sometimes deeply unpleasant) form of fandom from the sf and fanzine fandom I encountered back in the '80s and always regarded as an open and welcome 'safe space'. Although it may not always have been such given some of the 'dirty old men' stories I've heard since about some of the groping and leering (from both male pros and fans) that went on in the 1950s and 1960s. Thankfully I missed all of that, and my first encounters with sf fandom were only mildly tainted by a lingering milder form of snobbery between science fiction readers and fantasy readers, although that didn't survive too much into the 1990s before writers like China Mieville kicked it in the head with his debut novel *Perdido Street Station* and championing of the 'New Weird'.

I don't know much about comics fandom either. I stopped reading comics with the *Beano* and *Look and Learn* in my early teens and luckily (for my wallet) never caught the collecting bug for any DC/Marvel superhero or independent comics that filled most of the ground floor of Forbidden Planet. (Books were relegated to the basement, as if they, rather than the garish covered comics, were a shameful secret.) To date I only have the *Sandman* graphic novels, Jeff Smith's marvelous *Bone* and three or four volumes of *Cerebus the Aardvark*. The nearest I've come to either a gaming or comics convention was probably DragonCon, which was fun for a visit but seemed overly commercialized even then and not a place I'd want to live.

And of course, all that was largely before the internet and online gaming, blogs and chat rooms, and trolling. Did trolling exist on paper before the anonymity of the internet? I suppose something of the sort might have happened (I don't suppose the insecurities of 14 year old boys has changed anywhere near as fast as technology has) but it's hard to see how it might be sustained.

And of course, I'm writing from a male perspective. Things might have been different, even in sf fanzine fandom had I encountered it as a woman, although Vikki and I entered fandom as a couple and I didn't sense or hear of any discomfort on her part (apart from a few tiresome drunks, Vikki being a non-drinker) otherwise we would have stopped going.

So that was food for thought. I feel lucky I found the fandom I did, where it didn't seem to matter whether you were male or female, gay or transgender, white or BAME *[Black, Asian, Minority Ethnic]*, although even then I could probably count the number of non-white fans we knew on one hand.

There's a lot to enjoy and think about in this issue. I enjoyed Bruce Gillespie's article on Tiptree. I can't remember if I already knew of Tiptree's real identity as Alice Sheldon when I started reading her stories. I suspect I might have done, or the discovery came pretty soon after and added an interesting twist to an already fascinating and challenging writer. (I seem to have mislaid both copies I bought of Jeff Smith's Khatru 3/4,

167

and I must go digging in the boxes in the spare room sometime. Sorting these out might be a project for my continually deferred retirement if and when I ever get round to pushing that button. At the moment, though, things seem a little uncertain.)

I don't think I knew about Samuel Palmer, and Dale's article might well prompt me to a return visit to the Ashmolean, which is really just a 15 minute bus ride away. I haven't been back there since its makeover a few years ago. It's odd you can have something like that practically on your doorstep and not take advantage of it for years. I've been a Blake fan since I was in my teens. I have a fondness for maverick/visionary artists, and one of the highlight of Corflu FIAWOL was a trip with Steve and Elaine Stiles and Rich Coad and others to the Museum of Visionary Arts.

Sandra's 'I am a Computer' presses another of my buttons: a fascination with computer/ electronic music. I have a couple of fascinating documentaries recorded on my FreeView box on the history of electronic music, 'I Dream of Wires' and the rather more dubiously titled 'Sisters With Transistors' which goes back to pioneers like Delia Derbyshire and Daphne Oram. One of my best books read last year was Richard Powers' *Orfeo*, which similarly managed to press all my buttons at the same time, about 20th century music, electronics and computers, and was in part inspired by Alex Ross's brilliant and majestic overview of 20th century music, *The Rest is Noise*.

Although never put into practice, one of Ada Lovelace's comments in the extended notes (longer than the original article) of her translation of Luigi Menabrea's article on Charles Babbage's Analytical Engine was on the possibility of writing a program that would play music (one feels she would have loved MIDI, or even invented a precursor to it), although whether you would ever have heard it over the operation of Babbage's mechanical steam driven engine (had he ever got round to building it) is open to question.

What else? Cheryl Cline's 'Burrs Under the Saddle' follow up to her previous articles on sf and westerns was again fascinating and well done, even if I have almost no interest in westerns as a genre. That's the mark of a skilled and good writer. I don't think I'm anymore of a convert, or even wiser, but I am - as the saying goes - possibly now better informed.

I have read M. John Harrison's *Light* (like Gene Wolfe and John M. Ford, MJH is one of those writers who make me think I am always missing something important in my reading and if I were just a bit cleverer then it would cohere and come into focus.) I am on the side of those who think *Light* is astonishing, and also that *The Course of the Heart* and the *Viriconium* tales are works of brilliant and disturbing genius. (Although I really would love to learn more about Harrison's recurrent fascination - almost an obsession - with the disturbing image of the beribboned horse-skulled Mari Llwyd which reoccurs as the Shrander in *Light*.)

[Light *was my first taste of M. John Harrison's work. I have the collected* Viriconium *novels and stories volume on the shelf and do want to read the sequel to* Light, Nova Swing. *Wikipedia's description of* The Course of the Heart *sounds to me like Harrison has a set of obsessions he's continually working through; a few changes in description and it could be* Light. *A curious aside: I read* Light *because Paul di Filippo and Damien Broderick chose to include it as among the best in their book,* Science Fiction: The 101 Best Novels 1985-2010. *I read Ekaterina Sedia's* Alchemy of Stone *(see "review" this ish) for the same reason. I am finding that I am not much agreeing with their choices. I have several other of their selections on the shelf that I'll be getting to soon. It will be interesting to see if I ever wholeheartedly agree with them.]*

GARY CASEY

garycasey1701@gmail.com

Enterprise, Alabama

As promised here's the note about that half-baked idea I traded e-mails with you about. I wish this had occurred to me sooner, I would have loved to see it chewed over in the letters. Maybe it's for the best, like as not instead of this idea being chewed over, I'd just be chewed up.

I was reading John Brunner's *Interstellar Empire* a couple of months ago. About half way into it I quit. It's an okay read but once this *something* popped into my head it sort of ruined the story for me. The story is set in our galaxy. Thousands of years ago, humanity discovered the remains of a previous galactic empire in the form of thousands of ships complete with FTL drives scattered about space. We learned how to operate them but not to duplicate the technology. We quickly set about using them to establish our own empire. Now, thousands of years later, those ships are breaking down and we have no idea how to fix them. Naturally, the empire is starting to fall apart. But we are given hope that things may work out. There are rumors of a group of humans on the far edge of the galaxy that have learned to make their own star ships, just waiting for the chance to build their own empire after the current one has completely fallen. That, more or less, was what was holding my attention in the book. Just another case of the background being more interesting than the story itself.

All of it got me to thinking about the life span of galactic empires. Just how long could you expect one to really last? And is it reasonable to expect a new empire to rise from the ashes of the old?

Suppose we come up with a way to get around the light speed limit that we can actually make work and manage to build a bunch of FTL capable star ships. None too soon either. We need a new planet.

Even a small initial population can strip a planet of its resources in just a few hundred years. Look what we've done since the industrial revolution. Given how fast humans reproduce, if we started now with the current population of earth (so says an essay I found by Asimov) we can completely fill the galaxy in just a seven thousand years if each family has 2.3 kids. My bet is a few hundred years after that we will have picked it clean of resources and would revert back to the stone age if not die out completely. John Brunner's idea of a 10,000 year old galactic empire dying out to be replaced by a new one in short order is bunk. Same for Asimov's *Foundation* series. Any galactic empire that old would have left the galaxy a dead husk picked clean of every resource a technological civilization would need to have any technology beyond sticks and stones. I don't think even replicator technology like in *Star Trek* would help much...eventually the only thing left to feed into the system would be dead human bodies. That's right folks, *Soylent Green* IS made from humans...

It's an old idea. Any population will expand beyond its resources and die back. Put technology into the mix and said population will lose that technology, never to regain it due to lack of resources.

Then again, another old idea is that stuff you find on the periodic tale is made in the heart of stars and spread around when they go *nova*. So the good news is maybe another galactic civilization could arise; it'd just take a few billion years for enough stars to *nova* to restock the galaxy with the necessary resources. But 10K years? Forget it.

In any event, not new ideas, just viewed through a slightly dark lens.

Mr. Kitty Paws says to tell you 'Hi'

CY CHAUVIN

peterpumpkincat@juno.com

Roseville, Michigan

I missed an editorial from you, with a photo of Rusty licking envelopes and A.C. sitting back in her chair, thinking perhaps, "Gosh, I got those boys out of my hair at last!" But I enjoyed her "Going to the Pictures Final Showdown." It made me want to go (and I haven't in years). When I went regularly rather than for a specific picture, there was a bulk foods shop across the mall from the movie theatre, and I and my friend Pauline would select treats to smuggle into the theatre. The best of the movies we saw was *Shakespeare in Love*. (I tried to watch it recently and couldn't.)

Bruce Gillespie's "Her Fames Rises Up Forever" made me re-read "Her Smoke Rose Up Forever", and I realized what a clever title Bruce devised. The original Tiptree story is about someone whose most intense moments in life are captured, and replayed or relived again and again forever – just like Tiptree's own stories. I also thought immediately of "The Last Flight of Dr. Ain" at the start of the pandemic. Bruce's article is a very interesting ramble about Tiptree/Alice Sheldon and Jeff Smith. Strangely, I don't remember what I thought of the 'Great Reveal': instead I remember being very surprised when Jeff Smith said that Tiptree was in his late fifties, since the stories all seemed to be about much younger people, and written in a fresh, 'young' way. I couldn't imagine an old person in their fifties writing those stories. (Now, of course, I'm of a different mind.) Part of the interest in the Tiptree fiction is the disguise, that Alice Sheldon fooled so many people for so long. So perhaps we do have to judge her for herself, and not just for her fiction? (It's not an idea I'm enthusiastic about.)

I'm appalled by Gary Casey and his sly maneuvers to con the SF Book Club out of free books! In my underhanded moments, I just contented myself with re-using a postage stamps that weren't cancelled. But he joined the SF Book Club long before I knew of its existence. Instead, I recall my mother showing an atlas I had bought through a book club ("what he bought with his lawn cutting money") to my uncle, and I felt hopelessly embarrassed by this example of my bookishness.

Gregory Benford's heartfelt comments on Roger Zelanzy were unexpected and eloquent. Unexpected because we don't realize all the connections between authors in sf, and maybe too because their fiction was so different (the same was true with his connection with Brian Aldiss). I wonder how many of the new writers in science fiction have these connections?

When I saw "The Hubbard Problem" in The Mail section, I immediately thought, 'What has Gary Hubbard done now?" But Gary's problem is later in the Letters of Comment section, where he writes that James Blish ("of course") was a Christian. But that is not true. Blish was an agnostic (meaning he didn't know whether God exists or not; as opposed to an atheist, who is sure there is no God), but "profoundly sympathetic" to believers. Gary shouldn't take this misunderstanding to heart, since Blish's fiction has mislead other people. Perhaps like the careful attention to science in his science fiction, the detailed religious background and themes are more than usually convincing too.

My favorite part of Joe Pearson's three months of danger in Ukraine were the details of everyday life: Lisa having to search for food, the odd shortages, eccentric people. I'm surprised that he didn't have a harder time communicating. It still seems bizarre to spend three months in a far country to produce a nine minute animated short set in outer space! I'm astounded too at the revelation of how films are pitched.

Jeanne Bowman's tale of cracking trees was ominous: climate change, both drought and high winds, stalks the plains of Northern California. As trees in a woods die, their inter-connecting root systems die, and it becomes easier for individual trees to topple. They seemed to be getting closer and closer to Jeanne as her story progressed, like a haunting, only it was trees cracking. Crack, crack, crack, she wrote. Did she knock on wood? Do they have something against her? Or does she have some latent, negative sort of superpower that's only now being exposed – like the idea in physics that the observer affects the

outcome of every experiment? (Don't look at me Jeanne!!)*[Okay, can't resist: If a tree falls in the woods and there is no one to hear it does it still make a noise?]*

I think you may be on to something when you write in your review of M. John Harrison that "When a writer becomes a mixologist of the concrete and conceptual metaphor...the reader begins to falter, willing suspension of disbelief disengaging." The old pulp writer would hurry the plot along, bring in the guy with a gun, before you could start to think, and your belief system unravel. Most current sf I find difficult to read because it lacks convincing prose and characters, and substitutes the appeal of the strange for both. I did enjoy what I read of Harrison's *The Centuri Device*, with its hippie space jockeys and resplendent prose, but I set it down at one point and never felt compelled to pick it back up. I think I would hesitate to insist that "in real life that doesn't happen" (i.e. Characters/people that don't change) and then note that the same book has characters become the personality of a K-ship and dunked into tanks of viscous nutrients. 'Real', what? E.M. Forster wrote that plots were often distracting but a necessary part of a novel.

[What I meant about people not changing in life as opposed to a reader's expectations in fiction is that it is never that obvious in real life—of course we change, just not "transformed", as much as we would like to be. And: I would heartily agree with E.M. Forster when I'm getting sick and tired of genre fiction. It would have been interesting if Harrison had taken all the wild and wooly sf plot elements out of Light *and set it as a bizarre triangle in his beloved Peak District— but then we might have ended up with* The Course of the Heart! *]*

Michael Gorra mentioned in his letter that thanks to the way James Blish used Oswald Spengler ideas in *Cities in Flight*, he did not feel he would have to read Spengler. Well, during the past year, I actually was inspired to try Spengler, and so borrowed *The Decline of the West* from the library. I could not read very far in it; it read more like a work of philosophy or religion, rather than any book of history I've encountered. My favorite bit from what little I read was: "*....for whom is there History? ...history is for everyone to this extent, that everyone with his own ex-*

istence and consciousness, is a Part of history. But it makes a great difference whether anyone lives under the constant impression that his life is an element in a far wider life course that goes on for hundreds and thousands of years, or conceives of himself as something rounded off and self-contained. For the latter...there is no world history..."

--Oswald Spengler

Maybe it's lucky James Blish read it for us!

Cheryl Cline and Stephen Bryan Bieler give lots of interesting titles for possible reading later on. And the cover is a real beauty, with its aura of Frank R. Paul and steampunk modernity. I'm a sucker for that type of color blending technique used, too. In all, another fine issue. Red Boggs' photo doesn't match at all the mental image I had of him!

RICHARD DENGROVE

richd22426@aol..com

Alexandria, Virginia

Once again, William, you've done it with *Portable Storage*. Is it the longest fanzine now? Or are there ones longer? It certainly has delved into fannish themes. Over all, it is one of the most superlative fanzines around.

I understand that your zine concerns science fiction. However, you had an article by Cheryl Cline on Westerns. Or should I say anti-Westerns? She did not give her opinion much. However, she did discuss a number of novels and other media she considered anti-Western. In one way or another, they criticized Westerns as spreading untruths about the Old West. Of course, by the same token, most popular fiction, movies, etc. are untrue. Certainly, action adventure rarely follows the truth. The one exception is military pulps. Written for military men, authors have to know their guns or forget it.

There is a good reason why it is a fannish issue and found in your zine. Our part of fandom is old. We remember when the Western was everywhere. I remember when half the movies you saw were Westerns. Also, half the TV shows. When you went into a pharmacy, it was easy to find Western novels and Western pulp magazines. By contrast, there is no question that Westerns are a shadow of their former selves.

What are the grievances of the anti-Western? Cheryl presents anti-Westerns that fault the old Westerns for being prejudiced against Native Americans. How a lot of cowboys hated them, killed them, took away their land, and made them live on reservations. In addition, Westerns were prejudiced against other races. Cheryl presents one which faulted Westerns for being anti-Chinese.

Was this a reason for the fall of the Western? There was a lot of what we currently regard as racism in all genres in the '50s and '60s. Also, there were Westerns where cowboys and Native Americans worked together. That was not as much the case with Chinese. However, I remember Paladin in the "Have Gun Will Travel" series helping out a Chinese law man in San Francisco who was facing terrible odds.

Also, Cheryl presents anti-Westerns that fault the cowboy for being too violent. For shooting people at the drop of a hat. Maybe a hat did not need to be dropped. Is that why they carried their six guns everywhere? To prove this, lots of blood is spilled in some anti-Westerns. In addition, a lot of gore. In one TV movie I remember from when the Western was at its height, someone killing people for the hell of it – and I think he was the hero. On the other hand, there is a lot of violence and gore in all action adventure novels, movies and television. Particularly cop shows.

I think the reason Westerns are in the awful state they are in, whether movies, novels, etc. is this: the public decided that they preferred cop shows, cop novels, etc. There is a passage from a song about cowboys "Back in the Saddle Again," which went "You stay up all night and the only law is right." I think that that is what ruined the Western. People were more into law and order in the '70s and '80s. The lawlessness of the 19th Century no longer appealed to them. There was an increase in crime and they wanted it stopped. Apparently, even in their wish-dreams. I guess that's what I wanted to say.

Before I go, I would like to tell Cheryl this. I remember seeing "Lonesome Dove"; and I really liked it. Even when a Texas Ranger summarily executes some killers. Of course, out in the middle of nowhere where a trial and other niceties would not be possible. Also, I liked it when the Native Americans were going to attack the settlers. I found it weird, though, that a white man was their chief. In short, I can't follow the straight and narrow all the time.

[Be sure to check out Cheryl's final installment

on Westerns this issue. Take note of the section on novels vs. films.]

BRAD FOSTER

jabberwocky2000@hotmail.com

Irving, Texas

It's a new year, and sorting and clearing all the random stacks on the desk and drawing board because, damnit, I *am* going to do better this year, and what do I find... *Portable Storage Eight* from wwaaayyy back in October of 2022. Yep, time once again for the usual "sorry it took so long to respond to your sending me your amazing zine for absolutely free, but I am a scum" loc, that all fandom editors look forward to so much from me!

First, of course, super-cool wrap around cover from the team of Sung Woo Hong & Joe Pearson. Love the retro-future look. Maybe someday the project it was done for will find backers, and we can see more.

Kudos on the *New Yorker* design work. Nicely done.

Reading through all the wonderful articles in here, I get to the end of each and realize that I had nothing to add. Often, I am blown away by the amount of research and history that each author has put into each piece. At the analysis and gathering of thoughts on the subject being far beyond what I could do, or feel worthy of commenting on. Article after article, no notes to put into a pithy loc, just more amazement at all this great writing, this wonderful *thinking* about things.

And then it hit me, this is just what Cindy and I have been talking about for years in regards to the friends and acquaintances we have made in our various fandoms. We will never be bothered by having inflated egos, as we are surrounded by friends who are truly mega-levels smarter than we are. Who, amazingly enough, are still our friends and will even talk with us, and not just pat us on the head and tell us "That's nice" when we mumble something. I am so happy to have fallen into this group of people, so much smarter and cleverer than me, but still willing to share all of that with me.

Thanks for doing the work of gathering together this latest fat issue of engrossing reading and spreading it out to the world. It is appreciated, even if words fail in proper response.

And should you do another one this year, I swear that I will not take months to respond. (I also acknowledge the odds are that I will, once again, take that long, but one can always hope that one will do better in the future.)

FRANK VACANTI

frankvacanti@att.net

San Rafael, California

Wm.
Wanted to let you know how much I enjoy your publication.
Reading cover to cover I certainly get interesting tidbits which leads to more research... For instance, I'm now looking for computer music on vinyl!
I'm also starting a list of future reading material from reviews and recommendations.
So it's doing its job very well.
Cheers!
Frankie Vee

THERESE VANZO

Morgantown, West Virginia

I loved Kurt Erichsen's DIVA cartoon! I laugh every time I look at it!

JERRY KAUFMAN

jakaufman@aol.com

Seattle, Washington

Corflu Pangloss is mostly receding, except for mailing out membership materials to supporting members and those poor souls who had attending memberships but couldn't come after all. I've been there a few times myself. My memories will stick around a while longer. This means I have found the time to write to you, and maybe I'll think of a Corflu anecdote or two I can include, when relevant.

I'm glad to see how you carried the *New Yorker* theme all the way through. I was even able to read the smaller type you used (I think it was smaller). Your word count must have been astronomical. Sung Woo Hong and Joe Pearson's cover art is fantastic in at least two senses of the word, but I'm a bit wistful that it wasn't either of Eustace Tilley or a futuristic New York to keep with the theme!

In response to Bruce Gillespie's article about James Tiptree Jr/Alice Sheldon, I want to mention that I predicted the Big Reveal, though in jest. Suzle and I ran a series of fillers in an issue of *The Spanish Inquisition* I called "The Year That Flushing Won the Worldcon." Stu Shiffman had started a Hoax

WorldCon bid for Flushing, New York for 1980, so I was imagining a series of events that would take place. The revelation that Tiptree was a woman would take place, I thought, at the newest iteration of Susan Wood's "Women in SF" Panel. It was all tongue in cheek - until it wasn't.

Dale Nelson's piece on Samuel Palmer is a highlight of the issue; I know a little about some of the writers and other artists that Dale mentions, but nothing about Palmer. Thanks for the introduction and context.

Andy Hooper on Redd Boggs is also a standout. "The Bear and the Child" makes the point that Andy is aiming to put across; Boggs was an excellent writer. I'm glad that a lot of his zines are available at FANAC.org, making it much more likely that I will read more of Boggs's work.

Suzle always worries that the large pine in our front yard will fall in heavy wind, but the old oaks that line the street next to our property keep losing limbs and are more likely to topple over. We'll hear the "crack!" that Jeanne Bowman describes; then either the street will be blocked or the creek in the ravine will backup and flood our neighbors' house, as their place is thirty feet lower than ours.

I'm glad to see works from your old and new contributors like Alva Svoboda, Joe Pearson, Steve Bieler, Kurt Erichson, Cheryl Cline, et al. Lots of eye-pleasing spot illoes, which were also sometimes laugh-inducing.

What can I say about the letters? Possibly a lot, but I made the mistake of not marking the comment hooks. Still, it's a fine collection of writers.

I look forward to the next and final issue. Will it be safe to bind the set? *[With a fanzine you can never tell!]*

KEVIN COOK

vkcook@aol.com

Summerville, South Carolina

It is difficult to comment on *Portable Storage Eight* because you assembled a group of finely written articles, but none of them really set off any great emotion in me; better yet no alarm bells ringing either. After eight issues, though, I would have to conclude that Cheryl Cline is your best writer. What you

described as her sense of mischievous is probably the reason that I enjoy reading everything she writes, "Burrs Under the Saddle" being no exception.

A couple of other book comments are warranted. Unlike Steven Bryan Bieler I did find Thomas Wolfe's *Look Homeward Angel* to be transformative when I read it at age 21. Despite some beautiful passages, I will agree on the whole with his description of *Of Time and the River* as impenetrable. Regarding Arthur Machen, I really did not care for much of his fiction written after 1900. Now having stated that opinion, I must also state that I consider his autobiographical books, *Far Off Things* and *Things Near and Far*, to be the finest books of their type, only rivaled by Derek Raymond's *The Hidden Files*. The Brits seem to be more successful with author autobiographies than their American counterparts.

What resonated the most with me was the Letters of Comment and the whole sense of generational community that permeated the letters. Yes, we read the same science fiction and fantasy books and magazines, although with sometimes wildly different reactions, and we read and contributed to a variety of fanzines with different levels of commitment, but a larger umbrella still contains us all.

I recently had an interesting experience. We had to fly back to New York to attend a funeral in late September. It was the first time I had been back in the town where I grew up in several years, and as I drove through I passed the library where all my reading interests began, but alas the stores where I bought books and comics off the spinner racks are all long gone. It occurred to me that there were so many important personal moments in that town: what made me one day wander over to the section of the library labeled science fiction, what made me notice and purchase a copy of *Amazing Stories* from a luncheonette/candy store, what made me write away the first time for a copy of a fanzine? It certainly was not a Baby Boomer thing to do all three. I had friends who read science fiction, friends who read comic books, but that was the end of it for them. The group that Jim Jones described in his letter is gathered in the pages of *Portable Storage* as Jim acknowledged, Well done again, William.

GARY HUBBARD

n0rmalbeanster@gmail.com

Kalamazoo, Michigan

I found Bruce Gillespie's article on the woman

173

who wrote as James Tiptree, Jr. interesting in a number of ways. Like him, I didn't much like her stories initially, but I'm flexible and willing to give her more consideration. Actually, it seems to me she was coming into prominence at the same time as I was losing interest in SF. There was one story, though, that I'm reminded of that I'm not even sure she wrote or what the title was, but which my faulty memory associates with her name. It tells of a group of people stranded on an alien planet that's slowly killing them. It has plenty of air and water and the other necessities for them to live like Space Family Robinson, but there's something in the environment that's killing them. The usual trope in stories like this is that they will come together and prevail over the environment, like in one of my favorite Heinlein stories, *Tunnel in the Sky*. But in this one they don't and each succumbs one after the other. I'm generally not a fan of downbeat endings, but it was refreshing how this story turned the survival trope on its head. Besides, we live in a pessimistic age.

[Hmn. I've certainly not read everything Tiptree has written, but the basic plot you describe here sounds like Joanna Russ' We Who About To, *but that's a novel, not a short story, and it's the lone female character that is killing the male characters off, one by one, not the hostile planet they are stranded upon.]*

That passage from "The Last Flight of Dr. Ain" about how the Sahara was created by human activity struck me to the point to which I underlined the whole thing. Until now I'd assumed that the Desert had always existed, at least for millions of years (maybe it was underwater in the Cambrian), not caused by people and pigs. That seems like quite an accomplishment in a negative sort of way. But about the same time I saw a documentary on Curiosity Stream about how flourishing early civilizations were dicked away environmental changes Beyond Their Control, thus shifting the blame from people to Nature. In this case, the desertification of the Sahara forced nomadic pastoralists to settle along the banks of the Nile and found the Egyptian civilization. The theme of the series seems to be that environmental factors both created these ancient cultures and destroyed them. I wouldn't say the show goes as far as denying the role of human activity in the downfall as much as it just ignores it. If I hadn't been reading Bruce Gillespie's article, I wouldn't even have noticed the contrast.

Cheryl Cline's treatment of western literature was pretty interesting. I used to work in the Cataloging Dept of Western Michigan University's library and, as such, a lot of books came across my desk and one of these was *Blood Meridian* by Cormac McCarthy (and, I recall, *No Country for Old Men* was in the theaters at the time also). Cheryl says that: "something awful happens to the Kid at the end of the novel, but we're not sure what" but he dies in an outhouse, leaving an awful mess, which I'm pretty sure the Judge is responsible for. What puzzled me about the book was the epilogue, where we see a scene of a man walking along in the desert, periodically driving a spike in the soil, which creates sparks every time he hits it with a hammer. I have no idea what that's got to do with the rest of the story. Was it a metaphor? Metaphor is a game played by authors and critics, but as a reader I don't pay them much attention.

D. STEVEN BLACK

dstevenblack@gmail.com
Berkeley, California

Bravo Joe Pearson for—in the pages of *Portable Storage*—blazing a vivid picture of his fannish creativity guiding him into a life apparently very well lived, if not always the easiest or most remunerative. With Ukraine, he happened to be in the right place at the right time...for a brief moment, at least.

We met during Symposium '76, the day all the cool kids from Detroit and Brooklyn trooped to the Toronto Islands while I landed the afternoon at Mike Glicksohn's house. I must have impressed Joe too, for I received later by post a packet of his illos and a letter describing his itinerant life which I hope will eventually turn up in my correspondence archive.

Such wonderful memorials for recently departed eminences Robert Lichtman and Billy Ray Wolfenbarger. And what a service to read about Redd Boggs along with one of his resurrected essays.

So much to value here in this issue from old friends and new. I can see I'll have more pleasurable reading to come before putting these covers to bed.

DAVID M. SHEA

Ellicott City, Maryland

The cover immediately jumped out and grabbed my attention: and Joe Pearson's explanation of it also. Though not much alike in detail, it reminds me of a print I have, "walled City" by Paul Johnson, 1979, which I bought because it suggested to me a story (which I never wrote).

I was not familiar with the Robert Graves book described in Darrell Schweitzer's previous article. However, Cy Chauvin mentioned a detail: there was a mark people could put on their face "when they wanted to be invisible". There's a real SF idea!

Dale Nelson shows not only the skill of a detailed researcher, but a real empathy with a group of pastoral artists. A good footnote to art history, and neatly tied into SF by way of "sense of wonder".

Kurt Erichsen: I was Paul Simon and Art Garfunkel on their first major American tour. No electronics; Paul played his guitar, and they sang. Spellbinding. The playlist was mostly from *Wednesday Morning 3:00 AM* and *Sounds of Silence* albums. They also did a few other songs including "red Rubber Ball. Paul admitted he pretty much gave away the rights to the lyrics because he felt they were beneath his usual standards. I have to admit I thought of Herman's Hermits as a novelty act, not real musicians. As compared to, say, Chad and Jeremy.

[Sure, Herman's Hermits had some novelty songs but they were also a seriously good pop band. As one example, go back and listen to "No Milk Today". This song is as fully lush and beautifully produced as anything by the Hollies.]

Jon Sommer wants to discuss freethought from an isolated ivory tower perspective. Some of us have to get down in the mud and challenge religious intrusion into public law and policy where it happens.

Lynn Kuehl saus he gets customers looking for YA fantasy. Perhaps he should consider Diane Duane"s "Wizard" series that started with *So You Want To Be A Wizard*. At the 1983 Worldcon one of my staffers said she had come to the con mostly hoping to meet Diane, her favorite writer. I happened to run into Diane; she had some time, so I took her over to meet my staffer, who was delighted. We all do what we can.

Westerns, not so much my thing. In Fredric Brown's *Martians Go Home*, the central character Luke is writing a Western novel—

while he's a patient in a mental hospital. And in Nancy Springer's *The Hex Witch of Seldom*, Bobbi calls out to her black horse by name: "Shane". And he jolts to a stop, amazed that she see him for who he really is: the archetypal Dark Hero, Shane, Zorro, Paladin, Han Solo. . .

I did not exactly say that *A Canticle For Liebowitz*, by Walter M. Miller, Jr. is not SF. I do believe it's a book overpraised beyond its merits. It's an archetype: the one book about religion-in-SF that most people who have read SF (a diminishing minority in fandom) are aware of, whether or not they have actually read it. I did say *The Sparrow* by Mary Doria Russell is not SF for much the same reasons that *The Handmaid's Tale* by Margaret Atwood is not SF, and I stand by that. To Quote Cheryl Cline, "Literary fiction is. . .a genre. It has its own set of tropes, one of which is to make use of popular genre, like Westerns, Mysteries, or Science Fiction, to create a literary work." To which I might add: exactly my point!

JAY KINNEY

jmkinney@sonic.net

San Francisco, California

As stuck as I am in my GAFIA, I am grateful that you still send each issue of *PS* to me. I invariably find something of value in every issue, and the mix of contributors is just enough outside of the usual fanzine crew that it tickles my nervous system. Your Faan Awards the last two years are well deserved.

I loved the *New Yorker* design pastiche in this issue, and feel like you are (finally) getting a handle on the POD challenges of publication layout. While I am not a big fan of the quasi-professional POD publishing model — I mourn the decline of mimeographed fanzines, big time — I figure that you and Michael Dobson are exploring that platform about as good as it can get.

Part of my tilt towards GAFIA has been driven by the meagre egoboo produced by my admittedly sporadic offerings of writing and art over recent years in fandom. Granted, most of it has not been particularly fannish, and such topics as living in the same SF neighborhood for 40+ years or a book review of an analysis of Ataturk's influence on German far right Fuhrer-worship (in *Banana Wings*) are not bound to create excitement with fandom's reliable letter-hacks. Still, I found it rewarding — in a decidedly non-fannish way — that my piece on living on 16th St. for 40+ years in *PS*, several issues back, could earn me $600+

from a pro magazine, to which I offered it.

[I am glad that you were eventually able to place your piece on living 40 years in one place in the Mish in that paying market. However: that piece might have never been written if I had not commissioned it. It was an excellent piece and deserved that payment. I agree there is a dearth of egoboo and/or discussion administered by my mailing list. But at the same time I understand. The caliber of writing for this fanzine has been extraordinary, and I am very grateful. Being disgruntled is also understandable after sweating bullets over a major piece. I have been very lucky. I too, love the "homey" feel of old school fanzines. But print on demand just seemed like a no-brainer, regards costs. Just ask Andy Hooper or Nic Farey about local printshop expenses. Yikes. Thank you for the loc.]

Ten years from now, when we are all possibly dead or demented, I'm not sure who will still be around to ponder such things, but in the meantime, I appreciate *Portable Storage* and look forward to each issue.

CASEY JUNE WOLF

caseyjwolf@yahoo.com

Vancouver, British Columbia

I'm going to give a last hurrah to the LOC business around *Portable Storage*. It's weird to think that this lovely zine I have enjoyed so much will be no more. I have it in my mind that you must have come in with a plan, accomplished that plan, and put an end to it. That wasn't my original perception, but the last few issues seem that way to me. Or maybe it's just knowing that if this is the end that solidifies that thought.

I want to just generally say what a gratifying bunch of zines they've been. I've enjoyed the mix of writing, the mix of topics, the mix of voices, particularly in the later ones, where there are more women showing up, either writing or being written about. Oh, and the art. You have so much wonderful art in these PS. I enjoy the fannish humor I that shows up in many of the drawings. And your covers —also delightful. Speaking of images, I have really appreciated your enjoyment of photographs I have taken. I am thinking of the photos of that old lamp – I can't remember what they're called. It's a utility lamp of elder days, just a little aluminum cage and a light bulb on the end of a long cord, and you could hang it by the hook wherever you needed it while working. I set that lamp up for some seeds I was trying to encourage to sprout and then became taken with

the lamp itself and took some photos of it. I remember you also liked the photos of my dresses hanging in the graffiti laden room I was sleeping in at my brother's. You liked the photograph I took of my eyeglasses sitting on the cover of a PS zine. And you like the photograph of the pencil. When I take pictures like this, I truly enjoy the process but I don't expect anyone else to like the results, so it's been fun to send them to someone who has a taste for this sort of thing.

Actually, I think I'm going to go have something to eat before I carry-on with this conversation. This one-way conversation. And the sky is purple, just faintly purple, as the sun sinks slowly in the west, and I am looking east at the residue of its withdrawal. The other night it was a gorgeous, intense mauve. Tonight it looks like the edges of a watercolor.

[No, there was never any plan. This fanzine grew and evolved, over a series of intuitive leaps, each issue feeding the next. I have been a fan of photography since I was thirteen, when I first picked up an old Kodak Instamatic 110 camera. Your photos are— beautifully structured, evocative, moving.]

I read *PS Eight* more quickly than I normally do because this was the end and I wanted to do you the decency of a LOC before that final pulling up of the drawbridge. I'm just going to say random things and I won't be thorough.

I like that you put the contributors page up at the front this time. It makes it a forethought rather than an afterthought and of course, without these people there wouldn't be a zine.

I have a scribble here on page 8 —what does it say? Ulrika O'Brien says that she is hesitant to use the word misogyny because it's overused. I don't believe the word is overused, really. If misogyny wasn't everywhere you turned, the word wouldn't get used. And using it, actually identifying the quality of the thing instead of talking around it, is a really important act. So even if it is sometimes used in error, I wouldn't want us to be gun-shy of using it. Because Ulrika's name didn't come until the end of this piece, until she mentioned that she was a woman I thought it was William talking. Very strange sensation to suddenly find it was someone else, and a woman to boot. I wonder if I would've reacted the same way, if I had known that from the start. All in all, I enjoyed this article very much.

I'm sorry to hear of the demise of the last second-run theatre in Tucson. The pandemic did kill off many lovely businesses that were just hanging on as it was. It sounds like AC Kolthoff and you, William, had some great times there. I'm glad you did.

I love the piece on James Tiptree Jr. by Bruce Gillespie, and I was pleased to see something by him outside of his own zines, which, for the last, how long is it been since 1985? Well, since then, they have been pretty much the only fanzines that I have read. I've been struck by Tiptree's work since I first read it back in the olden days. And by chance I did read most of the biography that he refers to in his piece. Unlike Bruce, I am of two minds about this biography, and I suppose that I have conflicting desires when it comes to biographies in general. On the one hand, I want to know the truth about a person, and on the other hand, I think we all deserve some privacy. I can't remember the details now, but I remember feeling uncomfortable with this book, that the author went too far sometimes, either in her speculations or her reportages. But honestly, it's too vague to be sure.

I suppose I am in the minority in thinking that it's a pity that they took her name off of the award. She just seemed to me to be a person of integrity, which makes it hard for me to believe that she murdered her husband, rather than killing him in an agreed upon way. I could be very wrong about that, so I'm not putting any emphasis on that belief of mine, just explaining why I am sorry that her name has become mud. What I am more disturbed by than anything the biographer did is the decision that fellow made to let the world know that he, Tiptree, was a she. I don't really care what his reasons were or how difficult a decision it was for him to make. It wasn't his f*cking decision. I think a more responsible thing to do would have been to let her know that he knew and whatever fears he had about it coming to light and allow her to make a decision about how to handle it.

[I agree with you about the Tiptree Awards. I have absolutely no doubt in my mind that Tiptree did the right thing by her husband,

something that he had requested; a contract that they had agreed to. Jeff Smith did discuss the "reveal" with Tiptree and she said (para-quote) "It will be a relief, actually."]

I very much enjoyed Phil Paine's letter about Gord Downie. I am also a Canadian, and was touched by Downie's struggles and his decisions about how to use the rest of his life. This is an excellent tribute.

Dale Nelson has become a favorite contributor and the "Fields of the Extollagers" did not disappoint. Lovely to have the paintings to refer to, as well.

A favorite cartoon, also, which gives me a moment of amusement every time I look at it, is Teddy Harvia's "Scram kid. I wasn't cut out to be a mom." I love it!

Having Alva's piece right after Dale's, I thought, was a nice segue.

Jeanne Bowman's "Crack: When Trees Fall" is beautifully done. We read about these things in the abstract all the time, but having her itemize the process of losing known and beloved trees makes it all hit home. Very sad and very concerning.

I wonder if Steven Bryan Bieler would enjoy Margaret Atwood's *Blind Assassin*, in which we read the fantasy novel that is being written within the novel that we are reading, if you follow me. I can't say I am an enormous fan of Margaret Atwood generally, although I'm not an anti-fan, either, but I really did like that book. And tell Steve that he had bloody will better tell us how Avram Davidson changed his life. Or we may be coming after him...

I appreciated Bob Silverberg's speculation on what Stanley Weinbaum might have accomplished if he had lived longer. How different the world might have been!

Steve Jeffery mentions that he has a fondness for "books about other people's collections and their reading adventures," and I wanted to recommend librarything.com. I've been using librarything.com for much longer than I have goodreads.com, and I like it a lot more. Goodreads.com is great if you want to socialize around books, because the emphasis does seem to be on social connections more than on the books themselves. But librarything.com doesn't go in a whole lot for —actually, no. I just haven't explored the social side of librarything.com because that's not what I want it for. And you do have to look for it, with whereas in Goodreads.com, you can't avoid it, because it takes up most of your homepage. But I want it for keeping track of my books and seeing what other people are reading similar books, and so on. They have a number of listings of famous people's libraries. It can be interesting to see what books people who impacted us through their writing were once reading, books, by the very fact that they have kept them, which may have impacted them, in turn.

[One of the highlights of our trip to the National Mall in Washington, DC was getting to see Thomas Jefferson's library, which they kept intact—behind glass, of course!— and watching the crowd become engrossed and having aha! moments as they scanned titles.]

Kevin Cook remarks that he loves articles like Dale's because "the books we buy demonstrate the person we become as we mature and our tastes change." When Andre Norton died, I got out of the library *Cat's-eye* (the very edition I first read), which was the first book that I had read by her and one of the first SF novels I read. I was surprised to find that I liked it a lot still, although I was better able to see the flaws in the structure and so on. But it was fascinating how many different themes she brought up in that one little book that continue to be important themes in my life as an adult. So it isn't surprising that I liked it so much then and that it became one of the doors into speculative fiction, and eventually fandom, for me.

Is it the fannish thing to do to comment on your own letter? Well, I was very surprised to learn that I was one of the few people who enjoyed the staples in the previous zine. How could anyone not? Also, as you can tell by my perhaps new and improved comment making, I did take notes this time. I broke down and scribbled on the page in pencil, so I can erase them later if I want to. I want to mention a fantasy novel I read, actually a duology, that I thought was very interesting. They were big complex, beautifully realized books, to my way of thinking. They are NK Jemisin's *The Killing Moon* and *The Shadowed Sun*. I will certainly be reading more books by her.

[Funny you should mention that. I've been reading Jemisin's "Broken Earth Trilogy"; I have just finished the final volume, The Broken Sky. *She is a very unique writer. In a letter of comment to another fanzine Steve Jeffrey had commented that he'd never read anything like these books before, and I would have to concur. They are oddly written, with uses of both informal and formal writing, slang, and a second person narrative, mixed with complex and unusual ideas and structures, yet it is all very easy, even compulsive, reading. Just prior to his death Justin Busch sent me down the rabbit hole of 21st century sf/f writers, for which I will be forever grateful, as I have found all these authors very enjoyable:* **Arkady Martine, Ekaterina Sedia, Becky Chambers, Ailette du Bodard, N.K. Jemisin, Nnedi Okorafor, Sarah Gailey, and Theodora Goss.** *I don't think you can go wrong with any of these writers.]*

So now, a few words on *PS Seven*, which I haven't completely finished. I am not going to take as long with this because I'm quite tired and I need to stop. But I just want to give a brief nod to another good issue. I very much enjoyed your essay about your mother and Daphne du Maurier. As this one does, many of these pieces that I haven't even mentioned make me think about my own life and similar experiences — or wildly different experiences — in the same realm. I think that's one of the strengths of fan writing, because the writers touch on our own world, but they aren't the same worlds, exactly, and so they allow for both a sense of connection, of somewhat belonging, as well as enough difference that it leads to self-reflection.

Christina Lake's, "Uncanny Sleepers" is a wonderful gathering together of works of fiction that I hadn't thought of in quite that way before. I have a an enthusiastic note that I have written at the end of the article, but I haven't a freaking clue what it says. I can read the word good so let's just accept that it was a positive note. Sorry about that, Christina!

You know, I think I'm going to have to stop. But I will just say once more how much I've enjoyed tripping through the thought processes of yourself, William, and all your contributors over the last couple of years. Many, many thanks to you for putting it all together and especially for sending me *Rose Motel*, which was such a surprising and lovely gesture, and all the subsequent zines you've put out. It's been fun.

We Also Heard From

Paul di Filippo
Susan Breiding
Donald Sidney-Fryer
Michael McClure
John Benson
Michael Bracken
Leigh Edmonds
Tony Cvetko
Gary Mattingly
F. Brett Cox
Alan White

To These Fine Folks, Everlasting Gratitude For Financial Support:
Justin Case
Celia Kanth
Bobby Goodspeed
Kennedy Gammage
John Benson
Cy Chauvin
Kevin Cook
Richard Johnson

Contact!
portablezine@gmail.com

The Gorgon of Poses
G. Sutton Breiding

This Ink of Agates, This Emporium of Ashes
Notes Towards The Final Pose
or Working On a Poem For Months, I
Finally Get It Nowhere

*

O earthworms! space stations! donuts and
snow!.....Golden dragons leap with joy from
my golden pages, figurines carved from this
clay of fallen light.....

Look! grails of tomato soup, wheelchairs and
jackhammers, narwhals and seizures, the purity
of a city at 2 a.m., rain pouring like sentences from
RIDDLEY WALKER, sandworms, turntablism, the
Baader-Meinhof Gang, precious erections, possum
guts painting the streets, caterwauls and prophecies
and dogs that follow me through the twilight of almost
not quite death or consciousness.....

inkstained and half mad in pursuit
scribbling away in these shattered voices
the folklore of daily life
beneath our sacred power lines
the light of other Sundays
drifting across the river
a heron calling
a train heaving
the strange forlornness
of a derelict billboard
rotting in the woods

nothing is as I thought
where I have been
what I have done
all these long years
incredulous to have witnessed Time
in the bright hard hollows of the night
I come from beyond the cell towers
and bring you no messages

but coffee and forever
lost among the virtual shadows
and pylons raising their arms
into the the psychic sparkle
of these horrific days
I eat my memories
nutritionless as ramen
in another world
where leaves rustle
suddenly then don't
and I am full
of perturbations

still hoping even now to hear
a luminous incantation

in everything, everywhere
all the time

like the glass tongues of the poets
that never stop
breaking
*

DONALD SIDNEY-FRYER was born in 1934 in New Bedford, Massachusetts. After serving in the Marine Corps he attended UCLA where he began pursuing his lifelong love affair with Clark Ashton Smith. He lived in San Francisco during one of its seminal butterfly stages, 1965-1975. He has had three dozen titles published, many by Arkham House and Hippocampus Press. He was once bard to Edmund Spenser. DSF currently lives in Marblehead, Massachusetts.

GREGORY BENFORD is a Fellow of the American Physical Society, winner of the Lord Prize in science, the Asimov Prize for fiction and the UN Medal in Literature. His fiction and nonfiction has won many awards; he has published 32 novels, four volumes of nonfiction, and over 200 short stories and several hundred scientific papers in several fields.

Did **CY CHAUVIN** get hooked on the first sf book he bought, *High Vacuum* by Charles Eric Maine (1957), at a school White Elephant sale when he was ten? Or was it the copy of E.R. Burroughs' *The Land That Time Forgot* that his father had locked away with his Tarzan and Bomba the Jungle Boy books in the basement? Cy remembers thinking when he joined the Scholastic Book club that he could now get all the science fiction in the world! But he was for sure hooked after reading *You Will Never Be The Same* by Cordwainer Smith, and found his first copy of *Amazing Stories* in the same drug store. Soon Ted White started the Clubhouse feature, and he was writing away for fanzines, which seemed somehow a very natural thing. Cy didn't meet any fans in person until three years later, when he went to a club meeting at Wayne State U. Luckily John Benson asked for a ride home, since Cy was too shy to talk much at the meeting.

DARRELL SCHWEITZER'S latest volume of "ponderings and pontifications," i.e. literary essays and reviews, was *The Threshold of Forever* (Wildside Press, 2017), which means he is almost due for another one. He has been writing for fanzines since the late 1960s and more or less professionally since the early 1970s. He has published four novels and about 350 stories. Recently PS Publishing (UK) did a two-volume retrospective of his short fiction. His long association with British publishing – he was a regular in *Interzone* in the David Pringle era and his major novel, *The Mask of the Sorcerer,* was first published by New English Library in 1995 – has enabled him to claim to be a "famous British writer," despite lack of a convincing accent. His reviews and criticism have appeared in everything from Richard E. Geis's famous *Science Fiction Review* (where he was a columnist for many years) to *The New York Review of Science Fiction* to *Publishers Weekly* and *The Washington Post.*

CASEY JUNE WOLF is a poet and writer of occasional, mostly speculative short stories which have appeared in a variety of magazines and anthologies from *OnSpec* to *Room*. Two of her stories, "Eating Our Young" and "The One Who Gets Away," will appear in the upcoming speculative anthology, *Food of My People*, edited by Ursula Pflug and Candas Jane Dorsey. The first of these will also be featured in *Exile Quarterly*. Casey lives in Vancouver, Canada. Find short essays and links to more of her writing at her blog "Another Fine Day in the Scriptorium." http://finedayscriptorium.blogspot.com

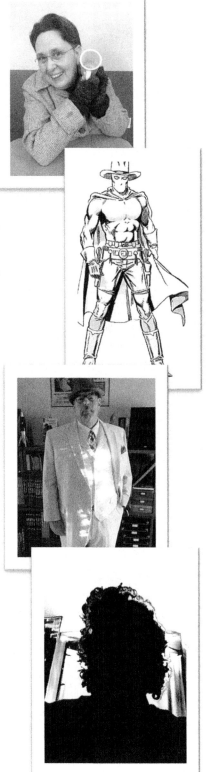

BOB JENNINGS was born in 1943, which makes him really old, but it means he also got to listen to a lot of great radio, see a lot of great serials and double feature B-movies, along with lots of classic TV while growing up that younger fans never experienced. Bob has been involved with stf fan2dom since the late 1950s, was one of the original founding members of comics fandom, founded and was the first OE of SFPA, helped develop Old Time Radio fandom, and published hundreds of fanzines in the process. He worked many years as a manager in mass market retailing, then many years as a salesman for Proctor & Gamble before starting a science fiction/comics/game retail store in 1979 that ran until 2000 when he closed the store and went all mail order, a business that continues to this day. Bob enjoy reading, listening, viewing, writing stuff, and vaporizing nosey flying saucers filled with obnoxious alien tourists with my cyclatrode. He and Dr. Doom are currently working to develop a similar device that will zap robo-callers and internet spammers.

RICH COAD has been in, or at least in close proximity to, fandom for about 45 years. Sadly his attempts to add sartorial splendor to the hobby have, at best, had mixed results. Over the years, Rich has produced a fannish fanzine, Space Junk, and a sercon fanzine, Sense of Wonder Stories, along with some lesser publications. He still enjoys reading science fiction and wishes that some of his favorite authors would achieve the sort of success that they deserve.

CHERYL CLINE is a science fiction fan and reader who lives in a house with filled with too many books. She's been married to fellow SF fan Lynn Kuehl for, like, forever, and he had too many books when she met him. Together they own a used bookshop, which only partly accounts for fact they have too many books.

JOHN FUGAZZI finessed the complex nuance of the segued mixtape in about 1976. He created worlds apart during his epic daytrips in Northern California searching for chocolate pie. His flat in San Francisco recently underwent the knife for an earthquake retrofit.

SANDRA BOND is a long time acti-fan, historian, and fan-publisher. Her novel *The Psychopath Club* was published by Canal Press in 2021.

Bon vivant and man-about-house **CARL JUAREZ** resides in the hithers of Seattle, where he enjoys gardening, making electronic music, and fishing in the latent space of all images. He currently tests Siri for Apple.

ANDY HOOPER attended the University of Wisconsin, where he studied anthropology, creative writing and theater. In 1986, his poem cycle on the *Challenger* disaster, *The 73 Seconds*, won a $500 senior thesis prize. To this day, this is the largest sum ever paid to a poet on the North American continent.

DALE NELSON is staff reviewer and columnist for *CSL: The Bulletin of the New York C. S. Lewis Society* and a frequent contributor to the Tolkien newsletter *Beyond Bree*. He often posts at Christopher Tompkins' *Darkly Bright* site, which features weekly reprints of Arthur Machen rarities. His work appeared in every issue of *Portable Storage*.

BRUCE GILLESPIE is an Australian SF reviewer, critic, and fanzine editor and publisher (SF Commentary since 1969, and other titles over the years), who for his trouble has been awarded quite a few Ditmar Awards, as well as Best Fan Writer (FAAN Awards 2009) and four lifetime achievement awards. He was Fan Guest of Honour at Aussiecon 3, the Worldcon held in Melbourne in 1999, and visited the West Coast of USA in 2004 (paid for by contributors to the Bring Bruce Bayside Fund.

JOE PEARSON is an animation producer, director, art director, writer and designer with a Hollywood and Pacific Rim career spanning over 30 years. He is the President of Epoch Ink Animation, an independent Los Angeles animation company that he founded in 1995. At Epoch Ink he was the show runner on two animated series and produced and directed on a number of shorts, pilots, specials, commercials and music videos including the animated music video "Do the Evolution" for Pearl Jam, earning him a Grammy nomination for Best Music Video that year. Joe was a co-producer on the anime film "Highlander: Search for Vengeance" for Imagi International in 2006. A few years later as a principal at Tripod Entertainment in Malaysia he served as the creator, director and co-producer/ writer of Tripod's animated feature film "War of the Worlds: Goliath". He was active in Fandom from 1970 to the mid-80's and credits his involvement with fanzines and conventions for nurturing his imagination and artistic chops. He lives in Long Beach with his wife, Lisa and two cats and is ramping up for one last entertainment hurrah with his partners in their new Entertainment Group— "Meta Cru". www.epochinkanimation.com

GARY HUBBARD is currently a retired librarian, but used to sell games in a hobby shop. He still cherishes a wide-ranging knowledge of the gaming world despite never having actually played any of the games. He spent the Sixties in the Army and it was not a happy experience. He didn't like the Army and the Army didn't like him. He wrote his first "Cracked Eye" for Frank Lunney in either *Beabohemia* or *Syndrome* (he can't remember which) and it's been an albatross around his neck ever since. Likes long walks on the beach and tentacle porn.

ALVA SVOBODA is a self-trained and largely unrecognized auto-archaeologist who aspires to create, before passing among the shades, a 3D-printed exact reenactment of his fannish pubescence composed entirely of vanilla fondant. Anyone with expertise in such matters is invited to contact him as soon as possible.

JEANNE BOWMAN is home at 38° 21' 19" N latitude 122° 31' 46" W longitude. Now and again she uses her grandmother's portable Singer sewing machine for perfect rolled hems and ponders the question of restore or repurpose for the treadle operated antiques in the barn.

CHRIS SHERMAN is an angel investor whose notable scores have included Silicon Valley startups Twitface, Shitsagram and I-Selftesla. He is currently the streaming media critic for SAG-AFTRA fave and Golden Lobes nominee Xenolith. His current recommendations (full disclosure: disavowed and not indemnified by RobinHood) include The Expanse, Altered Carbon, Rome, Grantchester, and Fawlty Towers.

Talking points for **G. SUTTON BREIDING,** a poet for our times, include siskins, deep green moss and Kate Moss, old age, amethyst, myrrh, space cowboys and lamia. His bio can be accessed at Wikipedia in all its fullness.

ARTISTS IN THIS ISSUE

2, 128, 163—Joe Pearson

4, 5—AC Kolthoff

7—Jude Falkerson

9—Marc Schirmeister

13, 15—Jim McLeod

17, 162—Wm. Breiding

36—Arlington Joseph

77—carl juarez

82—Ray Nelson

83—William Rotsler

94-101—John R. Benson

102—Dale Nelson/Kurt Erichsen

108—Samuel Palmer

123—Basil Palmer

146 —Wendy Victor

152—David A. Robinson

157—Jeanne Bowman

164—Casey Wolf

179—Harry O. Morris

122-144, the art of *War of the Worlds Goliath,* courtesy of Joe Pearson

Edited by William M. Breiding. Available in hard copy for the usual: letters of comment, trade, contributions of writing and visuals, or endowments of cash. Available at eFanzines.com & Amazon. Please send letters of comment to: **portablezine@gmail.com**.

Printed in Great Britain
by Amazon

18795829R00108